SONGS IN BLACK
AND LAVENDER

AFRICAN AMERICAN MUSIC IN GLOBAL PERSPECTIVE

Portia K. Maultsby and Mellonee V. Burnim, Series Editors

Archives of African American Music and Culture
Indiana University

A LIST OF BOOKS IN THE SERIES APPEARS AT THE END OF THIS BOOK.

Songs in Black and Lavender

RACE, SEXUAL POLITICS, AND WOMEN'S MUSIC

EILEEN M. HAYES

Foreword by Linda Tillery

UNIVERSITY OF ILLINOIS PRESS
URBANA, CHICAGO, AND SPRINGFIELD

Manufactured in the United States of America
1 2 3 4 5 C P 5 4 3 2
∞ This book is printed on acid-free paper.

Library of Congress Cataloging-in-Publication Data
Hayes, Eileen M.
Songs in Black and lavender : race, sexual politics, and women's music /
Eileen M. Hayes ; foreword by Linda Tillery.
p. cm. — (African American music in global perspective)
Includes bibliographical references and index.
ISBN 978-0-252-03514-2 (cloth : alk. paper)
ISBN 978-0-252-07698-5 (pbk : alk. paper)
1. African American women—Music—History and criticism.
2. Women's music—History and criticism.
3. Women's music festivals—United States.
4. Feminism and music—United States. I. Title.
ML82.H42 2010
780.82'0973—dc 2009038148

Some say feminism is dead. Others say black feminism stopped by but left in a hurry. A few claim that "women's music" is dull; "Besides," they say, "Bessie Smith is *so* last century." Others don't know any lesbians and would rather watch them on TV. It was chic to be lesbian—last year. They say you can't be black, lesbian, and musical at the same time. Maybe you can be black, lesbian, and love music—but if so, you probably can't dance, and if you can, you don't care about social change.

Lots of folks say all these things.
This book is not dedicated to them.

CONTENTS

FOREWORD

Linda Tillery

Songs in Black and Lavender is an ambitious undertaking that provides the reader with an incisive and thought-provoking analysis of a musical space that has been significantly reconfigured since its emergence in the early 1970s. As has been true with all major political or social movements, the concept of "women's music" was born out of a need for free expression and self-identification. Previously there had been no outlet for the cultural expression of woman-identified (lesbian feminist) ideologies.

The radical women's movement of the 1970s held out hope that women of all social, economic, and ethnic backgrounds would be able to measure themselves by their own standards and not those of the dominant male culture. Women who loved women could now openly express their passions and desires—an entire new culture emerged. For one glorious week at women's music festivals, lesbian, bisexual, and heterosexual women gathered to exchange political ideas, hawk their wares, make love, engage in ideological debate, and feel safe from the threat of domestic violence, rape, and the many challenges women face in the outside world. Lesbian identity and sexuality were validated. Transgenders raised their voices, too, and educated us in the process.

High expectations were associated with this new way of life. There were to be no stars, no dominant musical forms, and all artists would be given an equal chance to be selected for one of the performance stages. As the movement grew, so did the inevitable clashes of class, race, and privilege. Through ignorance or innocence—probably a little of both—there arose the assumption that every woman experienced the movement in the same way, that women viewed the world through the same lens. Nothing could have been further from the truth.

Could a woman who was raised listening to post–World War II blues and R&B be expected to fit into a culture that was dominated by a white, middle-class aesthetic? Could a singer from the barrios of New York City or Miami bring the music of Cuba or Puerto Rico into this new arena? Was there room for hard-core rockers? And what of European classical music and choral works? The lines of division had been drawn long ago by mainstream industry moguls—music was marketed by racial and cultural categories, and artists were labeled by terms of convenience like rock, pop, R&B, folk, gospel, folk rock, punk, grunge, classical, jazz, reggae, and so on. Not that cultural identification was, or is, a bad thing necessarily, but it was sometimes accompanied by an unfortunate exclusion or appropriation of the type that characterizes our country's histories, musical and otherwise.

There is something for everyone in Eileen Hayes's reckoning of black women's involvement in the women's music movement. Navigating between ethnography and interviews, trenchant analysis and laugh-out-loud humor, *Songs in Black and Lavender* will become a major resource for students and scholars—and if you were involved in the movement, you'll experience a myriad of emotions as the book addresses a most important period of our history.

SONGS IN BLACK
AND LAVENDER

Introduction

This book is about manifestations of black feminist consciousness in "women's music," which, as I argue here, is less a type of music than it is a site of women's thinking about music, a context for the enactment of lesbian feminist politics and notions of community. *Women's music* refers to a geographically dispersed network that arose from performances organized and produced by white lesbian, lesbian feminist, and feminist musicians and activists and was extended through their subsequent founding of women's music recording and distribution companies in the early 1970s.[1] Women's music was part and parcel of the women's culture, fueled by lesbian energies, that was associated with the radical feminist—as opposed to liberal feminist—politics of the period. As numerous scholars have noted, women who identified themselves as "radical" and as lesbian feminists envisioned transformation, rather than reform, of American society. Together, the two streams, "radical" and "liberal," comprise what is generally thought of as the women's movement.[2]

The women's culture of the 1970s held meaning for countless women, lesbian and straight alike, yet to date, scholars have not offered a framework for thinking about black women's collective presence in women's music. This book is offered not as a corrective to the omission of black women in a dominant narrative, although that, too, is important, but as a contribution to studies of black feminisms from the 1970s to the present. Women's music is a context for the emergence of ideas and ideals, musical and social. That this volume concerns black women's involvement in a predominantly white lesbian social field does not detract from its salience to the history of African American thought.

Toni Armstrong Jr., the editor of *Hot Wire,* an important women's music journal from the mid-1980s to 1994, described women's music as "music by, for, about, and financially controlled by women."[3] For more than two decades, Armstrong's concise definition figured centrally in the discourse of women's music, productively understood not as a coherent musical style but as a metonym for lesbian feminist values in terms of politics, identity, community, and music. In the aftermath of the dissolution of the women's music recording and distribution industry, women's music festivals are the legacy of what was formerly known as the women's music movement. These events are open to women identifying variously as lesbian, bisexual, and heterosexual, although the audiences, as well as the musicians, are mostly lesbian. These reductive labels are inadequate because, as anthropologist Kath Weston describes, they are "identity-based constructions of sexuality that cannot accommodate a range of intimacies and attractions"—nor, as I might add, music and politics.[4] Among the central figures of women's music are white musicians Holly Near, Margie Adam, Alix Dobkin, Maxine Feldman, Meg Christian, Kay Gardner, and Cris Williamson; often, the name of one of these artists is invoked to reference an era that many maintain has passed.[5]

Since the founding of the first festival in 1974, women's music festivals were or have been held annually (for longer or shorter runs) in numerous states, including Illinois, Indiana, Ohio, Michigan, New Mexico, California, Alaska, Wisconsin, Missouri, Texas, Delaware, Massachusetts, Mississippi, and Washington, DC.[6] Some festivals have remained in continuous operation (give or take a few years). Wiminfest, a project of Women in Movement in New Mexico, a nonprofit entity of Albuquerque, ceased operating as a festival but extended its legacy in other feminist-inspired (read *lesbian*) events sponsored by the organization. Historically, events such as the National Women's Music Festival (NWMF) have been held on college campuses over four-day weekends, giving festival attendees (or "festigoers") access to residence halls and other amenities of the university. Outdoor residential festivals extant at this writing include Camp Sister Spirit in Ovett, Mississippi; the six-day Michigan Womyn's Music Festival, and several more. With attendance in some years hovering around ten thousand, the Michigan Womyn's Music Festival (MWMF), founded in 1976, is considered by many to be the mother lode of those founded in lesbian separatism.[7]

Festival concert rosters are open to women of all races identifying variously as lesbian, bisexual, and heterosexual. The most celebrated African American women's ensemble to affiliate with the women's music circuit is Sweet Honey in the Rock (SHIR), the a cappella ensemble founded by Bernice Johnson Reagon in 1973. Sweet Honey was the first African American women's ensemble to collaborate through performance with artists associated with the women's music network. The ensemble came to the women's music circuit from years of association with leftist-associated causes.[8] Under the leadership of Reagon, a prominent public intellectual specializing in music of the civil rights movement, Sweet Honey has routinely been claimed by black women's music consumers and performers, in the words of singer/songwriter Melanie DeMore, as "the keeper of the flame," even as the ensemble has exhibited an ambivalent relationship to lesbian feminism.[9]

The cohort of professional black women musicians who have performed at women's music festivals or in women's music concerts in the past or present includes, but is not limited to, Edwina Lee Tyler, Linda Tillery and the Cultural Heritage Choir, Judith Casselberry/J.U.C.A. (Joy, Understanding, Creativity, Abundance), ASE, Regina Wells, In Process . . . , Deidre McCalla, Rachel Bagby, Melanie DeMore, Rhonda Benin, Vicki Randle, Ubaka Hill, Barbara "Wahru" Cleveland, the Washington Sisters, Mary Watkins, Pamela Means, Kim Archer, Gwen Avery, Nurudafina Pina Abena, Laura Love, Toshi Reagon and the Big Lovely, Faith Nolan, Afia Walking Tree, Bernice Brooks, India Cooke, Doria Roberts, Nedra Johnson, Debra Kenya McGee, Urban Bush Women, and Casselberry and DuPreé.[10] (A list of these musicians and others can be found in the section of this book titled "Dreamgirls.") African American sign language interpreters associated with women's music include Shirley Childress Saxton (SHIR) and Ariel Hall.[11]

Women's music has been jettisoned to the margins of critical study by scholars of both feminism and black music, but for different reasons. Because of its ideological foundation in cultural feminism, purveyors of feminist theory have regarded women's music as the anteriority of feminist performativity. Cultural feminism was based on an essentialist view of the differences between women and men and advocated separatism and women's institution building.[12] Women's bookstores, co-ops, coffeehouses, garages, health centers, and festivals were all part of the burgeoning women's culture of the period, and feminists of color contributed in significant ways to those institutions. When critics paint the cultural offshoot of radical feminism in broad strokes, or when they suggest that cultural feminism supplanted radical feminism, it makes it difficult for the roles of black women in this arena to be adequately assessed. The use of all-encompassing statements to characterize the experiences of white women and women of color means that the ways black women challenged essentialist notions that pervaded festival environments in the early years have not been brought to light.

Although black women were active as feminists in black feminist organizations of the late 1960s to the early 1980s, an even smaller minority of critics and scholars see black (predominantly) lesbian involvement in women's music as related to and part of the history of black liberatory struggle, and black women's activism in particular.[13] In spite of the florescence of writings critiquing and contributing to an interrogation of the essential black music subject, scholars have ignored women's music festivals as a site of African American music performance and black cultural production. This is as much because of masculinist and heteronormative modes of investigation and analyses in black music studies as it is because of the relative newness of ethnomusicological research into music scenes. Fundamentally, women's music as a site for the generation of critical theory by black women, many of whom identify as feminist, lesbian, or lesbian feminist, has been ignored. Critical scholarship should attend to doubly and triply minoritarian groups precisely because in doing so the interconstitutive nature of difference is revealed.

At issue for the ethnomusicologist also is that women's music has been declared over, even as some women's music festivals are ongoing. As Ray Charles puts it, "What'd you say?"[14] According to both movement founders and observers, women's music experienced its "golden age" from the early 1970s to the mid-to-late 1980s, a period that roughly coincides with the heyday of the women's movement. Nancy Whittier writes, "The 1980s saw the election of an overtly antifeminist President, Ronald Reagan, budget cuts for social services and social change organizations alike, and the rise of a grassroots Religious Right."[15] As women's organizations cut back or dissolved during the early 1980s, radical feminism "took new, less visible forms."[16] Women's music festivals were one manifestation of a radical feminism that continued—as it always had—"underground." Along a parallel track, the cultural feminism that fueled the women's music movement is also supposed to have failed: In the 1970s the women's recording industry provided opportunities for women, mostly lesbians, in music performance and all aspects of concert production. In spite of reaching thousands of audience members and consumers over time, the women's music industry was unable to transform mainstream music industry norms. Eventually, women's recording and (most) distribution companies went out of business. To some, women's music festivals are not only celebrations of what is, but also tangible reminders of "what might have been" in the future.

By the mid-1980s the gay men's and lesbian movements had moved closer together at the national level as lesbians assumed positions in previously male-dominated organizations like the National Gay Task Force, which in 1985 changed its name to the National Gay and Lesbian Task Force.[17] In the aftermath of the

HIV-AIDS crisis of the late 1980s, many veterans of the radical women's movement, along with lesbians who were new to activism, joined gay men in record numbers to present a united front against the epidemic.[18] Many women continued their involvement in "informal networks, service organizations, lesbian feminist institutions, cultural events, and assorted annual demonstrations."[19] Given this context, it is noteworthy that new women's music festivals were founded during the 1980s and 1990s. It must be remembered, however, that the social and political context in which women's music festivals exist today contrasts sharply with the set of circumstances that lesbian and lesbian feminist activists and musicians confronted in the early 1970s.

Though a number of women's music festivals ceased operation during the 1990s, the year 2000 marked the beginning of a surge in Ladyfest events, female-centered music festivals produced by a younger generation of queer-identified women who encourage attendance of persons identifying variously in terms of gender. Ladyfest events are not the music festival your mother warned you about, but then again, perhaps they are, depending on who your mother is. One young, black, lesbian-identified musician who has performed at several of the Ladyfest events related her disappointment at experiencing some of the same racial slights that her mother, also a lesbian, encountered, albeit at the older type of music festival. The persistence of racism—even in gay neighborhoods—is a reminder that the queer nation may not be as indivisible by race as some would like to believe. It is a truism that working out the operations of feminism is as messy outside academia as it is within it, and is as complicated today as it was yesterday, but its manifestations occur anew. Nonetheless, the musicians and organizers of the "next" generation with whom I spoke shared their enthusiasm for all that women's music offers and their plans for the future with a noticeable absence of nostalgia.

In considering alternatives to conceiving of women's music as a failed movement, I look to the work of social movement theorist Robin D. G. Kelley. Kelley suggests that if the success of radical movements is judged by whether or not they meet all of their goals, "virtually every radical movement failed because the basic power relations they sought to change remain pretty much intact. And yet it is precisely these alternative visions and dreams that inspire new generations to continue to struggle for change."[20] Although I do not disagree that the women's music festival as an institution did not and does not challenge state power,[21] I find valuable leads in the perspective Kelley offers. Women's music festivals should be appreciated not only for what they offer in the present but also for the valuable role they played historically in buoying women's spirits in the process of community formation and serving as the site for hammering out, in concrete terms, certain strains of feminist theory. For those who have come to take the decades-long institutionalization of academic feminism for granted, it is difficult to appreciate the significance of the women's music festival as an early site of radical feminist praxis. Scholars have noted that the collective efforts of radical feminists for social change occurred in the realms of culture, identity, and everyday life, as well as through direct engagement with the state.[22] Communities that formed around music making and consumption were an important part of the mix.

Whereas scholars writing earlier have debated whether efforts devoted to lesbian cultural effluence (visual art, theater, film, dance, literature, music), in contrast to traditional political activity, are retreatist or reformist, that is not my concern here. In preparing this book, I have tried to maintain an open mind as I explored the tensions between these two of several possible interpretations. As a result, I am most persuaded by the idea that involvement in politics, with its traditional associations with formal government, does not necessarily relegate activism in expressive culture to a position of lesser importance.

This book is based on interviews I conducted with black women musicians, festival organizers, and attendees—"flygirls in the buttermilk"—in a predominantly white lesbian social field. If some women I interviewed spoke to the tensions of representing blackness in this context, then so, too, do many black women experience cognitive dissonance identifying with the inclusive "rainbow flag" ideal that, through its color symbolism, effaces race while embracing all sexual orientations.

At the National Women's Music Festival, held at Ohio's Kent State University, I mentioned to another black festigoer attending the festival's annual Women of Color dinner that my book would be the first to devote primary attention to "black women in women's music." My interlocutor responded, speaking of mainstream writers or record company marketing personnel, "If they don't talk about the white girls, you know they don't talk about us [meaning African American women]." I laughed. Delivered with an intonation that often accompanies black comedic delivery, this sound bite of local knowledge was designed to inform and entertain. At the same time, however, the woman's comment deflected attention from a more accurate characterization of the scholarly literature on women's music. It is not the case simply that scholars have failed to acknowledge black women performers. Rather, when they have acknowledged them, some "inclusive passages" exhibit an add-and-stir quality that is reminiscent, as ethnomusicologist Ellen Koskoff reminds us, of early anthropological studies of women.[23] Musicologist Sherrie Tucker builds on this idea in her study of "all-girl" swing bands of the 1940s. Tucker suggests that the narrative inclusion of people of color does not "guarantee a departure from the ways in which race discourse operates" in music—and, I might add, in social analyses.[24]

Other women I met at festivals voiced delight that I would "tell our story." This is not precisely the work I carry out here. Rather, this is an interpretive study in which I meld interview data, participation observation, and critical social theory in the interest of black (and other) folks.[25] As I address issues of representation, my goal is to be as transparent as possible in the presentation of the insights uncovered and of my role in responding to and configuring the same. The contours of this book are shaped not only by my own identities as an ethnomusicologist, activist, and theorist, but by the equivalent of butchers, bakers, and candlestick makers in and outside the academy. Some of those to whom I am indebted in an intellectual sense engage in social movements from diverse locations.

During the course of this research, I became intrigued by the limits of identity politics, even as I participated in them, thereby blurring the lines between the observer and the observed. Scholars have questioned the virtue of maintaining that boundary since the 1970s. While some critics situate identity politics in the past, others remind us that this mode of thinking obscures the fact that "identity is central to all social movements, whether they claim to be about identity or not, and dissent over the borders of identity categories exists within movements, as well as outside them."[26] Individuals, too, can be intrigued and vexed by identity categories, some of which are more fluid than others. Before this book went to press, a black anthropologist colleague raised a timely question. All along, she said, she had assumed that women's music festivals attracted only the "baddest of the bad black sistahs," the "super-black, Afro-feminist, hair-as-big-as-Erykah-Badu, quote-Audre-Lorde-all-day-and-talk-about-revolution" sisters.[27] I will discuss the persistent and disabling equation of black feminist identity with the physical appearance of the "revolutionary sweethearts" of the Black Power movement later in this book.[28]

Several black feminist scholars have either commented on this phenomenon or alluded to it, among them Joy James and Patricia Hill Collins.[29] Still, I am glad my friend raised the issue, and I will make this clarification: *This book does not correlate black women's hairstyles with their musical styles or with their perspectives—political, social, or otherwise.* Women's music festivals attract black women, mostly lesbians, from all walks of life, but especially those who find and create resonance with the particular version of lesbian culture that the women's music festival, as an institution, represents. It would be wrong to assume that black women in a predominantly lesbian milieu do not exhibit heterogeneity in terms of class, erotic attraction, worldview, gender identity, and even clothing and hair texture. Although most women I interviewed shared the perspective that the oppressions black women experience are simultaneous, in terms of activism and politics (with a small *p*), their ideoscapes reflect greater, rather than less, diversity. This diversity also extends to the musical styles of black performers in this arena. Women's music festivals give participants a chance to see and hear outstanding black musicians and comediennes in performance who, as one festigoer put it, "look like us."

Is it reasonable to characterize nine thousand white women as "a bunch"?—EILEEN M. HAYES, DIARY ENTRY

CHAPTER I

Diary of a Mad Black Woman Festigoer

In the typical arrival story, a familiar aspect of traditional ethnography, the anthropologist acquaints herself with persons unknown and prepares to settle in so that she can begin her "real work." Although technically this diary does not do precisely that, my intent is that readers will find it a useful introduction to themes raised in this book. This includes, but is not limited to, the experience of festivals from the perspectives of black women.

Although some readers will be familiar with the women's music festival scene, most will probably not. Therefore, I sought a vehicle through which I could both describe and signify on women's music festivals from the perspective of a black attendee. This diary is the result. With an attitude reminiscent of Tyler Perry's *Diary of a Mad Black Woman,* the narrative genre of the travel diary provides me entrée to the representation of this different world.[1] At six feet, six inches tall, Perry, an Atlanta-based thespian, has made a career of portraying the African American wise-woman-cum-superhero Madea in the plays upon which his films are based, and some of her comedic spirit influences the diary I offer.[2] That many white readers are unfamiliar with Perry's work neither detracts from nor influences its success. African Americans who comprise Perry's target audience for live performances may experience a reality that differs dramatically, in their time away from integrated work sites, from the lived experience of whites.

A parallel sensibility might be acknowledged in regard to African Americans and the consumer base for women's music festivals. African American male friends and acquaintances with whom I discussed this book frequently posed the question "What about the [soul] brothers?" Therefore, I emphasize that these festivals are women-centered events—indeed, in the case of Michigan, women-born women events.[3] It would not be far off the mark to say that black male-bodied persons identifying as men don't count in these environments except as infrequent audience members. And as a comedian as sharp as the late Bernie Mac might say, "The brothers don't get to many lesbian events."

Within these pages, I do not presume to inhabit a black lesbian subject position. I say this not to disavow associations between myself and members of the community in which I conducted research, but rather to underscore, as Michael Awkward relates, that markers of identity ought not necessarily to be deemed sufficient grounds upon which to grant one authority to speak the cultural truths.[4] This idea undergirds my attempts to intervene in representations of blackness, black femaleness, black lesbianness, and black feminism, but it echoes a formulation put forth earlier by Valerie Smith and Hazel Carby.[5] I raise my own identities as a straight, black, and, arguably, old-school feminist activist precisely to question what these inflections mean, singly and in combination. Still, it is telling, as anthropologist Ellen Lewin and linguist William Leap suggest, that gay or lesbian identity is almost always attributed to scholars conducting research in lesbian and gay communities.[6] The diary entries, or field notes, that follow are a reminder that work in the field of identity politics requires care. The post–Stuart Hall generation has come to expect that positionalities align unevenly, and in unexpected ways.[7] This is as true in relation to race identity as it is for gender, sexual identity, class, politics, and so on. In none of these areas does this book assume a unitary subject.

My use of the first-person narrative in the diary that follows (and, indeed, throughout this book) is a mode of representation so fundamental to anthropological practice that it requires no justification. And while a number of influences are felt in these pages, that of John Gwaltney's *Drylongso: A Self-Portrait of Black America* (1981) must be credited at the outset. Gwaltney's recorded conversations with blacks living in a dozen black communities in the northeastern U.S. in the early 1970s reveal not only their perspectives about their own lives but also their perceptions of blacks as a people and of whites both individually and collectively. *Drylongso* was just one of Gwaltney's prescient studies in which he argued for a "native anthropology," an intellectual cause that was taken up by successive generations of anthropologists of color, women, and, later, scholars conducting ethnography in lesbian and gay communities.[8] In his comments for the dust jacket for *Drylongso,* the writer Ralph Ellison maintained that Gwaltney painted a portrait of "core Black America" (Gwaltney's phrase) that was designed to instruct and entertain. I have tried to infuse some of those qualities into this essay, nodding toward the African American tradition of indirect social criticism through humor.

For reasons that will become clear, some readers may never have the opportunity to attend a women's music festival. I offer the following polyglot (mis)adventures in feminism, lesbian identity, race matters, and music—replete with its reverberations of African American autoethnographical and oral traditions—in the hope that you, too, can experience a real vacation in lesbian utopia.[9]

The Diary

In August 1995 my friend Cindy Spillane and I drove from Maryland to the twentieth anniversary of the Michigan Womyn's Music Festival. In previous years I had attended the festival alone; now I was glad to have Spillane's company. She and I had met as members of the DC Area Feminist Chorus (Washington, DC), now called the Bread and Roses Feminist Singers.[10] Both of us dropped out eventually, for different reasons. I grew weary of being "the only one"—the sistahs know what I mean. Spillane felt strongly that the chorus's engagement with feminist praxis and music had, in her words, "petrified at about 1975." "How much Holly Near arranged for four-part women's voices can one take?" she would ask. I didn't begrudge the second-wave radical feminism sound track that the chorus's Near-Williamson-Christian repertoire evoked. Indeed, my own feminist resolve had been fortified by the music of women's music founders during the years of my young adulthood, and though those years were decidedly over, women's music was my music, too. Yet despite attempts to "multiculturalize" (is that a word?) the chorus' repertoire with the occasional song by Sweet Honey in the Rock, Spillane and I concluded independently that the group's raison d'etre was better fulfilled as a voluntary association for social networking than as a choir.

Our bond with each other was as feminist activists in the Washington, DC, area. Spillane, a white lesbian, frequently led workshops in the women's community on antiracism; she was also a fat women's activist—that is, a *fat,* fat-issues activist. My feminist organizing had been predominantly with other black women and women of color in reproductive rights advocacy and anti-sterilization abuse. I had been trained by lesbian feminists in the early 1980s and in part was still working out the repayment of a symbolic debt owed to the women from whom I learned feminist engagement. For the most part, Spillane "got it" about racism; I won't make it sound as though she didn't. I was a veteran feminist activist and didn't buy into narratives about black women not identifying with the f-word (feminism). It didn't take an Angela Davis to know that advocating on behalf of oneself as a black and as a woman was part and parcel of black women's activist heritage (although I'm glad Davis pointed that out).[11]

GENDER, PLAY, AND TRANSGRESSION

A source of our amusement during the road trip involved our speculating about how festigoers might assume we were girlfriends in the romantic rather than the platonic sense. There would be many couples at this festival, because for many lesbian and bisexual women this particular festival was a favorite place to vacation. Part of the pleasure participants derive from a large festival such as Michigan comes from attendees' opportunities to be both actors and audience members in the larger social drama that is the festival. In the festival arena, participants enact numerous social performances that contest, combine, and turn identity categories held by many to be fixed—particularly those of gender and sexuality—on their heads. These acts take place onstage, but even more often offstage, as festigoers, "virgin" (first-time attendees) and otherwise, conduct everyday life at the festival. I looked forward to highlighting in my study what was happening at the ground level in the lives of black women performers and festival attendees.

We were going to have a long ride. To pass the time in the car, Spillane and I constructed butch and femme personas for ourselves. Thwarting expectations about what some observers consider markers of butch and femme identities, Spillane and I adopted the aliases of "Bunnie" and "Lambert" respectively. Spillane performed "Bunnie" as overtly femme; I enacted "Lambert" as decisively butch. We were playing with stereotypes, but at the same time we understood that we would be subjected to an essentializing gaze while at the festival. Given the recurring trope of the "big, black butch," it struck us as clever that I, five feet tall and slightly built at one hundred pounds, would play that role, while "built for comfort" Spillane would occupy the femme space.[12] We took delight in our theatrics and enacted these personas privately throughout the festival for our own amusement.

We listened to the radio and to CDs we had brought along. Since we knew that Michigan, like some other women's music festivals, strongly encouraged women not to play men's voices over sound systems, we wanted to get in all the Mick Jagger, Elton John, Michael Jackson, Prince, and Luther Vandross we could. A self-conscious awareness accompanied our creation of the list. Every performer mentioned occupied, if not a gay positionality, an "in-betweenness" with regard to gender, sexual identity, race, or some combination of these. We also listened to Tracy Chapman, Joan Armatrading, Melissa Etheridge, and k. d. lang during our trip. They were our "girls," and we wished they were coming to Michigan, too.

BLACK AND LAVENDER

About halfway into our road trip, Spillane, who was driving, glanced in my direction: "How is our flag coming?" she asked. Before we left Maryland, I had described how women personalize their tents, recreational vehicles, and grounds in the immediate vicinity of their camps. Festigoers tack clotheslines in the woods so that they might hang beautiful/outrageous quilts, banners, and posters, many of which pay homage to women's history, lesbian/bisexual/transgender pride, and other politics. I had heard via the rumor mill that the Michigan festival would be conferring an award for the "best home exterior design" that year. I suggested we enter the contest. Spillane asked what we could do, since neither of us had talents in the domestic arts. I suggested that we take a flag and post it outside the tent. Spillane replied, "You mean a rainbow flag?" I shrugged. "Child, we need something black and lesbian," I said. "Where will you get that type of flag?" Spillane asked. Reversing herself suddenly, she exclaimed, "You're a het [heterosexual]; you can sew!" Little did we know it then, but our hand-sewn nylon flag, the design of which was a black triangle against a background of deep lavender, would become an object of admiration in our campsite neighborhood.

CITY ON A HILL

Though I had attended several women's music festivals previously, including Michigan, Spillane looked forward to her first one. She had wanted to be prepared, so before the trip she talked with me and her other friends about what she could expect. I am not sure if, once we arrived, she got what she came for or not. The Michigan ideal is that women will replicate an entire outdoor city—less Athens and more a poor people's tent city à la 1960s Washington, DC—into which some semipermanent structures, such as stages and commissaries, are introduced. Michigan is about long queues for food, open-air showers, ice cream, infrequent portions of meat, and a public transportation system comprised of flatbed trucks. These vehicles take festigoers from the registration site to camping areas, from the main stage concert area to the special constituency tents at which workshops are held. Each August, those who are familiar with the experience harbor a hope that is familiar to attendees at all residential music festivals, if not participants in utopian projects. "If we build it, they will come," the saying goes, and come they do: some alone, others towing babies and small children, male and female.[13] There are a fair number of two-mom families, crones, teens and young adults, and others in recreational vehicles, differently bodied women, interracial couples, dyed blondes and towheads, women with dreads and those with weaves, transgenders, femmes, straight women who remember what women-identified means, butches, wannabe butches, sexy women and others looking for sex or for Mr. Goodbar (the candy), and—I swear—several hundred men. A few "hopelessly straight" women come, too—some of whom have been lied to about what to expect. After a flash thunderstorm, probably hundreds from each identity group wonder why the hell they're there.

There is no "hill" as the word is used in military parlance, but if there were, we could take it. This is part of the Michigan experience, too: big talk, big Windy City, four-star-general talk by women who are fixed (as my grandmother would have put it) on doing big things. We had heard through the grapevine that more than nine thousand women (predominantly white lesbians) were expected for this outdoor, five- to seven-day event, billed as the largest women's music festival in the world. What was it about this festival that made it occupy a central place in the women's music festival imaginary?

WOMEN ONLY

In contrast to other women's (lesbian-oriented) music festivals, Michigan is a women-only gathering; men are not allowed. Indeed, at other festivals, men are now invited to participate both as audience members and sometimes as sidemen, though not as instrumental or vocal leads during performances. Addressing, in the course of Spillane's preparation for the festival, the various inconsistencies in festival inclusion policies that have arisen over time and location would have been too complicated.

Michigan welcomes women-born women of all ages and ethnicities and male children under the age of eleven. During the day, male youngsters go to the Brother Sun Boys Camp; the counterpart to the festival's day programming for girls is the Gaia Girls Camp.[14] The camps are age- and sex-specific. Brother Sun is for young boys ages five through ten; additionally, families with boys agree to reside in the Brother Sun camp for the entire week. The girls camp provides a range of activities and oversight for young females five and older. These accommodations for children are a festival offering that has evolved over the years—and not without debate by festival planners and attendees. Michigan also offers the Sprouts Family Campground for mothers and all children four years of age and under. I am afraid that given my "single woman with no children or nieces or nephews" centricity, I never sought to visit the boys or girls camp and don't know if it is possible for nonparents to do so.

DYKE SPOTTING

Toward evening, Spillane and I stretched our legs at a truck-stop diner in Hart, Michigan, the town nearest to the festival site in Walhalla, a small community in west-central Michigan. We were in a rural area and admittedly had been a bit spooked by a small flurry of anti-lesbian sentiment from passersby along the road. This was the last leg of the trip, and we had exhausted our supply of the best and worst scenarios that might befall us at the festival. We hoped our job assignments there would not be too taxing and that Spillane's tent, which she was borrowing from a friend, would not flood.

As we walked into the diner, Spillane joked nervously that the other customers could "spot us as dykes," a statement based on the belief that people engage in shared assumptions about visible markers of lesbian identity. She and I were temporarily relieved, however, by the proximity of three large, and as they say, dark-skinned, butch-looking black women in black leather jackets seated at a table near the door. "We are not alone," I thought to myself. Spillane urged me to approach the women for an interview because, in her words, they were "dykes going to Michigan." Her comment was audible confirmation that even my longtime feminist associate had lapsed into an essentialist notion of black lesbians.

ARRIVAL AND REGISTRATION

The festival was held on a plat of 650 acres of privately owned land in the woods. Upon arriving at the site and walking through registration, which included a brief orientation film, it was time for us to choose our work-shift assignments. From talking with her friends before the trip, Spillane knew that festival participants were required to complete three four-hour shifts as part of their Michigan stay. Various posts were available, but at least one kitchen stint was strongly encouraged. On the one hand, work shifts are voluntary, but on the other, they are vital to the functioning of the festival itself and help foster a spirit of community. At some festivals, attendees can pay a lower registration fee through work exchange. The rules of the workaday world don't seem to apply here. The work-shift leader may be given a list of her volunteer charges, but I've never heard of anyone getting in trouble for not showing up for an assignment. Still, it seems that most follow through on their commitments. Fulfilling one's work-shift assignments is a part of establishing one's festival cred.

Food preparation and serving occurs under large mega-tarps—the size of those big-ass tents rich people use for their wedding receptions, but not as nice. The kitchen, if one could call it that, is a wide expanse of outdoor grounds divided into areas for food preparation, cooking, serving, and cleanup. Rank-

and-file festival attendees service these areas. Paid festival "professionals" man (possibly I've used the wrong word here) the large cauldrons of cooking food: vegetarian chili, soup, tofu and vegetables, and the like. Noting the allure of ritualized infatuations that permeate festival environments, Spillane opined, "The pretty girls always get crushes on the *paid* staff."

SISTER (MAMMY) ACT

Unlike Spillane, I did not yearn to work in the "kitchen," no matter how "cute" the "girls" were. I especially did not want to volunteer in the dining area apportioning food to a bunch of white women. (Is it reasonable to characterize nine thousand white women as "a bunch"?) The possibility made me think not only of the numbers of black women, past and present, who earned their living in the food service industry but also of the career trajectories of two superb black film actors of the 1930s, Hattie McDaniel and Butterfly McQueen. Both were cast in David Selznick's *Gone with the Wind* as servants in the O'Hara household. McDaniel successfully parlayed the portrayal of an insubordinate mammy into a lucrative career. Less recognized today is McQueen, who, closer to my body type perhaps, left black audiences laughing and shaking their heads at her incisive portrayals of black house servants. The opportunity to staff one of the long conjoined tables in the dining area struck me as a little "too historical," and I was not sure I could play the role as well as either of those brilliant performers. If I could pull off the kitchen stint with style and the right combination of performative moves, that would be one thing. There was, however, always the chance that my act would pass unnoticed and that my role-playing would appear naturalized. How many times, after all, has a brother been caught holding the door for a line of whites because they think—granted, on a subliminal level—that he's the doorman? In the early 1970s my black piano teacher related that white parents would frequently appear at the front door of her home and ask her to announce their presence to the "lady of the house." From talking with numerous black women at women's music festivals, I knew that many brought a similar memory of place and race to the kitchen work-shift experience. "You don't look anything like Butterfly McQueen," Spillane said. "It's not about McQueen," I retorted. "Oh," Spillane replied, "I thought it was."

It's not that the white women were racists; I was too sophisticated to subscribe to that level of overdetermined analysis. In fact, such a sentiment is no analysis at all; it's the starting point for everyday conversation. "And besides," Spillane said, "a few of the white women here have black girlfriends." Okay, I'm thinking. Is that like saying that white folks aren't racist because they adopt Chinese national baby girls? I know it's controversial, but dang—couldn't they adopt some black kids? I did not give voice to these thoughts, and Spillane laughed before I had a chance to utter my usual "Don't get me started." To their credit, at least the white women of my generation who I passed at the festival extended a nod of acknowledgment. The same doesn't always happen in civilian life.

RACING THE IMAGINATION

On the evening of our arrival, we pitched Spillane's four-person tent, the capacity of which I questioned. I related that at my first women's music festival, a white woman attendee who I'll call Jerry warned me that a "cute gal such as yourself" should be careful "what with all the black studs around." I am not sure she attended the event first and foremost for the music—but then, many women do not. "That's so crude," Spillane said, reacting to the story I told her. She added, "But you are cute." "Yeah, right," I said. Though I was struck by the depth of Jerry's racialized imagination packaged in a well-meaning wrap, I do not mean to conjure her as a working-class fall guy for her silenced middle-class counterparts. Rather, I found Jerry's remark a disturbing, but perhaps also illuminating, peephole into some consumer perceptions of music, embodiment, and sexual identity.

This reminds me how broad the scope of this book project was in the first place. As my heart raced and my palms began to sweat, I resolved that next time I would narrow it down. How does one cover 650 acres in one week? What guarantees that by attending one event I won't miss another one of comparable value? These questions were symptomatic that I was in the middle of a breakdown—what Gayatri Spivak called "cognitive failure," or that moment when a project is faced by its own impossibility.[15] An exaggeration? Perhaps, but things were only going to get worse.

What about incidents I had only heard about but hadn't experienced—the alleged brothel set up for the festival's paid staff in the weeks leading up to the festival, for example? What operations of race were at play there? According to women I talked with, none of whom were black, the brothel event sparked controversy along the following lines. First, it was open only to those women categorized as festival workers, and not to festigoers in general. Second, it inspired concerns about the enactment of sadomasochism only in the brothel area. It's ironic that if the brothel had been situated in a heterosexual context, the nuances of its value might have been missed. The controversy revealed long-standing tensions in lesbian feminist communities between proponents of prostitution and/or sadomasochism between consenting adults, activists' concern with domestic violence in lesbian relationships or households, and other perspectives.

STRATIFICATION IN UTOPIA

The Michigan festival is a great communal experiment. Everyone eats the same food, and although it is apportioned buffet style, it is not cafeteria style: there are set menus for breakfast, lunch, and dinner. As the event is designed to be self-contained, it would be almost inconceivable for one to go off-land in search of kung pao chicken or a hamburger. Even if you could leave to find food, our experience driving down the road suggests that you might not feel comfortable doing so. After all, it's west-central Michigan, not the Bronx.

The only vendors at Michigan are the craftswomen in the festival marketplace, stretches of land devoted to the selling of lesbian- and feminist-inspired art and work by artisans. The store set up by the festival sells camping-related supplies (batteries, rain gear, personal hygiene products, candy), but festigoers can bring in supplemental food and other items,

Even in paradise, everyone is not equal. Musicians may have specific requests that the performer care staff can accommodate: special water; private accommodations in a recreational vehicle, tent, or two-star hotel room; or an extra piece of chicken on meat night. (The latter is no unsubstantiated conspiracy theory, although most of those are true, too.) When musicians aren't giving workshops or performing, they are seldom visible elsewhere on the land. But, then, how would one find them in crowds of Michigan's magnitude? My guess is that you can't be a star 24/7—not even in the promised land.

BREASTS AND MORE BREASTS

Michigan facilitates one of the largest aggregates of women's breasts in the world: boobs of all sizes, shapes, nationalities, and colors attached to bodies and minds of varied physical and political dimensions. There are indicators of the failed pink ribbon campaign: some breasts have been surgically removed. Others are enhanced, a few (about two thousand) stand at attention, most droop with pride. It's this wide expanse of bare-breasted women jamming or dancing together that is described in the literature as "nudity." In reality, it's that folks are topless; a much smaller number of women go bottomless, too.

The circumstances under which toplessness en masse occurs are interesting to observe. The large aggregates of boobs seem to occur spontaneously and are often spurred on or accompanied by music—say, an informal jam session begun by four or five (white) women playing *djembe* drums or congas. The combination of the August heat, the euphoria of a predominantly lesbian gathering outdoors, and a "what happens in Vegas stays in Vegas" attitude inspires some women to de-shirt ceremoniously, with a striptease flair. A few women look reluctant to disrobe. As though coerced by the will of the crowd, they also end up taking off their shirts. This is a reminder, as my mother always said, to wear clean underwear, and not just in case that car accident happens to you. The spontaneous combustion or performance of the crowd does not extend to evening concerts, where a greater sense of formality reigns. In the evening it's generally cooler, and festigoers wear clothes—sometimes lots of them in an effort to stay warm. At the concerts, whether held on the day stage (lesser status) or the evening stage (highest status), there is also a tacit recognition that the professionals provide the entertainment so that the audience does not have to.

At one point, Spillane hoped that her favorite musicians would go topless on stage. Outside of a white butch comedian, however, I had never seen one of the professional musicians—white, Latina, or black—go nude or disrobe to briefs and brassiere during a performance. To answer the inevitable question, yes, I have seen black women at Michigan, in a dancing crowd, enact the dramatic core of Sojourner Truth's reported speech at the 1851 Women's Convention in Akron, Ohio, and bare their breasts.[16] Alternatively, they might go topless in their campsite neighborhoods. If ever asked at a McCarthy-style Senate hearing, however, I can honestly say, "I am not now nor have I ever have been coerced by a crowd to de-shirt, nor have I chosen to do so." Simply put, going topless was never the way I enacted my feminist identity. That wasn't the only reason, however. I also had, as historian Mary Frances Berry might say, a long memory of crowd behavior gone badly, whether at a civil rights march or at an ostensibly peaceable demonstration. I could neither trust crowd behavior nor predict it with certainty.

THE CRUSH

Working around food makes me hungry. At Michigan, the predominantly volunteer kitchen staff serves meals for five thousand or more. By kitchen staff I refer not to the professionals paid by the festival, but rather to the supervisory personnel who provide instruction during the orientation sessions (that is, proper cutting of broccoli, efficient corn-husking, pan-scrubbing procedures). Competence in the kitchen, traditionally the domain of women, is highly regarded, especially by festival attendees, many of whom are participants in or spectators of outdoor mass meal production for the first time. After our breakfast of granola and yogurt the next morning—I know you know the joke: granola is the white lesbian national food, whatever—anyway, after breakfast the orientation team of which I was a member received corn-husking instruction from a tall, lithe, butchlike, levelheaded blonde. She had an attractive and appealing yet distant and unattainable look, similar to that of the lesbian-appropriated heroine of the television adventure series *Xena: Warrior Princess*.[17] I found myself getting a crush on a staff member, just like so many others. The uncompensated physical labor of my African American ancestors notwithstanding, I remember thinking that under our instructor's supervision, I could husk corn for the rest of my life.

PRESSURES ARE RISING

After my work shift, I wandered the grounds trying to gain my bearings, looking as though I knew where I was going and that it was my intention to be there. After lunch I washed my dishes (those nonbreakable camping sets work best) in the dishwashing trough—the kind of watering system you find on Texas ranches for horses. I was glad to have brought the biodegradable soap. Privately, I was already craving a Dove bar, a designer ice cream treat I don't even buy at home, but then again, there was a lot of stress. How was I going to get to the Women of Color tent, meet up with a potential interviewee I met briefly last night, see if it would be possible to visit activists protesting the women-born women admission policy outside the festival proper, and get a psychic reading at the Village Marketplace? For five dollars I could ask Lady Abundantia, self-named after a minor Roman goddess of good fortune and prosperity, if I would finish this book or not. Everyone knows that African American women comprise the highest percentage of American consumers who purchase the services of psychics, fortune tellers, tarot card readers, and crystal-ball seers.[18] Holding out hope against a sociological literature that suggests otherwise, black women collectively seem to believe that there is promise at the end of the rainbow, appearances notwithstanding.

DOING RESEARCH

What the fortune teller said is private. Afterward, I retrieved the clipboard and pen from my backpack; it was time to begin my interviews with black festigoers. After establishing a bit of rapport, I would ask the interviewee to tell me her favorite black women-identified musicians so that we could talk about them. "Women-identified" is the name proponents eventually used to refer to the genre; just one reason is that the term *women's music* seemed to invoke white, middle-class norms and inspired raised eyebrows. Responses I received initially included mainstream artists such as Janet Jackson and Tina Turner. "Oh, no," I said to Spillane later. "The women are giving me the wrong answers." Although we went on to have interesting exchanges, I had really wanted festigoers to talk about artists associated with the women's music circuit. "Maybe you should change your research design and write a book on Tina Turner," Spillane said, referencing the rock star we had loved since the days when Ike was a nice guy.[19]

IMAGINE MY SURPRISE

Imagine my surprise—that was also the name of my favorite Holly Near song—when Spillane and another woman, blonde and "well-kept for her age," trudged in my direction.[20] The searing heat would make anybody wilt. Though she was fit, Spillane looked beat; her white companion, on the other hand, chugged away as though powered by an Everready battery. "Kathy wanted to meet you," Spillane said. "Oh," I replied, "great, I'm Eileen," and extended my hand. "It's good to meet you," said Kathy. Her handshake was limp, like those of some of the undergraduate women I now teach. "Cindy said I could ask a few questions about what it's like for you as a straight woman at the festival. I'm straight, too, and it's soooooo different being here." "Oh, no," I thought, "I hope she gets to the ten o'clock workshop titled 'Heterosexual and Bisexual Support.' Spillane better not plan to bring me stray straight white women throughout our stay here."

I asked the visitor how she was finding the festival—not that I was interested, but she was Spillane's guest. "Everyone is pretty nice . . . I'm here with a couple girls who tell me that at the concert tonight the emcee will undoubtedly ask the straight women to stand so that everyone can acknowledge them. That's so cool." Spillane, who had been wiping the dirt from her hiking boots, raised her head, smirking under her Jane Deere baseball cap. It seemed that Kathy's friends had deliberately fed her misinformation concerning the benign nature of that "welcome," and Spillane knew it. Public humiliation via the punch line is a more accurate description of the event that would ensue. "Actually," I said, "I suggest that you don't raise your hand—or stand up, for that matter." "Why not?" Kathy asked. All of a sudden, Spillane rushed away as though she had to catch the last train out of Manhattan, leaving me alone to explain to her friend that her volunteer outing in the concert context would set her up to be humiliated by the comedienne, who routinely made a joke at the expense of straight women.

NO SHADES OF GRAY

At a concert held on the day stage the next afternoon, Spillane and I met some new festival friends, one white and three black lesbians, the latter of whom were an engineer, a firefighter, and a naval officer. I learned that only two of them had known each other before the festival. They were fit, fine—like brown sugar that wouldn't melt—in a word, cute. The engineer mentioned the cost of traveling to the festival: "Michigan is expensive. Every year you spend a couple hundred bucks on the ticket . . . then about eight hundred dollars to get here and be comfortable." The naval officer from Virginia asked if I were a "porcelain girl." She continued, "I just mean, do you like to camp? You either like to camp or you don't." Her question about my camping affinities—one that left no room for a middle ground—sparked the thought that I had met few, if any, black festigoers, or musicians for that matter, who identified as bisexual. Sure, a good portion of women had been attached to men at some point in their lives—their children were testimony to that—but no one intimated that such women were bisexual rather than lesbian.[21] The naval officer continued, "You either are the type who brings your TV and porcelain dishes to Michigan, or you rough it like the rest of us." I thought, "Geez, is there no space in between? I hate to camp, but I don't have any of the fineries advertised in upscale camping magazines." For the naval officer, there was no room for ambivalence. I excused myself.

LANGUAGE MATTERS

I found the PortaJane—but so had two hundred others. Lines moved pretty fast. The festival lexicon as we know it is a legacy of 1970s cultural feminism, when language was used as a tool to raise consciousness.[22] For feminist and lesbian participants in the women-identified music network, for example, the respelling of "women" as "womyn" or "wimmin" (omitting the root "man") was a marker of sexuality as well as of gender. I say "was" because people seem to apply the spellings with a greater sense of irony now. Maybe it's a sign that time is passing.

GENDER FLOW/RACE FLOW

Spillane was pleased with her work-shift assignments. After careful deliberations, she opted for three shifts: one in the kitchen, one that could employ her skills and experience as an antiracism trainer and activist, and one in security. Security detail included various functions, some pragmatic, such as parking, traffic flow management, and tending to emergencies, and others that were more symbolic. Security team personnel helped regulate and monitor the flow of gendered bodies onto the festival grounds, referred to by participants wistfully as "the land."[23] One of their duties was to enforce the festival's policy of admitting women-born women only, the effect of which meant that not only were men (and boys over age eleven) barred from the festival but also those who identified as male-to-female transgenderists.

The plethora of references to "the land," the multicolored dream-catchers on display at the festival marketplace, the burning of herbs, and an "essentialist vision of women's intrinsic connection to the earth," proves, as Philip Deloria observes, that anyone can "play Indian," to which I add, feminist or not.[24] Over the years, Native American festival attendees—not those whose heritage includes black, Scottish, Irish, and Cherokee, but women who identify as Indian 24/7—have worked to raise festival consciousness in regard to their inappropriateness of "Indian play" by non-Indian Americans. Something tells me they need to work harder.

Following our exchange about the Michigan admittance policy, Spillane asked me to share instances of exclusion women of color have experienced. I immediately thought of the Women of Color tent. Founded by Amoja Three Rivers, the Women of Color tent was one of the large networking tents sponsored by the festival.[25] For many years, Three Rivers, Blanche Jackson, and others advocated for a greater voice for black, Latina, Asian American, and Native American women at the music event. Participants describe being drawn to the tent because of the opportunities it provides to meet with other women of color. Moreover, it gives them a physical and discursive space that is separate from the madding crowds of white women. According to the African American women I interviewed, although festivals are generally thought to be lesbian-friendly places of recreation, women of color often experience what one black woman described as "white overload." Black women therefore may seek refuge from whites for a while. It is ironic that the type of white overload that black women and other women of color might experience at women's music festivals may in fact mirror their experiences at their workplaces or, possibly, in their neighborhoods. I made a note to ask someone about this.

Black women related incidents in which the politics of skin color were played out in the Women of Color tent a few years earlier. The ethnic/political allegiance of lighter-skinned women was questioned by women of darker hues. "That's deep," Spillane said. Next, I told her about an incident I had observed firsthand: an evidently white mother stood near the open-sided Women of Color tent, providing visual supervision for her mixed-heritage (biracial) daughter, who was participating in a drumming workshop for women of color. It did not take a mother to realize the poignancy of the moment. "Wow, this race s——t is f——d up," Spillane said. "I know," I replied, "I know."

WHITE LOOKS

Spillane learned that over the years, many white women have yearned for their own space at the festival, similar to that occupied by the Women of Color tent. "But the whole festival is white!" I said. In response, the White Women's Patio was accepted as a programmed event at the festival.[26] The Patio itself consisted of several chairs in a designated area of grass and dirt several hundred feet from the Women of Color tent. That year, the Patio sponsored antiracism workshops, in which activists worked with women on feelings of entitlement that inspired them—ironically, given the ratio of whites to nonwhites at the event—to yearn for a white-identified space comparable to that of the Women of Color tent. The Patio staff also worked as patrollers, encouraging traffic flow around the Women of Color tent, as visual surveillance by white curiosity seekers was frequently reported by those inside. Having experienced this type of visual surveillance at the festival as well as in public venues off-land, I remarked to Spillane that things were "better this year in part, because of the Patio's efforts." We laughed over the event's appellation and were smug in our recognition that Patio participants would be credited for their efforts in diverting the hard and steady gazes of white festival attendees from the Women of Color tent.

TO BE REAL

It surprised me that there were not more women of color at the Women of Color tent when I went there to hang out in the afternoons. On the positive side, fewer women at the tent gave me more time to spend with each person who was willing to fill out my survey. The questionnaire was my way of getting to know people so that we could talk more in depth at a later time. Most everyone, it seemed, assumed I was lesbian. In the festival environment, white women gave me a metaphorical lesbian pass; if black women didn't extend to me the same benefit of the doubt, they never let on.

APPROPRIATING AFRICA

Toward the end of the third day, it seemed as though I had walked for miles. In the late afternoon, I rested near the area reserved for stacks of watermelons. That simple gesture struck me also as historical, and I was awash in self-consciousness. Momentarily, I observed a trio of black festigoers begin to play a *shekere,* cowbell, and calabash—instruments often considered to be African—in interlocking patterns. Clearly, they were enjoying the interaction. Soon afterward, two white women playing African instruments joined them, and before long, many more white women joined the informal jam session. Some time passed, and eventually the three black women left the group. The next day, in the Women of Color tent, I overheard one of them talking about how the white women always take over. Another woman voiced a version of this sentiment in expressing her regret about missing a drumming workshop with Ubaka Hill, ostensibly, she suggested, because of its enormous popularity with white festival participants. Her question, "How come the white women get Ubaka and we don't?" reverberated in my consciousness throughout the festival. Later I learned that it was precisely the sense of exclusion festigoers described that prompted festival producers and the Women of Color series to schedule drumming workshops for women of color only. The incident revealed that group lessons with Ubaka Hill, a musician whom many festigoers, black and white, considered a drumming goddess, was also one of our civil rights.

GETTING READY FOR THE CONCERT

After dinner we dashed to the tent for a quick nap before the evening's show. Spillane was lying on her Snugpak mummy sleeping bag, a bag that supposedly could withstand temperatures of five degrees Fahrenheit. (My ultralight bag didn't have a name; I got it on sale at a local discounter.) Lying on her back, Spillane was absorbed in the festival program booklet, already so wrinkled it looked as though it wouldn't last the week. "Anybody black playing tonight?" I asked. Spillane shook her head. "You know they save the best 'til last," she said. What she meant was that the veteran black musicians would perform later in the week. I looked for a clean pair of socks; Spillane kept reading. Every once in a while, we broke the silence and talked about how we had slayed the dragon and survived for another day. To hear us tell it, you would have thought we had climbed Mount Everest. When we awoke ninety minutes later, we were almost late. Grabbing our blankets, insect repellant, and folding chairs, Spillane wondered whether she should go with the lavender or pink jacket. "Choose one," I said, and off we went to enjoy an evening of music and comedy with six thousand others.

LIGHTS OUT

We returned to the campsite on foot rather than wait in line for a truck. As we stuffed ourselves into our sleeping bags, Spillane reflected on our experiences leading up to our arrival. "I hope I meet somebody," Spillane said. "You'll always have me, just in case you don't," I replied. She continued, as though my words did not register. "Remember that diner we went to?" I nodded affirmatively, but really, I was dead tired. "You gotta admit they [the women in the diner] looked a lot like Bessie Smith," she said, referring to a narrative, frequently circulated in women-identified music spheres (by white women), about the popular black vaudeville blues singer and reports of her lesbian (but, significantly, not bisexual) identity. I was too exhausted to explore racialized elements of thought and feeling, identity politics and music. I squeezed her hand, said that we would "process" the issue in the morning, and rolled over.

Unpacking My Bags at This Location

To a certain extent, this book engages in the very project of processing that I promised Spillane we would get to the next morning—though what I aim to theorize is a much wider range of issues that emanate from black women's participation in the women's music festival scene. The diary is singular in the women's music festival literature in that it privileges the perspective of a black festigoer as opposed to that of a musician or white festival attendee. In fact, this book's underlying theme derives from an understanding I gleaned from black festigoers in the early years of my research: according to some black women I interviewed—a triangle that was half black, indicating black racial identity, and half lavender, indexing lesbian collectivity—was symbolic of their identities as black lesbians. Lisa Powell, an attorney and black activist I met at the now-defunct West Coast Women's Music and Comedy Festival (California), was one of the first festigoers to voice this formulation aloud. Powell shared her plans to reinvigorate with music a weekend retreat for the group she cofounded in 1990, United Lesbians of African Heritage (ULOAH).[27] Speaking of "sisters [black women] who don't pass" but who have not "assimilated into lesbian culture," Powell said, "I have to encourage them to like black *and* lavender."

Black women said that the colors of black and lavender spoke to black women's experiences "more loudly" than did those of the rainbow flag, the multicolored banner designed by Gilbert Baker in 1978 and adopted as the symbol of the gay and lesbian nation.[28] A critique of the queer nation's discourses of inclusion—and the skills in semiotics necessary to read the indicators of citizenship—emerges from my interviews. The firefighter I interviewed at the MWMF put it this way: "How come there is no black in the rainbow flag?" This statement alone was worth the price of the ticket. Who knows whether she had taken courses in African American history as part of her college degree? Indeed, I do not know that she had a degree, but in her critique, levied as a question, there were echoes of Fannie Lou Hamer's speech before the Credential Committee of the 1964 Democratic Convention held in Atlantic City, New Jersey. The civil rights leader and former sharecropper is remembered for her powerful entreaty that the Mississippi delegation seating be opened to include blacks. Hamer's address, punctuated with the phrase "I question America," was a scathing indictment of the failures of participatory democracy.[29] As black political philosopher Joy James observes, African American attachments to historical figures such as Hamer and Emma Lou Baker have deep political and emotional resonance and rootedness.[30] I heard the firefighter say all of that.

In the chapters that follow, I attempt to unpack my interactions with women at festivals I attended and interpret them alongside interviews and other research that I conducted over a number of years.[31] In its tendency to eschew conventional distinctions between musicians and consumers, this book contributes to discussions carried on by those who are fascinated by the complete range of black women's "musicking," a term coined by ethnomusicologist Christopher Small to refer to everything and everybody in the music environment.[32] In light of that understanding, now commonplace in ethnomusicology, I draw attention to the aesthetics of women's music and intervene in the politics of representation of those same systems. While this book might knock on the door of leisure studies, I do not hold out hope for that, outside of the literature on tourism. By and large, studies of African American leisure attempt to correlate and quantify risk factors, such as heart disease, with certain leisure activities, such as bass fishing.[33] The women whose participation facilitated the completion of this book experience a different type of risk.

One of the goals of this book is to connect the black pathways in women's music to larger processes of African American life in terms of music and community membership. In shedding light on salient issues, I take the discursive liberty of making festivals the center of a much larger world. Throughout this book, I refer to women's music festival sites as *metropoles*—a redeployment of a term some postcolonial scholars use as a gloss for the urban centers to which they migrate from their native countries.[34] I also borrow from U.S. voter theory when I propose that gay and lesbian cultural geographies and examinations of African American musical soundscapes be redistricted so as to inspire greater representation of black gay and lesbian cultural and social life. Both black music studies and gay and lesbian studies can benefit from a centripetal force of such magnitude that previously marginalized or spectacularized voices are catapulted to the epicenter of theory and analysis. This effort entails decentering not just whiteness but also received ways of thinking about women's music culture, the workings of race, and, as numerous observers contend, notions of citizenship in overlapping and competing communities.[35]

To many living in predominantly Latino or African American communities, the suggestion of redistricting is tantamount to the issuance of fighting words. I draw on the notion of "fighting words" articulated by both philosopher Judith Butler and sociologist Patricia Hill Collins as the conceptual bridge to ameliorate two manifestations of a neglect in scholarship.[36] The neglect of black gay and lesbian life in all aspects of scholarship outside of literature and film is paralleled by the omission of black women, and women's music in particular, from the history and discourse of black cultural production, including music. The music scene that is the focus of this book is a reminder that not all facets of African American musical life can be neatly accommodated through a historical lens or through examinations organized around notions of stylistic development. The latter is evident in curricula that suggest that the blues evolved into polyphonic New Orleans–style jazz, which transitioned into the big band sound, which morphed into bebop. The latter mode of analysis might make for efficient pedagogy, but it actually sheds less light on the persistence of musical styles over different time periods and music making that falls outside of contexts typically investigated by scholars. The privileging of stylistic development tends to elide musical influences from unanticipated sources, and it places certain types of musical hybridity outside the master narrative of black music. These modes of analyses also render the music making of black women invisible, wherein their experience of gender is treated as an afterthought.

While it is true that the music of the vaudeville blueswomen of the 1920s gave voice to a sexual politics that reflected and influenced the lived experience of working-class black women at the time, it would be wrong to assume that the musicians of this study are the "daughters," or, to carry the metaphor of the family further, the "granddaughters," of those earlier musicians. Although inspiring and useful in building broad arguments, assumptions of the latter are reductive and belie the numerous influences and differences that distinguish the context for the emergence of classic blues in the 1920s from that of women's music in the 1970s.[37] Moreover, metaphors associated with the family prove inadequate for unraveling the threads that contribute to black women's subordination.[38] An overemphasis of lines of continuity between the sexual identity politics of the vaudeville blueswomen and the musicians of this study fails to shed light on the specificity of factors, musical and political, that account for the presence of black women collectively in women's music.

The redistricting I offer in the presentation of this book has been influenced by postcolonial, African American, and white scholars whose challenges to received epistemological frameworks have enabled many to imagine new vistas in theory and retool old ones. Taking an investigatory road less traveled would mean that the Michigan Womyn's Music Festival would be decentered in analyses of women's music culture. To discuss the Michigan festival as though it is representative of all women's music (lesbian-identified) festivals underestimates the significance of those that are regionally based and attract women from more localized geographical areas. A focus on the Michigan festival to the exclusion of others deflects attention from sites of all-black women's lesbian festivals, or all-Chicana women's music events, or other women's music festivals geared toward different constituencies of lesbian-identified women. As critics have said for more than three decades, there is no unitary and homogeneous lesbian culture. Even if women's music festival purists insisted that newer festivals (such as those that started in 1995 or later, for instance) needed to demonstrate a political or cultural connection to the other festivals before they would be officially considered part of the network, reinscribing a smaller, rather than broader, palette of lesbian festivals would serve the "women's community," if this term has valence anymore, in ways that run counter to its own goal of inclusivity.

This book is organized by theme rather than by chronology or festival location. Perhaps sociologist Howard Becker says it best: "The ideas within are not a seamless web of logically connected propositions . . . but they are an organic whole."[39] Indeed, the book's organization underscores that this is not a study of women's music but, as Clifford Geertz might have reminded us, is one that has been done *in* that context.[40] The next chapter, under the guise of "reconnaissance," offers a discussion of my research methods and approaches, as well as a look at how women's music and black women's participation in it figures as a vanished subject. I take care to distinguish the festivals of this book from some other women-centered events in popular culture because of my belief that greater rather than less orientation is necessary for the general reader—especially those who are familiar with the logics of black feminisms that have, in the public sphere, been commodified, mainstreamed, or de-radicalized, as argued by Joy James.[41]

The third chapter offers a way of thinking about black women's involvement in women's music in the aftermath of the passing of the golden age. I propose an approach to understanding differences between an early generation of musicians and audience members and more recent arrivals to the scene. In a section that might otherwise have been titled "How I Got Over," first-generation musicians share their assessments of the women's music ideal in both sonic and political terms. Headliners critique and participate in the circulation of nostalgia as they address the musical underneath or musical aspects of a white cultural feminism. The fourth chapter maintains this focus on perspective but shifts to consider the "nappy roots" of women's music—that is, an American music discourse that is richly imbricated by uneven exchanges between black and white musical cultures and rich, intertwining, and contested feminist legacies. This chapter's exploration is predicated upon multiple streams of musical and political influence. The point is that numerous musical traditions have mattered to black women in women's music—from soul, pop, and funk of the sort that Spillane and I listened to in the car on the way to Michigan—to the African-influenced drumming of artists like Ubaka Hill, the urban folk-infused music of an artist like Tracy Chapman, and the fusion of many of these traditions in the performances of Sweet Honey in the Rock. The chapter concludes with the "coming out" stories of several musicians of the first generation describing how, through involvement in various social and musical networks, they became involved in women's music. This section reveals and is revealing of how these overlapping histories at the local and national levels are entangled with their own lives and musical careers.

Far from being a project of the past, activism in the women's music scene is emphatically a large part of what continues to draw women to festivals and to make their participation as festigoers and musicians meaningful. The outcome of these efforts, however, reveals ambivalences and disjunctures. The fifth chapter considers both the ideals and idealism that continues to animate the women's music scene—utopian ideals of community of the sort expressed in the very creation of a "city on a hill" like the Michigan festival. Some of the fissures in the women's music community that persist despite (and in some cases because of) these ideals are present as well. I devote particular attention in this chapter to attempts to promote multiculturalism at women's music festivals and how they fall short or fail, as well as to how black women have responded to the open invitation of festival organizers to join them—meaning white lesbians—often in the woods.

In chapter six, I dream of a world—an all-black lesbian world, that is—and explore ramifications of dreams that actually come true. The focus of this chapter is twofold: a music festival for queer women of color and an all-black lesbian retreat. Themes include relationships between different political generations of black lesbians and the familiar trope of returning home. The reconstitution of the feminist project in a changed social and political context reverberates in the last three chapters of this study, the first two of which take up issues of identity politics, feminist activism, and the future of women's music festivals through interviews with two groups of women who are largely invisible in the Michigan diary: a younger cohort of musicians and festival organizers. Chapter 7 weaves a set of interviews with a "next" generation of black women musicians in which they address how they came into the women's music scene; their relationship to an earlier political and musical generation; and their understandings of feminism, queer identities, blackness, and music. Chapter 8 uses interviews with women to reveal their roles in supporting festival production, whether as board members, volunteers, or festival "workers."

Chapter 9, finally, considers the phenomenon of "drag kinging" (the staged performance of masculinity) and the decades-long controversy over the Michigan festival's exclusion of male-to-female transgenders on the grounds that they are not "womyn-born womyn." Here, I interrogate the central role that the Michigan festival played in the community's definition of the boundaries of membership, with special attention to black women musicians' and festigoers' views on these subjects. The events recorded in the diary make clear that sexual identity is often at least seemingly on display at the Michigan Womyn's Music Festival, with butch- and femme-identified lesbians performing and searching for visible cues of sexual identities, as Spillane and I anticipated with our "Bunnie" and "Lambert" personas, and as Spillane reinforced with her statement about the "dykes going to Michigan." It is worth asking how such understandings map onto drag king performances, which make the performance of masculinity (by women) a spectacle to be enjoyed by festigoers (almost always women, usually lesbians, and often self-identified feminists), as well as onto the controversy over Michigan's now-relaxed admittance policy, which denied the rights of festival citizenship to male-to-female transgenders.

The book concludes with some final reflections on the contours of the study and a few words about areas for future research. Although true appendixes are typically held to be tangential to books of this type, the list of artists that appears in the section titled "Dreamgirls" will be of particular interest to those who are intimately familiar with this music scene. While the hopes of some women's music festival culture veterans might be thwarted by the lack of pictorial references, I would offer that the latter can be accessed via musicians' Web sites. For decades, women's music festivals discouraged the taking of photographs or video at festival events, a directive that bears on the researcher's ability to offer visual (and aural) ephemera that attest to being there. Even so, visual images are not transparent vehicles of representation. Given that this book does not address musicians' roles in producing such images, I thought it best not to ignore the rhetorical ambivalence that pervades black women's relationship to visual culture or to reinscribe its practice, however well-intentioned.[42]

Songs in Black and Lavender reveals women's music festivals as sites of black women's musicking and theorizing about gender, race, sexual identity, and other issues that fall broadly under the rubric of politics with a small *p*. If this book exhibits a multiple address, it is because it is directed to a readership comprised of different, and sometimes overlapping, factions of interest. It is now a widely adopted convention for authors to assert as much. While I do not wish for otherwise, I admit to having a more specific audience in mind as well. I write thinking of a young black man in my life, college age, who maintains that he is "homo-tolerant, but not homo-friendly." I think of young adult women of all backgrounds, who, in contrast to the ways their collective political consciousness is represented in the media, seek a way in—to feminism, lesbian cultures, activism on their own behalf, and, yes, perhaps, to guitar lessons. A black Marxist scholar friend of mine insists that there is no place for examination of gay and lesbian cultures in African American studies. As scholar Charles Nero points out, gay neighborhoods are still white, and, I add, it is worth inquiring what kinds of political distresses are reflected in segregations of all types.[43] I believe that there is hope for the hopelessly straight kin among us to grasp the significance of the issues discussed herein and to go forward in the quest for justice. These potential readers, known and unbeknownst by me, are members of the families I choose, and I write with them in mind.[44]

Recalling the vignette sketched in the diary entry, the hand-sewn flag peeks out from behind a cabinet in my office. This flag is symbolic of a special journey—one that has been traveled by more "brave" women than I can acknowledge here.[45] This book builds on early touchstones in the continuum of influences along my path of intellectual and activist engagement with this topic. My intent is not to contribute to an African American cultural analysis that is overdetermined by an emphasis on black women's activism and resistance, even if it is through music. All too often, black women's "racial awareness," as scholar Paula Stewart Brush calls it, is represented as though, like Topsy, it also "jes' grew."[46] In the complex field of politics, resistance is by no means always subversive of power, and so in all of these matters a more nuanced approach is warranted.

A productive way to think about women's music is through the lenses of containment and possibility. The improbability of black women "coming to voice" through women's music is as sobering as the potential for doing so is inspiring.[47] Through music performance, consumption, and their involvement in women's music festivals, predominantly black lesbian musicians and music consumers enact their affinities with both lesbian (lavender) and African American (black) communities. Over the years, African American women identifying in various ways have performed at or attended women's music festivals. This book argues that their collective experience in those venues represents a significant moment in the history of African American thought.

If you are thinking about going skydiving you should know some things about the sport. The first being what the risk is. Speaking statistically, parachuting is a very safe sport.
—WWW.SKYDIVING-PARACHUTING-GUIDE.COM

CHAPTER 2

Reconnaissance

ENTERING A MUSIC FESTIVAL SCENE

Parachuting In

Songs in Black and Lavender unites interview-based research with multisited ethnography carried out at eight different women's music festivals held during the summers of 1992–1995 and 2003–2005. I attended the Michigan Womyn's Music Festival, the Gulf Coast Womyn's Festival (Ovett, Mississippi), the National Women's Music Festival (Bloomington, Indiana, and Muncie, Indiana), the Northampton Lesbian Festival (Northampton, Massachusetts), the West Coast Women's Music and Comedy Festival (Yosemite National Park, California), Wiminfest (Albuquerque, New Mexico), Sistahfest (Malibu, California), and Serafemme: Women of Color Music Festival (Los Angeles, California).[1] I conducted open-ended interviews with more than thirty black women musicians and festival attendees and had informal conversations with many more women of all backgrounds.[2] This study is shaped not only by my own interests as an ethnomusicologist but also by the location of black women in women's music, and by the latter in scholarly discourses and in popular culture. This chapter effects a theoretical and practical exploration of these contexts, leading the reader through the reconnaissance necessary for understanding and interpreting the chapters that follow.

My own interest in women's music festivals is less as a site of women's music making to be recovered (although this, too, is important) than as an underexamined site of black women's production of critical social theory. Like many other researchers, I teased out some of these formulations through conversations with participants. While interview-based research may exhibit some similarities to oral history, these modes are not in every way congruent. Moreover, early on, I experienced confusion myself about the mode of inquiry that would figure more prominently in the book. As I made the rounds of festivals, the question put to me frequently by festigoers was "What are you finding out?" Given my orientation to the research, I was less able to relate to this question than I might have been had I been engaged in a study that was more quantitative in nature or focused on normative ethnographic description. It was not that I was not taking in new experiences and learning new information; rather, it was that the underlying assumptions about knowledge creation that the question represented contrasted with my own view that knowledge is dynamic, collaborative, and emergent.

This study departs from traditional anthropological accounts in which the ethnographer lives in the community he or she studies over a period of many months or, sometimes, years. Scholars continue to engage music cultures in this manner, but the thinking about such research since the golden age of the classic ethnography has changed considerably.[3] Departing from models of older ethnographies that focus on the culture of a specific geographical region, this book exhibits commonalities with the work of other scholars, such as sociologists Andy Bennett and Richard Peterson, whose research encompasses "widely scattered local scenes drawn into regular communication around a distinctive form of music and lifestyle." Bennett and Peterson describe this type of phenomenon as a music scene and designate it further as one that is translocal: "While [music festivals] are local, they are also connected with groups of kindred spirits many miles away." A distinguishing feature of this book is that it is informed by my participation at "festivals . . . that periodically bring together scene devotees from far and wide in one place, where they can enjoy their kind of music and *briefly live the lifestyle associated with it with little concern for the expectations of others*."[4] This definition of "music scene" is significant in that it closely reflects the understandings of festival attendees regarding the phenomenon of women's music.

A number of consequences follow from conducting research into a music scene as opposed to a centralized locale. In contrast to those working in more localized communities, establishing rapport as one conducts interviews in a translocal network requires a different set of criteria for evaluation and possibly a different range of interpersonal skills. Whereas it is possible for one to establish situational rapport with an individual over a period of two or three hours, this contextual social bonding does not necessarily make the researcher and interviewee friends or mean that interviewees will recognize the interviewer not in situ two years later. In other words, working on a translocal network seems to ensure that researchers and interviewees will be "professional strangers" even more so than usual.[5] Research into a music scene characterized by a star system, albeit on a smaller scale, means also that while I have met the musicians interviewed for this book at women's music festivals, our conversations were often held over the phone, since their festival schedules could not accommodate an interview on-site.

Over a period of many years, I have had to balance my own research interests with a sensitivity for the situatedness of musicians who are prominent within a relatively narrow sphere. It was necessary for me to comply with musicians' requests for confidentiality and not act in ways that might diminish their standing in the women's music community. As one veteran musician put it, "Don't mess with my mystique." She was joking—I think. Following one researcher's admonition to feminist interviewers, however, I tried not "to elicit a repertoire of attention-getting monologic narratives, especially narratives that originated in previous communication contexts and are well-polished from repeated rehearsals."[6] This proves to be a tall order, especially in contexts in which musicians have managers and evoke their own representational strategies in carrying out their public relations agendas.

Several of the musicians or festival organizers I spoke with requested anonymity; in these cases, the interactions between the interviewee and me involved a certain level of trust. The nature and depth of this trust is difficult to quantify. Over the past thirty years, scholars have written extensively about the positionalities of researchers and subjects and their relationship, especially in regard to the overdetermined notion of working in one's own culture, or what John Gwaltney referred to as native anthropology.[7] Anthropologist Mitchell Duneier puts it this way: "Fieldwork is presumed to require trust. But one never can know for certain that he or she has gained such trust, given the absence of any agreed upon indicator of what 'full' trust would look like. In this case, I think, some level of trust was shown by people's readiness to provide access to information, settings, and activities of the most intimate sort."[8] Although I would like to think that I succeeded in establishing rapport with the women I interviewed, it is wise that I not overestimate that success.

While the importance of reciprocity between researcher and interviewee is emphasized, if not idealized, in some social science literatures, I admit to being given arguably more than I gave; busy interviewees shared generously their time and hospitality. Adhering to an ethical research practice meant neither discussing details of musicians' private lives (including love interests) with festigoers nor taking sides in disagreements or conflicts conveyed to me by narrators in conversation. Rather, like all researchers, I strove to be a good listener and to remain sympathetic to the narrator's point of view; in other words, through music listening and listening to talk about music, I tried, in Philip Bohlman's words, to "become an ethnomusicologist."[9]

The Black Ethnomusicologist Speaks

It makes sense that as the researcher I would also address my own relationship to this field of study, a phenomenon that was formerly framed in the familiar binaries of insider/outsider.[10] Inspired by social movements within and beyond the academy, anthropologists have critiqued received notions of objectivity in knowledge acquisition and creation since the early 1970s. The move to decolonize the discipline included arguments that the homeward gaze—that is, researching what eventually became glossed as "one's own society"—had significant value.[11] Even so, the model of the scholar showing her cultural membership card at the door, and hence, establishing her ethnographic authority, has been supplanted as scholars have advanced more nuanced positions in terms of these debates.

My own introduction to women's music was similar to those recounted by a sizable number of women of my generation who worked in feminist organizations during the early 1980s. Like many straight women, I took refuge in and thrived in women-only spaces: coffeehouses, women's centers, and women's bookstores. White women with whom I worked in feminist reproductive rights organizations in Philadelphia introduced me to the music of Holly Near, Meg Christian, Cris Williamson, Linda Tillery, and, later, Sweet Honey in the Rock. At the age of twenty-one, I was younger than most of my fellow activists; I sensed that I was catching the tail end of second-wave feminism. Later studies by feminist historians verified that assessment. The goals of radical feminism articulated by black feminists, predominantly lesbian, and other feminists of color slightly before this period resonated with my own commitment to the transformation of society. Given that I lacked skills in organizing (canvassing, leafleting, picketing, marching), several older lesbians (one black and two white) taught me the mechanics of "doing politics."

Before moving to Philadelphia at the age of twenty to continue my degree in music, I had already been greatly influenced by my mother, an advocate for black women's advancement vis-à-vis "racial uplift," and my father, a minister and local civil rights leader born in Alabama. It is to my great benefit that along the way my father had absorbed the lessons of early black Communists based in Alabama in the 1930s and passed those lessons on to me informally at every opportunity.[12] More than anything, growing up in a black activist household made me aware of what African American anthropologist Faye Harrison calls the "multiple subaltern statuses and bases of Otherness, combined with the apparent irreconcilability between them and the ideals and normative expectations of 'the free world.'"[13]

As a graduate student in ethnomusicology, I returned, in terms of music listening on my own time, to the music I had listened to during my early years of feminist activism. I spent hours listening to "Song of the Exiled" by Alice Partnoy, a Latina poet who at one time was disappeared for months within her native country of Argentina. Partnoy read "Song of the Exiled" at an early Sisterfire (1985), an ambitious but short-lived multicultural music festival showcasing women performers. I remembered it well, as they say, although I was not there. Innumerable times, I fast-forwarded *Sisterfire,* a recorded compilation of diverse performances, to Partnoy's recitation as it segued to Sweet Honey in the Rock's "Chile/Biko/Venceremos," which became the object of my listening desire.

In the advent of queer musicology, scholars have explored the valences of listening to music from gay or lesbian subject positions. According to that logic, what does it mean that early albums by women's music artists affected me deeply and yet I was the Other to the lesbian norm of women's music consumers? Was there, as feminist musicologist Suzanne Cusick puts it, a "bleed-through" of a lesbian listening sensibility?[14] This might suggest that oppositional hearings of music in terms of gender and sexuality can be explained only through the listening subject's avowal of lesbian identity. I offer the years I listened most avidly to recordings of Sweet Honey in the Rock as a counterargument. How can I explain those times when performances of that ensemble spoke to me as a woman-identified, political lesbian in a way they did not to my black woman friends who exhibited more mainstream and straight sensibilities? Occupying similar subject positions in terms of race, gender, and sexual identity, we each responded to an idea of feminism, yet we heard the music and responded to one of the communities with which it was associated differently. The questions I raise are a strong reminder that it is increasingly difficult to posit one-to-one correspondences between the labels we use to describe our subject positions and the meaning we derive from our musical encounters.

Flygirl Demographics; or, Race and the Habits of Bird-Watchers

Musicians and festigoers are not the only ones steeped in the expressive practices of talk and verbal art; social theorists, for example, frequently use metaphors to show "how a set of relations that seems evident in one sphere might illuminate thinking and action in other spheres."[15] This section uses metaphors—and quite a number of them—to help theorize the involvement of black women in women's music. Thinking through political theory via the use of metaphor has been useful as scholars have come to replace facile understandings of coming to voice with the more complicated reality of its limits.

"Flygirls in the buttermilk" is the first of these tropes; this is followed by demographics of the same, bird-watching, black-specked birds, and lastly, jelly beans. Would that I could take credit for all of them, but I can not: only one is my own, another is borrowed, while still another I stole from a relative. "Flygirls in the buttermilk" is a regendered riff on the title of Greg Tate's compilation of essays on race, politics, literature, and music.[16] The parameters of my romantic imagination were assuaged to think that in deploying the title, Tate unearthed a gem that writer James Baldwin cast more than three decades earlier as "a fly in the buttermilk."[17] Baldwin's essay concerned the experiences of his black school-age friend as he integrated an all-white grammar school in the American South; in this section, I use the term "flygirls in the buttermilk" as a metaphoric lens through which to examine the location of black women in an arena in which they are outnumbered by whites.

The narratives of women I interviewed confirmed my own experience on the women's music festival circuit—that is, it is possible for a black woman festigoer to be one of only two or, at the most, three women of color at a women's music festival. (This observation applies to the smaller festivals of thirty to fifty attendees. Although a larger festival such as Michigan will have more women of color, the percentage of African American women may be even less—at two percent.) The experience of being "the only one," meaning the only black or the only fill-in-the-blank minority, pertains not only to workplace environments, as numerous scholars have illuminated, but to vacation destinations as well.

Ebbs and flows in participation are to be expected in networks of many types; scholars write at length about black women's participation patterns in organizations predominated by white women.[18] Women's music festivals are no exception. African American women, however, are not the only ones whose attendance of festivals may wax and wane over the years. At the individual level, white women and others may also find that whereas at one point in their lives or political life cycles festivals were the mainstay of their vacations, they now make other choices. For many women who are now middle-aged and older, involvement with women's music coincided with the wide-eyed optimism of their young adulthood and the heady days of the women's movement. With the passage of time, some have opted to shift their attention away from these events. A consideration, therefore, of what I am calling "flygirl demographics" is critical for an understanding of both the turnover and continued presence of black women in women's music festival culture.

Speaking of flygirl demographics, one day in July 2000 I was reflecting on my research with my closest aunt. We were seated at her kitchen table, just the two of us. I related that while I attend numerous women's music festivals, it is always the case that, in spite of the presence of one or two acts comprised of African American musicians, the number of black women attending these festivals is "abysmally low." "Even," I said, "in the case of a large festival such as Michigan, which, in its twentieth-anniversary year, boasted an attendance of ten thousand. Two hundred were said to have been women of color (Asian American, Latino, African American, Native American). Half of them were black."[19] My aunt glanced up from her coffee mug, looking at me thoughtfully. "That's not bad, honey," she said. "If I could get one hundred black women to come to our meetings at church, I would be thrilled." "But it's not as though all the colored girls gather together for dinner or something," I said. "We're spread out over 650 acres—each woman has her own tent, or maybe she shares with her friends or her partner. Then, when you see somebody you'd like to interview, she is either in the chow line, rushing to a drumming workshop, working security, or naked. It's all so humiliating." "Well, don't give up," she said. "It sounds like you're bird-watching."

The conversation with my aunt crystallizes some features of a reception study that in retrospect now seems rather strange. Since my focus was, in part, black women's experiences of racial identity in women's music, for me to be on the lookout for racially marked bodies was at odds with now-commonplace thinking of race as a social construct. During my off time, I resist essentializing people in precisely this way. The only thing that separated my approach from that of a tourist, or a bird-watcher, perhaps, was that I did not carry a pair of binoculars. Whereas I had identified lesbian music festivals as a popular vacation destination for many women, in fact I was the one who had adopted the "tourist gaze" in the sense that the phrase is used by John Urry.[20] Scholar Jane Desmond illuminates these processes to vivid effect: "Although this looking varies somewhat in different historical periods, it is always performed in contradistinction to everyday looking—it looks at 'difference,' differently. As Jonathan Culler notes, the 'tourist is interested in everything as a sign of itself.'"[21]

Whereas Desmond devotes part of her book to an examination of animal tourism, my attempts at identifying and meeting (with some modicum of grace) black women attendees of women's music festivals seemed to exact from me as the researcher a range of bird-watching behaviors: "First, I study migratory patterns of the 'black-specked bird' (as I soon came to think of the women for whom I searched), a rare and precious find; second, I wait in relaxed fashion for the species to appear; third, I identify the species (Does she look like a first-timer, or does she exude an air of someone who will know what she is talking about?); fourth, I identify her location (Is she nearby? Will she be there by the time I return from the PortaJanes?); fifth, I prepare for approach."

This bird-watching vignette exhibits an underlying tension about the engagement of black women's studies. African American feminists in the humanities and social sciences have noted that these are vexing times in which to conduct studies of "the black woman object." On the one hand, black women are a cultural phenomenon, a "hot commodity," as critic Ann duCille writes.[22] On the other hand, as she observes, this popularity has a double edge: "I am alternately pleased, puzzled, and perturbed—bewitched, bothered, and bewildered—by this, by the alterity that is perpetually thrust upon African American women, by the production of black women as infinitely deconstructable 'othered' matter. Why are black women always-already Other? . . . To myself, of course, I am not Other; to me it is the white women and men so intent on theorizing my difference who are the Other. Why are they so interested in me and people who look like me (metaphorically speaking)?"[23]

DuCille's observations apply to African American women in the social field of research, whether or not they consider themselves subjects for study. The truth of this assertion became all too clear to me during the preparation of this book. Occasionally during the course of a festival, a young, white, middle-class female graduate student stopped to ask if, "as a black woman," I would be willing to participate in a survey or interview about women's music. Sometimes these requests were accompanied by statements that discounted or underestimated my agency as a feminist or women's activist. What was the expected response? Should I have said, "Wait for my book," or, in feminist solidarity, should I have shared my thoughts freely, offering to review the research designs of strangers? Should I have pretended to be unknowing or new to the scene? My experience illustrates anthropologist Terence Turner's observation that researchers who share overlapping experiences or statuses with their subjects often become part of the process one is trying to record.[24] Other researchers have addressed instances of misrecognition that they have experienced during the course of their fieldwork, though in a different vein. Conducting research among the BaAka in the Central African Republic, white ethnomusicologist Michelle Kisliuk recalls being confused for a nurse at the site of a village dancing ritual. Anthropologist Maureen Mahon, author of a compelling study about the Black Rock Coalition, writes of her frequent misidentification by male musicians as the girlfriend of one of the coalition members.[25] These examples demonstrate that misrecognitions of various types take place in multiple contexts, feminist and otherwise. Still, it is odd to be a black-specked bird.

Returning to looking at "difference" differently, I have drawn attention to the quandaries of the researcher on the lookout for persons of a particular background—in this case, black women. This apparent collapse of culture into race and onto bodies masks an important issue: This book accepts the heterogeneity of black women's individual experiences, musical and social. At the same time, it contributes to studies that contemplate black difference in a context in which the intransigence of African American collective identity rules. These two presuppositions might initially seem contradictory or come as a surprise to those who have grown accustomed to postmodern suggestions of the fluidity of gender and sexual identities. These fluidities have not been extended to operations of racial statuses, in large part because race is held, in many ways, to be foundational and therefore intractable. This distinction is of particular value to those whose research entails coming to terms with the workings of minoritized genders and sexualities in communities of color.

Modes of analyses that privilege the contingent nature of identities fall short as social theories and therefore fail to explain the continued workings of black women's location as a group, within a hierarchical field of power relations.[26] Groups, Patricia Collins says, become defined largely by their placement within historically specific power relations, not from choices exercised by individual group members concerning issues of identity and belonging.[27] Achieving social justice means attending to the relationships between groups. To illustrate black women's distinctive history in relation to that of other groups, Collins paints a picture of the "black jelly beans in the bottom of the jar." The challenge for African American women, she says, is "constructing notions of a Black female collectivity that remain sensitive to Black women's placement in distinctively American hierarchal power relations, while simultaneously resisting replication of these same relations within the group's own ranks."[28]

Taking the metaphor a step further, I am interested in the various hues of the black jelly beans in the jar—in other words, black women musicians and diversity within perceived sameness. While this book theorizes black women's involvement in women's music, I do not suggest that the music of the performers interviewed comprises a subgenre within this small field. The musicians who figure largely in this study should not and indeed cannot be dismissed as merely black girls with guitars, the inverse of the ubiquitous "white girls with guitars" that also circulates. Blackness alone does not a musical style make; that black musicians exhibit styles that exemplify cultural hybridity is now a commonplace of black music scholarship.

Singer/songwriter Melanie DeMore pursues this line of thinking further. The veteran musician raises the concern that she, Afro-Canadian Faith Nolan, and lower-forty-eight artists Deidre McCalla, Rashida Oji (now Regina Wells), and even Tracy Chapman, might not be seen as unique individuals because the "one thing" they have in common is that they are "African American women who play guitars," electric and acoustic. Therefore, I shared with DeMore my search for an understanding that accommodates the idea of diversity within perceived sameness as discussed by Collins. Noting other black musicians who are active on the women's music circuit, not all of whom play guitar, DeMore said: "We probably have some common experiences being African American lesbian women. . . . So we have all of that, and the fact that we also have to deal with homophobia within our own community. So there are those things. But our approaches and our subject matter is really very different. We may have all sung about the same thing, but it sure doesn't sound like it. So I'm really glad that all those sisters are out there."[29]

DeMore is wise to expand on the diversity represented by these musicians. As social movement theorist Kimberly Springer identifies, women working in black feminist organizations of the 1970s encountered ideological disputes that were rooted in an initial assumption about the homogeneity of the lives of black feminists. Although many of these organizations emphasized race and gender, "black women had their own individual identities based in class, sexual orientation, and color differences."[30] We would do well to remember the lessons of the history that Springer uncovers. As chapter 4 will demonstrate, it was the failure of black women's feminist organizations in the 1970s to address issues of heterogeneity that was partly responsible for their demise.[31]

"Vanished": Women's Music Festivals and Popular Culture

The term *women's music* is confusing in that it invokes flashpoints of associations with previous notions of the "universal woman." The confusion is compounded exponentially by the ways feminism's legacy suffuses popular culture, even as the efficacy of feminist movement is denied or forgotten.[32] This is as true for the lasting contributions of radical black feminist activists working in the late 1960s and early 1980s as it is for mainstream feminists. In order to clarify the focus of this book, I draw attention to two tours of women musicians that black women I met outside of the metropoles of the festivals frequently confused with the women's music festival scene of this book. *Reconnaissance* is an apt word to describe my attempts to distinguish the music festivals of this study from others in popular culture.

The women's music festival scene that is the subject of this book predates by more than twenty years Lilith Fair, the traveling tour founded in 1997 by singer/songwriter Sarah McLachlan. Just one way that Lilith, with concert rosters of all-women performers, differed from the Michigan Womyn's Music Festival is that Lilith's admission policy was inclusive, without regard for the gender or sex of attendees. Although the tour featured black musicians such as folk rocker Tracy Chapman and jazz singer Cassandra Wilson, Lilith, like its precursors in alternative culture, was criticized for its relative lack of cultural diversity.[33]

The predominantly lesbian women's music festivals that inform this study also predate concert tours by black women performers directed toward an African American target market; Verizon's Ladies First Tour and the Sugar Water Festival are two examples. Both of these events drew on updated tropes of the "strong black woman," a mode of presentation that critic Joan Morgan outlines in her discussion of hip-hop feminism.[34] The 2004 Ladies First Tour featured black pop performers Alicia Keys and Beyoncé Knowles, as well as hip-hop artist Missy Elliott. Borrowing its name from Queen Latifah's 1989 single (and the same-titled track from her album *All Hail the Queen*), the evocation of "Ladies First" recalled and paid tribute to the Afrocentric feminist ethos that pervaded the earlier work of Dana Owens (aka Latifah).[35] Described by one blogger as the "quasi–Black Lilith Fair," the Sugar Water Festival (2005 and 2006), which was less a festival than a multistop concert series, featured Latifah, Erykah Badu, and Jill Scott.[36]

I mention these two black women–centered musical events because they borrow a page from a more widely circulated type of black feminism in popular culture. One of the consequences of recognizing black feminisms is that the density of the field makes it difficult to distinguish various strains. Which black feminisms function as "radical?" Which are more market-driven or -inspired? Which have a foundation in or connection to a political movement?[37]

At the same time, it can be argued that since most everyone is an outsider to the women's music scene, and particularly to black women's place in it, it is relatively easy for this realm to be confused with others that, on their surface, seem similar. Indeed, a lingering question remains: Why does the music of these artists receive little airplay, a phenomenon that lends credence to the assertion that women's music boasts some of the world's best musicians you've never heard of? Ironically, the collective repertoire of black performers in women's music reflects a wide range of musical styles, including those that typically fall under the rubric of "black music" (R&B, redeployed spirituals, gospel, blues). Therefore, strictly from a groove perspective, at least some of this music should be attractive to programmers of urban music; lyrics are women-centered and may be socially concerned, yet they do not reflect a lesbian-separatist philosophy. This is as true for tracks that are black-identified as well as those that fall in the interstices of "musical blackness and whiteness," contemporary ideological categories that, as Christopher Waterman writes, have tended to confine the complexities and contradictions of people's lived experience (including their experience of racism). The implication of Waterman's point is that "performers, genres, texts, and practices not consonant with dominant conceptions of racial difference have often been elided from academic, journalistic, and popular representations of American music."[38]

While Waterman's statement speaks to racialized hearings and interpretations of music histories, there is limited radio airplay also of nonnormative musical expressions of gender and sexuality politics. That women's music was founded in lesbian separatism helps explain some, but not all, of the disconnect between a broader black music market and the recordings of performers of this study.

Rhonda Benin, who became a part of the women's music scene in the early 1990s, addresses the fact that even concerts that Linda Tillery and the Cultural Heritage Choir give outside of the festival metropoles still draw predominantly white audiences:

> RB: I feel like blacks don't have the opportunity to know that we exist. I don't know whose fault that is. I'm not sure if African Americans do enough reading, if they have the same access to knowing about their own culture as much as whites. I think a lot of times it has to do with not reading . . . I think that if we'd work at getting the audience, we'd get them in a minute. We've all talked about this.
>
> EH: And you haven't arrived at anything different yet?
>
> RB: No, the majority of our gigs are not in town. I was hired to do flyering for this last concert, did a lot of footwork. I still didn't see enough blacks in the audience. So I think we may have to perform in the black churches.
>
> EH: That sounds good. I'd love it if more blacks were exposed to your music.
>
> RB: As I was putting the flyers on the cars, I was wondering what folks were going to do when they go to this "lesbian event."[39]

This is where the model of Sweet Honey with its African American, gender-inclusive audience base in Washington, DC, is instructive. The bottom line is that although only some of the music performed in women's music settings is overtly politicized in terms of gender and sexuality, its reach into a broader consumer market via recordings, distribution, and broadcasting has been circumscribed. The marginalization of women's music by the mainstream music industry means that in spite of its appeal to women, a very small consumer market has been—and will be—exposed to women-identified music or the ideals of this community outside of women's music festivals. This is especially true in the aftermath of the dissolution of the women's music recording industry.

If it is the case that higher education is the primary site for the articulation of black feminist theory, then the fact that women's music has such a low profile—even in contemporary popular culture and black music studies—is of concern. The extent of the elided knowledge about black women's participation in women's music was brought home to me forcefully when I attended a Feminism and Hip Hop Conference held at the University of Chicago. The roster of speakers and the open call for graduate student papers inspired more than three hundred participants, mostly black women scholars, graduate students, and community activists. Sponsored by the university's Center for Race, Politics, and Culture, participants were encouraged to imagine a hip-hop culture void of sexism, one that could embrace a wide range of representations of black femininities and masculinities.[40] Conference organizer and black political theorist Cathy Cohen asked rhetorically whether hip-hop and feminism were indeed compatible or if they were mutually exclusive. Prominent black cultural critics pointed to hip-hop's situatedness in global capitalism. Speakers questioned the representation of hip-hop as a counterhegemonic enterprise and referenced the limits of hip-hop's liberatory potential.

Although the current period has been described as post-post-feminist, the tone of discussions was not nearly as gloomy or resigned as that pronouncement suggests. Presenters, male and female, refused to capitulate to the misogyny and preoccupation with materialism and violence that characterizes a good deal of hip-hop produced in the United States. Indeed, participants spoke eloquently about the need for African American communities and the music industry to address black (hetero-) sexual politics, real and imagined, as they are mirrored by and reinscribed through hip-hop videos, films, and rap music.

At a time when black women—young black women in particular—are represented or represent themselves as having an ambivalent relationship to feminism, including black feminism, the enthusiasm of those attending was refreshing.[41] Scholars captivated the attention of participants with pyrotechnic displays of high theory; activists spoke to the material conditions of black girls and women "on the ground"; community advocates appealed for collective intervention in the lives of the next generation. A doctoral student urged audience members to bridge the breach between those identified as "black feminist" and others who hold to "womanist" values. Delivered without preacherly overtones, the speaker's admonition was right on time; those who have only a passing acquaintance with African American cultural politics often use the terms interchangeably and without discernment.

Since feminism was the conceptual, if not political, frame of the hip-hop conference, in conversations with attendees I spoke of black women's participation in the women's music scene, an obvious source of data for projects focused on black women and feminism. No one with whom I talked was familiar with this area of musical activity. The reaction of conference attendees was vexing in that this was an audience that presumably was deeply familiar with the feminist literature, including contributions of black feminist thinkers. What had happened so that black experiences in women's music were minimized both in lesbian cultural studies and in studies of African American music? Black musicians who are active on the women's music scene include Grammy award winners, humanitarian award recipients, college professors, workshop leaders, choral conductors, master drummers, full-time musicians, singers, composers, lyricists, bass players, and guitarists. And yet my conversations with attendees of the Feminism and Hip Hop Conference reinforced a perception of which I was always-already aware: black women and women's music have passed under the radar not only of those who are interested in black music, black cultural studies, and African American anthropology, but also of those who are interested in black women's studies.

A complex of factors helps explain the persistent inaudibility of women's music to popular music enthusiasts, the subjugation of black women's experiences in the discourse of women's music, and the almost complete unfamiliarity of African Americans with women's music festivals as sites of the production of black expressive culture. The remainder of this book is devoted to pumping up the volume.

This is another day! Are its eyes blurred with maudlin grief for any wasted past? A thousand thousand failures shall not daunt! Let dust clasp dust, death, death; I am alive!—DON MARQUIS

CHAPTER 3

After the Golden Age

NEGOTIATING PERSPECTIVE

According to both movement founders and scholars, women's music experienced its golden age from the early 1970s to the mid-to-late 1980s, a period that roughly coincides with the heyday of the women's movement, 1969–1984.[1] As liberal feminism became more institutionalized, explicit antifeminism emerged in the late 1970s as a major foundation of the ultraconservative New Right; the election of President Ronald Reagan reflected the influence of that countermovement.[2] The halcyon days of the women's movement gave way to a period of abeyance or suspended activity. Scholars point out that it is possible for members of social movements to feel they are still a part of those movements, even during periods of individual or collective inactivity.

The suggestion of endism implied in this chapter's title is appropriate for a number of reasons. By 1990 one of the early signposts that the women's music movement was in a state of flux was the demise of most of the women's music recording and distribution companies that had sustained the women's music network during the 1970s. Recording companies like Olivia Records (1973–1989); Redwood Records, founded in 1972 by singer and peace activist

Holly Near; and Women's Wax Works, founded by Alix Dobkin, had ceased operation by the late 1980s. During the same period, the number of independent women's music distribution companies, including Women's Revolutions Per Minute, shrank from sixty to only a few, the best known being Ladyslipper and Goldenrod.[3]

Another signpost was that musicians who performed at women's music festivals early in their careers—white rockers Melissa Etheridge and Michelle Shocked, and black neo-folk-rocker Tracy Chapman among them—became mainstream sensations and, to the disappointment of many fans, did not credit the community that gave them their start.[4] In the end, women's music as a lesbian feminist project did not change the mainstream industry as some of its proponents had hoped. Many women, however, were provided with hands-on experience in lighting design, sound engineering, performance, and concert production. Countless more women, mostly lesbians, benefited from the *communitas* and feminist esprit de corps that women's music concerts and, later, festivals inspired.

Given these signs of decline, a question sounds throughout this book with ostinato-like frequency: How can black women's collective musical experience be integrated into an examination of women's music without positioning their participation as supplemental to a narrative in progress, or even tangential to an era that has been memorialized by cultural insiders and scholars alike?[5] It is tricky to suggest that an era is over and at the same time argue not only that its activities are ongoing but that they matter, yet this is the work I carry out here.

Constructs of golden ages are as interesting for what they tell us about the designators of such eras and the modes of discourse through which such pronouncements are made as they are for the periods they characterize. Refuting suggestions that women's music has lost its relevance or that it is dead, veteran musicians and cultural insiders, black and white, have marked the end of an era in particular ways while at the same time continuing to perform at festivals. *Radical Harmonies,* an award-winning film by ethnomusicologist Boden Sandstrom and director Dee Mosbacher, is a highly visible example of the framing of women's music as an era in the past. The film, situated as a retrospective, is described as a history of a movement that paved the way for today's new wave of musicians in rock.[6] It consists of interviews with prominent musicians, festival producers, and heads of the former women's record labels interspersed with performance footage. In part because of its medium, celebratory tone, and rockist frame, Sandstrom and Mosbacher's film will dictate the way women's music is perceived for decades to come. *Radical Harmonies* subsumes the literature on the topic, which to date consists of several dissertations, articles scattered through the literature of various disciplines, this study, and Bonnie Morris's *Eden Built by Eves.* Morris, a women's historian by training, is well known in the festival community as both a performer and a chronicler of women's music festival history. By her own admission, Morris's book is a "soaring tribute" to women's music festivals and not a scholarly examination, a fact that does not detract from its insights. At the same time, it is unfortunate that Morris counterposes her book against an alternative she describes as a "dry scholarship of festival culture."[7] I would have liked to have read her version of the latter, certain that had she eschewed positivist historical description and problematized issues of women's historiography, the final product would have been anything but dry.

That cultural insiders would frame women's music is both strategic and preemptive. Veteran black producer Linda Tillery describes herself as the "queen mother" to women's music. For some, this description constitutes a rhetorical maneuver by which the esteemed musician attempts to deflect the tendency of women fans to consider her a love interest or sex object.[8] For others, the appellation of "queen mother" recalls the term's honorific association in some African cultures. Holly Near, the well-known white peace activist and singer/songwriter, describes the "women's music era" as a phenomenon of the 1970s and 1980s. No matter how the pie of periodicity is sliced, it becomes clear that time has passed and that lesbian feminism and society as a whole has been affected, a phenomenon that recalls the title of Cris Williamson's *Changer and the Changed*.[9] Cultural insiders have been inspired to put their own spin on the history of an alternative industry that was poised to "change women and music forever."[10]

This chapter explores the effects of the passage of time on the women's music scene. Drawing primarily on interviews with "first-generation" black women musicians, I consider how musicians' lives and attitudes have changed over time, their responses to the ethos of cultural feminism, and how we can most appropriately conceptualize the differences in perspective between the scene's first generation of black musicians and more recent arrivals. After analyzing certain common features in how first-generation musicians conceptualize their multifaceted identities as musicians, feminists, black women, and in some cases lesbians, I conclude the chapter with a consideration of strategic silences and the politics of sexual identity disclosure.

Nostalgia and Hope

The focus on endism calls forth the circulation of nostalgia that accompanies the closure of various projects or perceived ends of eras. This structure of feeling pervades not only recent writings about women's music but also classic rhythm and blues.[11] Ironically, champions of periodization in black music studies often decry the end of a genre while acknowledging or participating simultaneously in its perpetuation. What helps interpret this phenomenon is the suggestion that nostalgia is a cultural practice, not a given content. Its forms, meanings, and effects shift with the context, writes Kathleen Stewart, and one's point of view depends on one's position in the present.[12]

Insiders to women's music also participate in this selective reframing of the past, invoking a discourse of nostalgia, referring to "passed torches" or to the vast numbers of (white) "graying heads" at festivals. The ever-increasing numbers of recreational vehicles in a landscape where tents once predominated, as well as comments that "the music isn't the same as it used to be," or "festivals aren't as political as they were in the past," dramatize nostalgia's role as an "essential, narrative, function of language."[13] Musicians in particular prefaced stories of festival history with "back in the day," a phrase that at one point circulated in African American communities almost exclusively but is now ubiquitous. If the comments of my undergraduate students are any indication, there is little cross-generational agreement as to the temporal dimensions of "the day," meaning whether it was decades or months ago.

Phase one of my research, which was comprised of interviews with musicians of the first generation, was characterized by the selective framing of the past I have described. Conversations I had with black festigoers, both during and after phase one, gave voice to the hope for the future incorporation of more black musicians into the women's music fold.[14] A black woman engineer from West Virginia put it aptly, "Ten years from now, we could have a whole slew of artists in the mainstream." As an African American researcher talking with other black women, I interpreted this point of view as a racialized hope for inclusion. Yet, more than ten years have passed since that declaration, and the interlocutor's hope of witnessing an exponential increase in black lesbian artists in the mainstream has not come to pass. The career trajectory of a Tracy Chapman indicates that it may not be possible or even desirable for black woman artists to maintain a presence in both camps, by which I mean the pop music industry and the alternative social space of women's music based in lesbian separatism.

Within women's music festival culture, temporality is marked by the distance from one memorable event (whether pleasant or rancour filled) to the next. Paradoxically, however, black musicians seemed little inclined to revisit the bad "good ole days," preferring to focus on the present. I spoke about this reluctance with Judy Dlugacz, who in 1973 founded the women's music recording company Olivia. Dlugacz referred to the activities of Olivia during the early period as "a great experiment." She elaborated: "We made incredible music and we put it out there. And we cared about each other and wanted it to work, and the truth is, we couldn't really pull it off." As she articulated later, Olivia made "real attempts" to record diverse music and artists of various ethnicities, but "the economics" weren't in their favor. "The reasons are many," Dlugacz said, "but the main one is that there were not very many women of color out of the closet in the mid-seventies, and so while the R&B [Linda Tillery] and jazz records [Mary Watkins] sold well for an independent label (over ten thousand copies), there was not enough to sustain the economics of the record company." Returning to the reluctance of some musicians to talk about past incidents, she elaborated: "Do we want to be disappointed in each other? Do we want to say 'somebody hurt me'? It's not as though anybody meant to hurt anybody. It's just—what are you going to do?—it didn't work . . . That's why I would say people don't want to talk about it. That would be it."[15] For the reasons Dlugacz describes, part of what I experienced in conversation with "first-generation" musicians (an analytical category I will detail momentarily) was long pauses when I followed certain paths of inquiry. Perhaps some of the reticence alluded to by Dlugacz can also be explained by what a small world women's music is. Although some black women artists have since moved on, many are still performing and enjoy working relationships, if not friendships, with other musicians and festival producers on the circuit. Dlugacz's allusion to the selective lens of memory is compatible with my own interests, for it is not my intent to present a seamless narrative of women's music festival history, a titillating exposé, or a longitudinal ethnographic account of any one festival; rather, the essays of this book are conceived as a contemplation on race and the politics of sexual identity in the women's music festival community.

The Changers and the Changed

Generational fissures figure prominently in public and private debates about the future of the (black) race, feminism, black feminism, and lesbian feminism. How can we reconcile the continued involvement of veteran musicians, some of whom are now in their late fifties or older, with the contributions of musicians who comprise a much younger cohort? This book posits the involvement of two generations of musicians in women's music, a perspective that applies to the white musicians in this arena as well.[16] Indeed, age is a less productive mode of categorization than the distinctive features separating the periods in which musicians came of political age. Both cohorts have exhibited a wide range of musical sensibilities over time and have advocated for themselves as blacks, women, and, in applicable instances, lesbians. The task is to reconcile the involvement of all these musicians with the changing manifestations of racism and the evolution of sexual identity politics from the mid-1970s to the second decade of the twenty-first century.

Musicians who readily identified with the modes of feminist thought exhibited in the political legacy represented by Bernice Johnson Reagon and Sweet Honey in the Rock (SHIR) comprise the "first" generation of musicians.

Under Reagon's direction, SHIR brought a civil-rights-protest-era-inflected music and sensibility, as well as a history of radical women's politics, to the women's music scene. Although there is an age difference between Reagon, Linda Tillery, and singer/songwriter Deidre McCalla, for example, within this framework they are all members of the first generation. In an observation into which one can insert politics and musical style, Nancy Whittier writes, "At some point, separate micro-cohorts cohere into a distinct political generation when the similarities among them outweigh their differences."[17] A newer cohort of musicians negotiates feminism and lesbian feminist identities with the advent of queer nation politics emerging in the early 1990s—hence, singer/songwriter/guitarist Doria Roberts's appeal to a constituency that is very different from that of the first generation.

The generational mode of analysis has a practical use. Thinking along the lines I suggest can help temper the propensity of middle-aged adults to despair at the ways members of the next generation "do politics" and, for that matter, music. At the same time, it helps members of the next generation understand the considerable investment of members of a prior generation who, still active, also responded to the complexities of their time.[18] The first and second generations of black women musicians in women's music made commitments to the women's movement, to feminism, and to lesbian feminism at different times and therefore exhibit different frames of reference. In the field of identity politics, coming to terms with the understandings of differently positioned subjects is crucial.

The newer cohort of black musicians, some of whom incorporate sampling into their musical compositions, pay tribute periodically to members of an earlier generation of central figures in women's music, black and white. Nedra Johnson's rendition of Maxine Feldman's "Amazon Woman Rise," originally written in the 1970s, is an example. The tribute to Feldman and to "Amazon history" became a tradition wherein each year musicians performed the song at the opening ceremony of the Michigan festival.[19] I asked Nedra Johnson to talk about what the song meant to her. Her response indicates the appreciation of one generation of black women musicians and feminist activists for paths forged by women of an earlier generation. She speaks to a discourse in which women's music is projected into the past as a sonic reverberation of lesbian feminism and to the importance of contextualizing the contributions of radical feminism to the women's movement:

> Yeah, she [Maxine Feldman] called me crying and was like, "Thanks for not forgetting me." I was like, "Are you kidding? I hear this song every year. We definitely haven't forgotten."
>
> This is where I hear the younger folks being like "old school, lesbian, folk

music, blah blah," but I have my own opinion on that. I am like, "This is gangsta. It's not radical?" It's not radical because she did it thirty years ago. It wouldn't be radical to do that today, because young folks are doing more crazy things and they are like, "Look, I'm out; I've always been out of the closet," and they take that for granted. It is great that people can be like that, but it is disappointing, because it's like they think they are Christopher Columbus or something—like they discovered America and didn't nobody live there before.

[Along another line,] I remember twenty years ago, I had her [Alix Dobkin's] card, and it said "International Lesbian Folk Singer." It was dangerous to have a business card that said "lesbian" on it. It might not seem all that deep now.[20]

Johnson critiques the tendency of a newer generation of queer-identified consumers to distance themselves from the music, if not the politics, represented by white musicians Cris Williamson, Margie Adam, Holly Near, Meg Christian, Alix Dobkin, and Maxine Feldman. Ironically, many middle-aged music consumers also both claim and distance themselves from the era evoked by the names of these musicians.

In recent years, black women within and beyond the academy have engaged in an intergenerational exchange of thinking about black feminist identity. These conversations have taken place over coffee, at kitchen tables, in scholarly journals, and in cars while hip-hop music plays at high decibels. Proponents from various camps, discrete and overlapping, maintain that young people—women in particular—care little about inroads into black liberatory struggle or feminism made by members of a generation before them. My conversation with Malika, twenty-five, belies this suggestion. Here, the musician talks generally about the debt her generation owes the preceding one in terms of black feminist activism, lesbian feminism, and so on:

First of all, I think that the younger generation are really perceived as taking a lot for granted. I think that this might be true, but on the other hand, all the fighting [the older generation did] was so we could take these things for granted. I mean—not to say we should take things for granted—but so we don't have to think about stuff. The idea was to remove discrimination as much as possible so the next generation wouldn't have to deal with it. So now we're not dealing with it as much, so we are just kind of carefree and very loud about our sexuality, which makes the older generation very annoyed, because they are like, "We fought, and all you guys are doing is just throwing parties." But the freedom that they granted us by the work that they did was so that we could throw parties out in the open, and celebrate our music. It's kinda like how—I had a friend whose landlady was annoyed because we weren't going to gay churches, because they had fought for that, when the reality is that they fought to give us the option of going to gay churches. It's like the black college situation. It makes me mad that more of us are not going and that they are closing, but the reality of it is that the civil rights movement was about us being able to go to school wherever we wanted. That's what is happening, so I think you definitely lose some culture from that, but you know, things move on—even when sometimes they probably shouldn't.[21]

Implicit in the observations of both Johnson and Malika is that social movements are not static; nor, over the long haul, are they propagated by the same activist leaders. These understandings can be missed in modes of analyses that pit generation against generation, as the next generation sets its priorities and puts its own spin on the legacy it has been bequeathed. This is as true for the radical women's movement as it is for black liberatory struggle in its current manifestations. In an observation that has relevance for women's music festival culture, Whittier rightly suggests that differences between feminist generations result in generational politics that are more relevant to the resulting debates and shifts within the women's movement than to young women's decisions to become feminists in the first place. In putting conflicts between generations of participants in the women's movement in context, she prosaically says something that others have said more plainly: "A movement remains alive as long as there is struggle over its collective identity, or as long as calling oneself or one's organization 'feminist' means something."[22] These are issues that resonate with insiders to women's music.

"But I Never Believed That": Reactions to the Musical Underneath of Cultural Feminism

Given that women's music festivals continue to this day and that consumers purchase cds and attend concerts by the musicians discussed in this book, it makes sense for me to clarify more precisely what has ended with the passing of the genre's golden age, unpeeling some of the layers to examine the ideologies of cultural feminism that held sway in women's music during the mid-1970s.

Cultural feminism has been defined as "the ideology of a female nature or female essence reappropriated by feminists themselves in an effort to revalidate undervalued female attributes."[23] Although cultural feminism in its early manifestations was by no means homogenous, its ideals were rooted in essentialist notions about gender, sexuality, politics, and, in this case, music. The latter is a complex that, in mapping essentialized notions of sexual difference onto inanimate objects, can be described as an excess of lesbian feminism that emerged during this time period. Among the manifestations of cultural feminism in women's music were the idea that musical instruments had gender associations (e.g., tubas are coded male whereas harps are coded female), the notion that lesbian separatism was the only viable way for women to achieve autonomy and liberation, and the conviction that gender and sexuality were the epistemological centers of lesbian feminism.

When I broached these issues in conversation with musicians, many of their responses indicated that they never subscribed to these ideas in the first place—hence the title of this section. Musician Vicki Randle addresses the impact of the ideas about instrumentation on musicians: "Instead of defining women's music in the obvious, confrontive and controversial way—as music by lesbians for lesbians, which would have been the most honest at the time—the spokeswomen for this movement tried to sidestep this overt declaration by attempting instead to define what 'female-oriented' and 'male-oriented' music was."[24] While the prescriptive notions Randle mentions were broad enough to include (acoustic) guitarists under the rubric of acceptable musical acts, musical genres adopted by women of color, which often incorporated a wider range of musical styles, such as jazz and funk, as well as instrumentation—horns, for example—were deemed to fall outside of the boundaries of "women's music." Implicitly, according to the logic of this tenet, it was easier to determine the women-identifiedness of a song with lyrics than it was to assess the same of a composition for instruments only. This presented problems for some black women musicians. Composer Mary Watkins, who recorded with Olivia Records (*Something Moving*) at the end of the 1970s, put it this way: "What is women's music? If that's all they're looking for [meaning women-identified lyrics] in women's music, then I guess it [my music] doesn't have anything to do with women's music."[25] Crediting Linda Tillery for the observation that follows, she continued, underscoring the fact that a reified musical structure does not have a gender identity: "I'm telling you, 'a triad is a triad.'" Later, Watkins said:

> I'm an American composer, an African American composer. Anytime I have the opportunity to express the soul of the African American people, I'm going to do that. I love classical music, and I also love the music of my people. I understand where it comes from. I am not bound by a combination of instruments . . . if you want to use strings, use them. I'm saying this because there is a history of "this is what you should use" in women's music. I don't have much patience with it—with women's music or whatever that is. I'm not invalidating the need for an identity, but I don't take well to being dictated to. You don't win popularity contests that way.

Yet, I might add, Watkins is highly esteemed and popular on the festival circuit.

Essentialist perceptions of the sort I have outlined, however short-lived they were and however embarrassing they are now, had long-lasting effects. Another musician, Tara Jenkins, a pianist, addresses attitudes of exclusivity that she perceived in the women's music community: "I could never do music just for lesbians. They reminded me of kittens huddled together, clinging to each other, and anybody who didn't fit their idea of what lesbian feminist was—they were out. This turned me off. Someone decides what femininity is—soft, nurturing—and what's female—usually white, by the way. I saw that they were not particularly supportive."[26]

One of the areas in which black musicians experienced nonsupport initially was when their music was performed as a reflection of their religious heritage. For many white women, feminist spirituality encompassed revisiting patriarchal constructions of Christianity and emphasizing goddess culture, a construct that critics such as Audre Lorde faulted for its racially exclusionary framework. Conflict within women's music festival culture arose when white members of the festival gospel chorus changed male pronouns to female ones. Melanie DeMore explains:

> Because, you know, we're going to do music which is very African American–identified. I like to include in my shows spirituals and things like that, and the thing is that as an African American woman, I cannot ignore the spiritual influence of my people. So when I do the gospel choir at Michigan, I tell them from the jump [from the start], "If you have a problem with the word 'God' and 'his' and all this other stuff, this is not the group for you to be in, because I refuse to diminish this music because it may feel politically incorrect to you. Get over it. If you don't like it, don't sing in the chorus." So I try to pick music that is universal. I tell them that this is the music that has literally saved my people, and I am not going to change it to make it politically more comfortable for you.[27]

Echoing or rather foreshadowing DeMore's warning to the Michigan festival's gospel choir, the 1992 program booklet describes the choir, led by Linda Tillery: "The repertoire will draw from spirituals and gospel standards and the workshop will include a discussion of the cultural roots of gospel. The music will be sung *exactly* as it is written (no gender substitution of pronouns or names)."[28]

In a separate conversation, musician Sandra Washington elaborated on the point made by Tillery and DeMore. Although recordings of the Washington Sisters, produced by white musician Teresa Trull, do not evidence the performance of songs in idioms typically considered black, the duo fused awareness of their African American heritage into their act by singing "Lift Every Voice and Sing" at festivals: "I'm not going to sing 'she is my Saviour' at one of my concerts. We do let them know that it's not negotiable with us. People have said to us, 'How can you sing this, because it's so patriarchal?' I've heard all this. But we sing this because it has meaning for us. We say it so that people are educated about why we perform it. Hopefully people will be prevented from trying to 'educate' us afterwards."[29]

The one black festigoer I met who had participated in Michigan's gospel chorus said that the fact that musicians such as Linda Tillery and Melanie DeMore had the musical authority to caution choir members against changing the pronouns meant a lot. The examples musicians offered are within an arguably Protestant frame, and not within the context of Yoruba traditional religious practices that some African American festigoers and musicians have introduced to the women's music festival scene. Although beyond the scope of this book, it is worth interrogating the operations of class, generation, region, religion, and musical genre in festival programming by women of color. Some of the excesses of lesbian feminism can also be identified in the expectations some white feminists had of black women in the earlier years of the movement. Jenkins offers the following:

> I hate to say this, but . . . some of it had to do with racism—race . . . people get in their minds what represents what and that's that. You are worthy of acknowledgment as an African American as long as you are accusing them of being racist, lecturing them . . . on their case, making an obvious and distinct difference between what they are and you are. You are supposed to be black—angry, expressing the anger—you grew up underprivileged . . . they [whites] are going to guilt-trip. That is not the way for me to grow and become who I am. I'm not going to say that there isn't somebody who should be doing that—it's just not me. Don't let people get away with shit and be disrespectful. I want to expand. To me, a lot of that bogs you down. It leads to high blood pressure.[30]

Musicians also revealed the cognitive tensions they experienced in earlier years when women's music festivals encouraged more stage performances by amateur musicians, many of whom were not very good. Speaking on the down low, a veteran black musician said that what bothered her most was the lack of musical and performance standards fostered by the women's music community in those years: "The difference," she said, is that "the black women musicians can *play*."[31] White women's music founder Sue Fink underscores at least part of that sentiment: "In many ways I'm disappointed that we don't have a more educated audience to tell the difference between something which is really musically and lyrically art versus something that is just fun entertainment . . . I just feel that if you're going to do something, do it with art. And there's so much that isn't."[32]

Jenkins and Fink were responding to part of the ethos of early 1970s lesbian feminist culture about which Lillian Faderman comments: "At the first National Women's Music Festival in Champaign, Illinois, in 1974, singers who appeared too professional, like stars, got a cold reception. The audience wanted to see their own declassed, unslick image onstage . . . In fact, 'professionalism' of any kind was considered undesirable hierarchical behavior: It represented artificial and destructive categories, barriers set up by the patriarchy that limited the possibilities of women 'creating a vision together.'"[33] Drumming workshops and the occasional guitar workshop notwithstanding, there are fewer opportunities today for the truly novice amateur to take to the stage at women's music festivals.

Time Passages

Many changes have taken place since the early and mid-1990s, when I conducted interviews with first-generation musicians; some of these transformations are more difficult than others for festigoers to accept. Veteran Linda Tillery comments on how her relationship to such audience expectations has changed: "We also change with time. And what we look for as expressions of gratitude and admiration becomes real different. I am in a period now where what I want is to see clearly what my goals are in life for the next, say, 20 years. I know how I want to live my life, and I know what I need to do in order to live it that way. It certainly doesn't include gratuitous sexual admiration, as in former years. So, as we change, our audiences change as well."[34]

At the time of our interview, Tillery had launched Linda Tillery and the Cultural Heritage Choir (CHC), an all-women's a cappella group that specialized in what one member called "African American roots music." While the all-female ensemble was popular on the women's music circuit, several years later Tillery reconfigured the ensemble to include two male members. Explaining that she wanted to "do something new," the CHC did not often perform at women's music festivals in that configuration again.

Still other changes have ensued over the years. That certain audience favorites such as Casselberry and DuPreé and the Washington Sisters had stopped performing on the circuit by the time I began my round of interviews is testimony that career paths vary, especially in music scenes beyond the big tent of the popular music industry. Composer Rachel Bagby and dub-poetry artist Lillian Allen, though still active in other creative ventures, are no longer involved, and singer/songwriter Regina Wells now devotes her energies to the women's drumming circuit, regarded by many as an offshoot of the women's music movement. The career trajectories of musicians worldwide exhibit ups and downs over the decades: A beloved artist falls upon hard times financially, and the women's music community responds with a fund-raiser; capping off an illustrious career in music and activism, Bernice Reagon Johnson retired in 2004 from SHIR, the ensemble she founded thirty years ago, and has moved on to other projects. (The elder Reagon still makes appearances with daughter Toshi Reagon and her band, Big Lovely.)[35]

Few of us have exactly the same interests as we did a decade or two ago, and, as the careers of numerous artists indicate, it is natural for performers to at some point decide to come off the road.[36] In contrast, there is something to be said for the longevity of certain artists; many continue to reinvent themselves and expand their consumer base. It is enough that many of these musicians took to festival stages during critical and formative years of the women's music festival scene. In fact, given a mainstream popular music industry characterized by a fixation on youth, women's music is remarkable for the number of middle-aged women performers it has supported—and continues to support, even after the demise of the women's music recording industry.

Musicians who have contributed to this project include headliner and solo performers, such as Deidre McCalla, as well as members of bands (referred to as "sidemen") or ensembles, such as Bernice Brooks. While soloists or leaders of ensembles are well known to audience members, musicians who figure only as members of ensembles often are not. Many of the performers listed in this book's "Dreamgirls" section maintain significant musical careers beyond the women's music festival circuit; after all, festivals are held typically from May to September only, and artists have to make a living. Some, like Rhonda Benin (CHC) and Emma Jean Foster (former member of CHC), both of whom came into the circuit in the 1990s, enjoyed careers as professional musicians before their paths intersected with the women's music scene.

My use of the term *professional* indicates a high level of musicianship and not necessarily a devotion to the craft full-time; it is true, however, that most of those who are active on the scene make their livings, full-time, as musicians. For some, like veteran Linda Tillery, this means maintaining a career that includes conducting workshops on African American music, producing the albums of other artists, and performing both with the ensemble she founded and with others. Pianist and composer Mary Watkins is the recipient of numerous awards for composition; she recently completed a concert piece titled "Queen Clara," and her latest cd, *Who Has Not Been Touched,* was released in 2004. Musician Vicki Randle was the first and only female member of the Prime Time band, led by Kevin Eubanks. Tillery, Watkins, and Randle have worked with some of the finest musicians in the business. Drumming masters Ubaka Hill and Afia Walking Tree head drumming institutes, offering workshops at women's drumming camps, and at festivals. Judith Casselberry performs with her own band, J.U.C.A., and as a member of Toshi Reagon's Big Lovely.

First-Generation Commonalities

Three salient points emerge from interviews conducted with first-generation musicians. First, in light of the African American feminist legacy that preceded them, it makes sense that members of the first generation, when asked about their identities as musicians, emphasized the totality of their persons as blacks, women, and, in many cases, lesbians. Although it seems almost redundant for me to linger here, we are reminded that historically there have been—and still are—strong cultural expectations that black lesbians and gays express allegiance to one identity over another, meaning the African American community or the (white) gay and lesbian community. Therefore, that narrators consider their identities in terms of race, gender, and sexual orientation as integrated is critically important. Musician Judith Casselberry put it best when she described her identities as a "package deal."[37]

Second, the rhetoric and focus of musicians in women's music suggest that many black musicians have felt compelled to advocate for a heightened awareness of African American culture in these contexts. They have done this through their music, insights they have shared from the stage, and the work they do in festival organizations behind the scenes. This heightened sense of black consciousness might seem paradoxical, given that some artists, such as the Washington Sisters and Vicki Randle, report being reared in environments that were not necessarily or typically black-identified. The trope of returning home to one's roots in terms of music, later rather than sooner, is recurrent also in narratives that appear in the promotional material of Randle and singer/songwriter Laura Love, both of whom discuss their black identity and biracial heritage.[38]

Third, in spite of their contributions to lesbian feminism through performance, and in ways that might not be appreciated by those who came of political age in the aftermath of the emergence of queer nation, performers revealed that they wished to be regarded as musicians first.[39] These revelations were often tacit. This does not mean that performers resist representation as activists, feminists, lesbians, or anything else; it only suggests that although some of these women enjoy iconic status in women's music, they are aware of the complex social fabric in which their positionalities are read. Musicians pursue careers in multiple contexts—on the folk music scene; in creative music circles; and in jazz, film, and gospel music. Given the intricate set of circumstances faced by members of their political generation, it is understandable that they have chosen not to privilege sexual identity in their music—or even in speech about music. First-generation musicians continue to appeal to the lesbian consumer base of women's music festivals while nurturing careers that are more inclusive in terms of audiences across gender, race, and sexual orientation.

Out and About

Based in Los Angeles, Out and About is the name of a special events planning company for lesbians of color. I use the phrase to draw attention to two related issues: my use of the word *lesbian* instead of *queer,* and nuances of sexual identity disclosure. Although my decision to use *lesbian* rather than *queer* puts me at odds with self-identified queer theorists, activists, and other scholars who, in part because of their own backgrounds, apply the term with greater frequency, it is consonant with the preference of the majority of women I interviewed for this book and with the labels adopted by the National Black Justice Coalition (NBJC).[40] My decision not to use the two words interchangeably is made with deliberation and provides a strong counterpoint to those who are concerned with text-based studies, whose context for scholarship, along with, perhaps, their own political commitments, inspires them to use the word *queer* with greater frequency.[41]

The second issue pertains to sexual identity disclosure. During my research, star-struck festival attendees voiced surprise that musicians who seemed quite "out" within the festival environment were not out in the same way under all circumstances. While outness as a lesbian might characterize the choices made by some of the better-known musicians and comediennes associated with women's music (such as white musicians Alix Dobkin, Cris Williamson, and Diane Davidson, and comedienne Kate Clinton), the same is not a given in terms of black performers. Several black lesbian musicians granted me interviews with the caveat that I neither disclose their sexual identities nor reveal their names in publications issuing from my research. Emphasizing the need for her lesbian identity to remain undisclosed, a violinist explained she had "to make a living," and that since she gigged also for musical theater and symphony orchestras, she had to "keep her reputation intact." Moreover, her first love was contemporary, experimental music, but like so many musicians, she had to meet her financial responsibilities: "I want to play what I feel. I don't want to play Bach right now. I don't want to play Andrew Lloyd Weber, but I've got to do that to pay the mortgage. So what's happening now is that I'm prostituting my music—that's what I have to do."[42]

The circumstances this violinist outlines have been discussed by scholars who have suggested that sexual identity disclosure is situational and may emerge over time.[43] This is particularly true in terms of those from or relating to African American communities. Patricia Collins writes that members of the black LGBT community seem "less likely than their White counterparts to be openly gay or to consider themselves completely out of the closet."[44] Of course, the operative word in Collins's observation is "completely."

Interviews revealed that black women organizers of women's music festivals and, in some cases, second-generation musicians think strategically about sexual identity disclosure. Consider Tanya Ray, a festival organizer who articulates the parameters that she and other black lesbians from her region must take into consideration in regard to "coming out": "When we talked about trying to bring in more musicians of color, we quickly realized that a lot of women did not identify themselves as lesbian because—especially here—there's a stigma attached to being black and lesbian in our city [Midwest location]. Most of the women I know in the city are not out in that sense." Here, I interjected a reality check intended to help us move forward: "Right, well, not just in your city, but in a lot of places." Tanya replied, "Okay, sometimes it feels like the rest of the world is proud and gay and we're, like, scared." Recalling Sherrie Tucker's discussion of black women subjects who "don't come out," the contrast between the shortsightedness of some who maintain that everyone should be out all the time and the organizer's reticence was familiar but nonetheless moving. Tanya continued:

> TR: Like, you meet women and you know they're gay. "Girl, where you work at?" They won't even tell you where they work for fear that it will get back to their workplaces. It's a phenomenal thing. It was very different in Chicago. There, it was like, "Okay, I'm out and gay—deal with it." . . . The people I associated with—we were out. Not that we were, like, "Hey, how you doin'—I'm a lesbian"—but it was much more free than it is here.
>
> EH: Yeah, Chicago is, what—the third largest city in the U.S?
>
> TR: Yeah, that's part of it. There was no fear of someone finding out I'm a lesbian at work [in Chicago], but here, there is the fear that "I may get fired," or "I'll be ostracized—whatever—kicked out the church."
>
> EH: And do you think that works for gay men the same way it works for lesbians?
>
> TR: No, I think it's much more difficult for us.
>
> EH: I do, too.
>
> TR: Every black church I've ever been in, has a gay musician—I mean, flaming, and no one says anything. I think it's much more difficult for us.[45]

Monica Falls, a second-generation musician in her twenties who works full-time as a middle-school teacher illustrates some of the tensions that even black women of the second generation experience in regard to being out at the workplace:

> I am also considered "out" as far as that, even though that is kind of tough at my job, because it can be dangerous. When you are working with kids, people have a lot of misinformation. I ended up on the second page of the metro section in the [newspaper] holding a bullhorn at the black gay Pride march. I was pretty much

out at the school at that point. I was really scared about it, honestly, even though [name of city] public schools protect—under their laws they can't discriminate based on sexual orientation. But I know that when they want to get rid of you, they can. I was afraid that parents were going to call and that there would be this really big backlash, but there really wasn't. The kids teased me, which was kind of funny, once I stopped being traumatized and afraid. I guess once you're out, you're out, and you can't really go back in. So there was no point in my being afraid, but I think that's just part of living in this society.[46]

Although the theory the festival organizer and musician articulate has circulated in African American communities for many years, it is rare that the insights of black lesbians and gays are reflected in the ethnographic literature. If blacks and Latinos experience instances of everyday racism, then it is also true that gays and lesbians of color are subject to everyday homophobia, whether or not they are out.[47] The risk of this exposure is something the women of this study have contemplated.

In contrast to the well-considered responses of some lesbians to questions about sexual identity disclosure, replies of some straight women did not always reveal a high degree of forethought. The black leader of a popular percussion ensemble, for example, said she was unaware that white lesbians comprised the majority of the ensemble's audiences at women's music festivals. I was not quite sure how to process this level of what could only be termed denial. In contrast, Chandra Foley, a straight musician in another ensemble, was up-front about her degree of (dis)comfort in women-identified space. Describing her first experience attending a women's music concert, she said, "I saw all these white lesbians—and left the concert! . . . Homophobia runs high in the black community." Interestingly, Chandra explains or links her individual response to a generalization about African Americans. I asked her to elaborate on how she felt about the women's music scene initially, since before joining the band she had no previous experience in the women's community.

CF: Strange. Uncomfortable initially. Eventually, I was able to look at it from a music side instead of from a homophobic side.

EH: So you think of yourself as being pretty homophobic at the beginning?

CF: Real [homophobic]. I never made any bones about it . . . the girls helped me through it. We used to sit down and talk about it—about being straight and being gay. But I found it to be uncomfortable.[48]

The separate cases of straight women coming into their identities as the Other in this lesbian-dominated world provide a glimpse into the journey some must take in order to function successfully in this field.

In this chapter, I asked musicians to think back and blackward—in other words, to share their reactions to the musical manifestation of cultural feminism in the early years of women's music. I offered a conceptual framework that responds to the passing of the golden age with a mode of analysis that accommodates the ongoing presence of two black feminist generations in women's music. The efforts of musicians to intervene in their own representations figure prominently in the way we are to understand this musical scene. Framing the chapters that follow in this way was a necessary undertaking, given the ongoing prominence of the first generation of musicians in women's music and the nostalgia that permeated the festival circuit during the early phase of my research. Chapter 4 takes up the prequel to these issues—that is, the roots of black women's collective and individual participation in the women's music festival circuit.

All that is gold does not glitter,
Not all those who wander are lost;
The old that is strong does not wither,
Deep roots are not reached by frost.
—J. R. R. TOLKIEN,
THE FELLOWSHIP OF THE RING

CHAPTER 4

Nappy (and Deep) Roots

STREAMS OF MUSICAL AND POLITICAL INFLUENCE

In this chapter I address streams of musical and political influence that loom large in the genealogy of black women's collective involvement in women's music. In doing so, I attempt to reconcile a complex of musical styles and political influences that does not fit easily into traditional histories, whether they concern black music, black women's history, black feminist organizational history, or lesbian feminist politics.

Three musical histories converge in women's music. The first is a broad category of music generally identified as African American, including the entire range of black musical genres, from spirituals to funk. The second category, related to the first, includes African and Afro-Latin influences. The third category is comprised of stylistic influences stemming from the urban folk music revival of the 1940s and 1950s. This last category is less clearly defined stylistically than the others and includes pop music styles of the 1960s and singer/songwriter styles of the 1970s.[1] These traditions are conglomerations of various musical innovations that have drawn heavily from one another. Each reveals an internal crosscutting of influence from one genre to another. They have at their foundation a contradiction inherent in American popular culture as it emerged in the antebellum period and continued in the aftermath of slavery. Historians of American popular music frequently refer to an explicit "borrowing" of black cultural materials by whites for mainstream white dissemination. By this calculation, even without the visible and aural presence of black musicians, women's music would owe a debt to the creators of black popular and religious music.

Ironically, and for various reasons, many women's music enthusiasts have both claimed and distanced themselves from the model of the singer/songwriter with acoustic guitar practiced by artists such as Cris Williamson, Holly Near, Meg Christian, and Alix Dobkin. Scholar Arlene Stein describes this style, which has been characterized as "white girl with guitar," or "wgwg," as being thoroughly based in a European tradition. This mode of thinking belies the fact that the wgwg folk style Stein references derived from post–World War II folk revival groups such as the Weavers and incorporated the influence of black performers, including the Mississippi-born singer Leadbelly (aka Huddie Ledbetter) and African American folksingers like Odetta. In other words, the "white" folk style from which so many women's music enthusiasts seek to distance themselves draws on black traditions—or, to borrow a phrase from writer Greg Tate, "it draws on nappy roots."[2]

The suggestion that women's music as a "sound object" is white requires the eliding in historical memory of those musical styles typically regarded as black, as well as the awareness of those performers who, according to ethnomusicologist Christopher Waterman, exhibit styles that are "suspended between dominant conceptions of whiteness-as-performance and blackness-as-performance."[3] This selective forgetting of American music history resonates in discursive strategies that position musicians such as Jimi Hendrix, Tracy Chapman, or, to invoke a musician from an earlier time period, string bandleader Bo Chatmon outside the boundaries of black music. At the same time, however, performances that are steeped in notions of "blackness-as-performance" in a gendered frame, such as SHIR, are also frequently not regarded as typical black music, a topic that first-generation musicians addressed in chapter 3.

Sweet Honey in the Rock

A significant point of entry for black women's regular participation in women's music as performers was the West Coast tour of Sweet Honey in the Rock. It has been difficult for some observers to gauge the influence and impact of this ensemble within the women's music festival community. The relationship between SHIR and the women's music community has been glossed by some commentators so as to obfuscate the different cultural perspective that SHIR brought to it. While it is true that the ensemble changed the political landscape as well as the soundscape of women's music, this did not occur overnight, nor did it occur in an isolated political—or musical—context. Sweet Honey in the Rock was not the first "black act" to appear at a women's music festival. Rather, SHIR was the first black women's ensemble to appear, maintain a presence as black women musicians, and make a lasting impact on the women's music scene. In 1977, Sweet Honey in the Rock became the first black ensemble whose performances intersected nodes of the women's music community.

Founder and artistic director Bernice Johnson Reagon, an African American cultural historian, was leader of the ensemble. The daughter of a black Baptist minister, Bernice Reagon attained musical experience growing up in a region in southwest Georgia that had "developed a strong sacred-music singing tradition."[4] She obtained her early political experience during the 1960s as a member of the Freedom Singers, a mixed-sex a cappella ensemble that participated in the campaign for desegregation and voting rights in Albany, Georgia. Noting that by the time of the Albany desegregation movement, schisms had emerged between the various civil rights organizations, historian Paula Giddings observes: "It would take a special effort to keep the disparate elements of the Albany Movement together, and SNCC [the Student Nonviolent Coordinating Committee] discovered a key to that unity . . . Albany became known as a 'singing movement' and it was the rich, darkly timbred voice of Bernice Reagon, an Albany State College student, who joined SNCC, that evoked the resonance of centuries-old memories and strength."[5]

Almost a decade later, Reagon conducted vocal workshops for the women and men of the DC Black Repertory Company, where she served as vocal director beginning in 1972. Sweet Honey in the Rock emerged from one of Reagon's vocal workshops in 1973.[6] The ensemble had its first performance at a conference held at Howard University in November of that year and produced its first concert in 1974. Reagon writes that for that concert, Sweet Honey sang "the full range of what would mark the group's performances, such as traditional songs like 'No More Auction Block for Me,' gospel songs like 'Traveling Shoes,' a blues medley of Jimmy Reed's 'You got me run / hide, hide / run anyway you want it let it roll,' and 'See See Rider,' and songs depicting struggle, like Len Chandler's 'I'm Going to Get My Baby Out of Jail.'"[7] After its formation as an ensemble, Sweet Honey in the Rock performed in racially integrated venues inclusive of women and men. The singers performed for predominantly black audiences and also for racially diverse audiences at concerts held at churches, schools, theaters, folk festivals, and political rallies.

A significant event in the history of both Sweet Honey in the Rock and the women-identified music community was the performance of Sweet Honey with women's music founders Holly Near and Meg Christian in association with

Olivia Records. In 1977, Reagon, scheduled for a residency at a university in Santa Cruz, decided to launch a West Coast tour for Sweet Honey in the Rock. After anticipated funding sources failed to materialize, Sweet Honey agreed to collaborate in a recording with Olivia Records in exchange for financial support for the ensemble's tour.

This tour facilitated the ensemble's introduction to the "radical, separatist, white-women-dominated, lesbian cultural network in California," a network that differed radically from that which had nurtured the formation and development of Sweet Honey.[8] Although the Olivia activists were varied in sexual orientation, they described themselves as "political lesbians." This naming practice had been adopted by radical feminists across the nation, especially during the 1970s, when heterosexual feminists frequently identified under that label. The appellation signified women's commitment to other women as a political entity. The term's use was short-lived, however; few references are made to it today outside of women's studies classes.

Reagon recalls that she found important congruencies between the black nationalist sentiments with which she was familiar and sentiments of the radical women's movement, to which she was introduced through Sweet Honey's West Coast tour. Nonetheless, conflicts highlighting both race and cultural differences arose between Sweet Honey in the Rock and the West Coast women-identified music community. "Many of these conflicts," Reagon writes, "came from our being 'people-identified' (which included men), rather than 'women-identified.' We were working in a community [California women's network] that excluded men. The communities we moved among did a lot of checking; they wanted to be sure that they protected themselves and that they were dealing with women-identified women. I think we came up short, but they took us in anyway."[9]

Reagon relates that another source of conflict was that early sponsors of the concert tour questioned the ensemble's collective identity as a feminist group, so much so that Sweet Honey's name was called into question: "When we insisted on our name, Sweet Honey in the Rock, an ensemble of Black women singers, we were asked what was wrong with being called feminist. I would answer, 'What is wrong with being a Black radical woman and calling your organization an ensemble of Black women singers?' I explained that our radicalness was rooted in our history and models, and that the words and phrases we used were used by our mothers and our mothers' mothers, and we wanted to always name that connection."[10] Reagon's response is not unique among members of black women activists' organizations in the late 1970s.[11]

According to Reagon, the character of that connection recalls the name of the ensemble that references "the legacy of African American women in the United States." Her father, she states, related to her a nonbiblical parable about "a land that was so rich that when you cracked the rocks, honey would flow from them." Reagon compares the sturdiness of black women to rocks and mountains and the sweetness of black women to honey.[12]

Part of the subtext surrounding the conflict that Sweet Honey experienced with members of the West Coast women's music community had to do with the widespread perception, even among women of color activists such as Reagon, that the women's movement was foremost a vehicle for perpetuating the interests of white middle-class women.[13] References to black feminist organizations of the time do not appear in her narrative. As a black woman who had grown up with numerous strong African American role models who worked both inside and outside the home, Reagon relates, for example, that she did not immediately share the feminist call for women to become gainfully employed. What, then, inspired Reagon's political consciousness, already sensitive to racial issues, to become inflected with gender concerns? A turning point seems to have come when Joan Little, a black woman in North Carolina, was arrested on a burglary conspiracy charge in 1974. The highly publicized case involving rape, retaliatory murder, and escape galvanized black feminists and allies. Reagon composed "Joan Little" in response, and the song became the first by Sweet Honey in the Rock to be played on black-oriented radio. Sweet Honey produced its first recording, self-titled, in the autumn of 1976.

In 1977, inspired by Sweet Honey in the Rock's experience with the radical women's movement, Reagon composed "Every Woman," the text of which calls for honoring the various roles women play in relationship to one another ("mother, sister, daughter, lover"). Reagon's penning of "Every Woman" coincided with the increased influence of religious conservatives in U.S. politics. Former pop singer Anita Bryant, a spokesperson for Florida's orange growers, led a campaign to repeal Dade County, Florida's nondiscrimination ordinance, which included sexual orientation in its list of protected minorities in hiring and housing. A national boycott of orange juice followed; the song, celebrating the many ways that women love and bond, was, as Reagon suggests, "important to that struggle."[14]

Reagon recollects that prior to the song's debut before Sweet Honey's East Coast–based, black community audience in the spring of that year, she was concerned about its reception. Although she does not elaborate, perhaps it was the last verse that caused her the most anxiety: "Woke up this morning feeling fine / rolled over, kissed a friend of mine." Admittedly, the song's text is not particularly radical by today's standards; however, for a black women's ensemble to perform such a song in the late 1970s before a gender-inclusive black audience most certainly was a transgressive act.

In 1982, SHIR founded Sisterfire, an urban festival open to men as attendees.[15] Spearheaded by Roadwork, a multiracial women's production company founded by Amy Horowitz that produced concerts in the Washington,

DC, area, the multicultural, gender- and sexuality-inclusive community that it forged around SHIR was unprecedented. Numerous black women artists took to Sisterfire stages, including Elizabeth Cotton, Flora Molten, Tracy Chapman, Toshi Reagon, Alice Walker, June Jordan, Lillian Allen, In Process . . . , and Yolanda King, among others. While trying to embrace a wide range of musical styles and political affinities, SHIR found "herself" pressured to negotiate and conform with a more narrow political agenda in terms of gender by white lesbian activists. Without the support of the white women's music festival community, Sisterfire was forced to cease operations after a series of cultural/racial/sexual clashes proved too big a burden for the festival infrastructure.[16]

The ensemble continues to incorporate songs in its repertoire that advocate for respect and justice for women and same-sex partnerships. With its trenchant voicing of women's concerns through a wide range of African American musical genres, Sweet Honey has been described as providing a cultural bridge in musical style and thematic content between the aftermath of the civil rights movement and the women's movement.[17] As Reagon states: "To sing a Sweet Honey concert, it is necessary to sing songs in the nineteenth-century congregational style, as well as the performance styles required for arranged concert spirituals, quartet singing, early and classical gospel, jazz, West African traditional, rhythm and blues, and rap—all in the same evening."[18]

Varied Voices of Black Women Tour

African American women's critique of the universalization of white women's experience was manifest in the emergence of independent black feminist organizations throughout the country in the early 1970s. In addition to their perspectives on race and gender inequity, black women who had been active in the "New Left" incorporated class analysis into their organizational framework. The term *New Left politics* refers to the fusion of "the personal and moral optimism of the southern civil rights movement with the cultural alienation of educated middle-class youth."[19] Sara Evans writes, "The intellectual mode that dominated the early years of the new left operated to exclude women as leaders, and only those with roots in an older left tradition ever thought to raise the 'women question' before the mid-sixties."[20] Black women activists of this period advocated on behalf of themselves as women in the civil rights movement, through the period of a heightened black nationalism, and the Black Power movement. The National Black Feminist Organization (NBFO), founded in 1973, articulated the need for political, social, and economic equality, especially for black women. Within a year of its founding, the NBFO had a membership of two thousand women in ten chapters; similar groups followed in its wake.[21] In 1974, members of the Boston chapter of the NBFO decided to form an independent group, the Combahee River Collective, emerging "to contest the liberalism of the National Black Feminist Organization that preceded it."[22] The collective expressed its "serious disagreements with NBFO's bourgeois-feminist stance and their lack of a clear political focus."[23] In 1977 this small group of African American women outlined a black feminist politic emphasizing the simultaneity of black women's oppression as blacks and as women.[24] Members of Combahee described themselves as "political lesbians," a term that referenced women's affinity with lesbian concerns and not necessarily their sexual identity.[25]

The Combahee River Collective called for the eradication of homophobia and a rejection of lesbian separatism, because a philosophy that does otherwise, "A Black Feminist Statement" reads, "leaves out far too many people, particularly black men, women, and children."[26] This stance is similar to the one taken by Sweet Honey in the Rock. Explicit in "A Black Feminist Statement" was a prescient class critique, hence its publishing in 1979 in an edited volume on socialism and feminism.[27] Individuals within Combahee pursued multi-issue activist involvement in lesbian politics, abortion rights, and sterilization abuse prevention. (The mainstream women's movement was curiously silent on this latter abuse of women's reproductive rights.) On a national scale, the early commitment of black lesbian feminists such as Margaret Sloan, Pat Parker, Audre Lorde, and Barbara Smith was crucial to building the movement in the 1970s, when many heterosexual black women were reluctant to identify themselves as feminists.[28]

In October 1978 the Combahee River Collective decided to "illuminate the specificity of the feminine" and to connect it to the constitution of "class, race and ethnicity," through sponsoring cultural (art, music, dance, and film) events.[29] This initiative resulted in Varied Voices of Black Women, a concert tour by San Francisco Bay Area women-identified composer/pianist Mary Watkins, pianist/singer Gwen Avery, rhythm and blues/jazz vocalist and string bass player Linda Tillery, and poet Pat Parker. The tour demonstrated that white lesbians were not the only ones creating a new women's culture: "Though the concert [tour] was first and foremost a celebration of Black lesbian feminist identity and culture, it was also an attempt to broaden the white feminist community's understanding of feminist and lesbian identity."[30] Varied Voices of Black Women toured eight cities in the fall of 1978. Although the event failed to receive the support of the predominantly white women's audiences, it was a watershed event in the history of women-identified music, a term, now defunct, that I use deliberately here in light of its resonance for those for whom it had meaning in earlier decades.

The eliding of black women's involvement in women's music from dominant discourses of African American music parallels another type of erasure that has occurred; put simply, the alternative name for the genre, "women-identified music," seems to have been supplanted by "women's music." In chapter 3 I highlighted some of the different sensibilities that black women musicians brought to festival and recording environments suffused with the norms of cultural feminism. Many second-wave feminists maintained that the term "women's music" reinforced the notion of the universal woman, ignoring the specific ways that female-gendered experiences—including those of lesbian feminists—were inflected by race and class. Accordingly, many activists, including women of color, began to refer to themselves and to their politics as "women-identified." Their decisions to do so made tangible Adrienne Rich's suggestion that same-sex bonds among women—heterosexual, bisexual, and lesbian—be established in a mutual "woman-focused vision."[31]

Toni Armstrong Jr., a prominent white women's music activist, characterizes the thinking of black festigoers and others about the term "women-identified": "Being women-identified may or may not have anything to do with being lesbian, but it's always focused on the female sensibility, and on relationships between females. The specific topic could be mothers and daughters and grandmothers, friends, sisters, the women's movement, lesbian love relationships, the love between women musicians, the relationship a woman has to the world at large, 'the woman in your life is you,' whatever. Being women-identified means by, for, and about women."[32]

Between the time I began preparing this book and the present, a change has occurred. Black women musicians use the term "women's music" with greater frequency than "women-identified," or so it appears. When I have used the phrase "women-identified music" in conversation with festigoers more recent to the scene, it has been difficult to tell whether we are proceeding from a common understanding. Anecdotal evidence of this is revealed in on-screen interviews conducted with black musicians for Dee Mosbacher's *Radical Harmonies*. Although musicians raised aspects of the different cultural values they brought to the festival network, there seemed to be, as ethnomusicologist Charles Keil might say, consolidation of identity under the name of women's music.[33]

Coming Out and In to Women's Music

Life history narratives of first-generation musicians reveal that personal networks as much as musical expertise were determining factors in their engagement with women's music culture. The telling of life stories is part of "an ongoing reconstruction of experience, providing continuity between the past and current action and belief"; the latter is demonstrated in the remembrances of these musicians.[34] In some cases, there is a convergence of experiences and sentiments facilitated by proximity; in others, the specific areas that narrators choose to emphasize is unique. This section contributes to studies that examine the emergence of black women's feminist consciousness—through music performance—in the contemporary period. I chose to include just some of the musicians who, during the period of my fieldwork or immediately before it, were prominent in the women's music community.[35]

Rather than identify a single point of introduction to women's music, musicians recalled events and interpersonal encounters that were influential. Impacting multiple instances of musicians' contact with women's music is the distinction made between women's music (the genre) that was recorded, marketed, and distributed by the women's music recording industry well into the late 1980s, on the one hand, and women's music festivals, which emerged slowly in the 1970s and increased in numbers in the 1980s, on the other. Musicians and festigoers often report exposure to recordings first and attending festivals later.

Women's music was only one aspect of the women's culture that flourished in the wake of the radical feminist movement of the 1970s. The alternative institutions that early radical feminists founded, contributed to, and derived sustenance from included rape crisis centers, garages, health-care centers, bookstores, newspapers, support groups, domestic violence shelters, and other women-owned businesses.[36] Recording companies were an important part of the mix; reference to what became known as the "women's music coffeehouse circuit" is revealed in my conversation with musician Judith Casselberry:

EH: You mentioned that you became involved in the women's music scene around 1979 or 1980. How did that come about?

JC: I was living in San Francisco—the first place we [Casselberry and DuPreé] performed was the Artemis Café, which was in the women's music coffeehouse circuit. It's not there anymore, but it served as a nurturing ground for a lot of women performers. Lots of folk, including Mary Watkins, Linda Tillery, and Gwen Avery, played there. Anybody who was in the Bay Area during that time played there if they were at all involved in the women's community. That's where we got started.

Informal networks such as those developed through performances at women's music coffeehouses and through direct actions were characteristic of the lesbian feminist community during the late 1970s and into the 1980s. Casselberry remembers the Women's Building, serving the Mission District in San Francisco, as a site of her political engagement during this period. The Women's Center (housed in the Women's Building) served as the locus of black feminist readings by Gwendolyn Brooks, Nzantge Shange, and others. Festival gigs followed: "I think the first one we [Casselberry and DuPreé] did was 1980: Michigan was the first. After that, we started finding out about the others: Indiana, New England,

New Mexico, Northampton, California, Southern Fest, Rhythm Fest, Ohio Lesbian Festival, and Pacific Northwest."[37]

Women found affirmation not only in the political work in which they were engaged but also through their music listening practices. One of singer/songwriter Melanie DeMore's many introductions to the genre was her purchase of *Something Moving* by Mary Watkins. DeMore, who was already familiar with Meg Christian and Cris Williamson, among others, said: "Yeah. It was a great album . . . I bought it because it [Watkins] was a black woman. And I loved the album. It has the original 'Brick Hut' [a track on the album]. And that's what got me started listening to women's music—what they called women's music. And I played that album into the ground. Years and years later, when Mary and I got to write something together when I did my album, it was a thrill for me."[38] In DeMore's response—"what they called women's music"—are inklings that the definition of the genre is contested. Her comment is a reminder that the commonly used term "women's community" emphasized access for all women even if feminist institutions failed to include women of every race, class, and sexual identity.[39]

The chronicle of events DeMore recounts is significant in that various sites of contact with women's music emerge. A "movement's culture is more than a formal ideological position," and DeMore's recall of people and places along her career path illustrates the interconnectedness of feeling and shared values that brought her into the women's community and enabled her "to stay."[40] Like many lesbian feminist activists of the late 1970s to early 1980s, DeMore was living in a large communal house that was shared with a number of women in Austin, Texas. The house frequently welcomed overnight guests, particularly those in the women's community. Several members of Alive! (an all-women's jazz ensemble) stayed there, and DeMore asked if she could play with them even though, to that point, she had been playing with men. That is how DeMore, playing flute, was introduced to white musician hand drummer Carolyn Brandy, a leader in the women's hand drumming circuit. She also met Mary Watkins and Linda Tillery, who were in town to perform in the first and only Austin Women's Music Festival. DeMore recalls that when she first heard Linda Tillery, she was highly impressed. "That's how I first became connected to women's music," she added. At the time, DeMore was singing in Scintilla, an a cappella group, through which she met musician Elouise Burrell, now a member of Linda Tillery and the Cultural Heritage Choir. Elaborating further on what emerges as a dense layering of encounters with musicians, DeMore cites a joint concert Scintilla did with SHIR as her first performance with Bernice Johnson Reagon.

In the early days of women's music, concerts were frequently held in smaller venues—coffeehouses and, indeed, women's homes—not necessarily always in large concert halls. DeMore, who later opened a concert for Meg Christian, recalled attending her first concert by Christian: "My girlfriend at the time was this African American woman who was in the army, and she used to play with Meg in Washington, DC. It looked like the recreational room of an apartment complex. There must have been about thirty people. We also heard a talk by Del Martin among others."[41]

After playing a women of color music festival in Austin in 1984, DeMore moved to Oakland, California, at the encouragement of musicians Judith Casselberry, Jacque DuPreé, and Toshi Reagon. Eventually, DeMore, who has a bachelor's degree in music, began making her living full-time as a musician and became conductor of the Bay Area Lesbian Choral Ensemble, with whom she stayed for four years.[42] At the time of our interview, she had been with the Oakland Youth Chorus (OYC) for six years and was strongly committed to the development of music and arts programs for young people.

The Oakland Youth Chorus is also how CHC member Rhonda Benin met Linda Tillery. At the time, Benin was working as the chorus manager for the OYC, a period she identifies as being around 1994. Benin was recommended to Tillery by Elizabeth Min, then director of the OYC. The Cultural Heritage Choir was still in its formation. Others she knew at the audition included Louise Robinson, Michelle Jacques, Rachel Bagby, Melanie DeMore, Judith Casselberry, Vicki Randle, and Regina Wells. Says Benin: "We were startled that the performance was that good. The first to leave the group because of other commitments were Casselberry and Randle, then Bagby. Then Michelle and Louise left. Later, the group picked up Elouise [Burrell] and Emma Jean [Foster]."[43]

The narratives of musicians who function as members of ensembles but who in other contexts are solo artists or bring to women's music a history of performance with their own bands often go untold. The coming out story of Emma Jean Foster is a case in point. After touring with several bands, including her own, Emma Jean and the Soul Sots, Emma Jean Foster joined Linda Tillery and the Cultural Heritage Choir. At the time of our interview, she had been with the ensemble for two years. Foster recalls she was singing with the Glide Ensemble when Tillery invited her to join the CHC. Said Foster of joining the ensemble, "It was one of the best moves I ever made."[44] Linda Tillery and the Cultural Heritage Choir is an example of a group that has persisted over the years in spite of changes in personnel as members pursue new projects while maintaining an independent performance schedule.

Hailing from the East Coast, hand drummer Ubaka Hill reveals that her early exposure to women hand drummers occurred also through various types of networks. Hill credits Edwina Tyler as an early source of inspiration, beginning in 1982: "I played a lot of house parties in New York, so here in the city there were a lot of women living together in brownstones. In one particular house, everyone was an artist, and one of the drummers living there was Edwina Lee Tyler, who has been drumming for many years. She was and actually is my earliest inspiration as far as being a woman drummer is concerned . . . I had seen female trap drummers, but not hand drummers." Through personal networks, Hill began to interface with the women's community in New York City, adding, in a qualifying nod, "At that time, it was predominantly a lesbian community."

In the late 1980s, Hill cofounded RhythmFest, a trio of women drummers with whom she performed on the women's music festival circuit from 1987 to 1989: "First, I would go to the festivals as a festigoer and bring my drums to play, to share. From that point, I began to be recognized and invited to perform." Later, she had an opportunity to realize her dreams about teaching with the formation of the DrumSong Institute.

> The vision came to me about five years ago when I knew what I needed and wanted to switch gears. Working with the funding problems of nonprofits made me think that I should shift my focus. Also, women's interest in drumming began to grow. As a drummer, I began to recognize that there were many men drumming and that a lot of them were not encouraging women to do so. . . .
>
> As I developed my political savvy, I came to have a greater understanding and analysis of the politics of music, of feminism, and of the various ways that we [women] are oppressed and have been oppressed systematically through various institutions and systems, so as all of this is coming together, as I am becoming mature in many ways and my awareness broadened, I began to notice that women were not being invited to learn to drum and gain opportunities to experience drumming for themselves.[45]

In many ways, the women's drumming and music festival circuits are quite different, not only in terms of the emphasis, at women's drumming camps, on the transmission of world percussion styles, but on the numbers of opportunities attendees have for hands-on involvement in music making.[46] This book makes no attempt to cover women's drumming camps, rock music camps, or drumming institutes. In listening to musicians relate narratives of their musical development, however, it became clear that their exposure to music during their formative years exhibited gendered contours, a phenomenon that is consistent with the literature on the gendered experiences of girls and women in music learning. In the 1990s, Wahru Cleveland began leading drumming workshops at the National Women's Music Festival after taking lessons with Nuradafina Pel Pina. She described her experiences with music in her youth:

> I can't tell you the year I started. I'm from a Pentecostal background, so I grew up playing tambourine in church. Then I had a set of bongos. I loved to play those. In my teens, we were still experimenting with what it meant to be

boyfriend/girlfriend. I thought it meant that you dated the boy with the bongos. I played those and got pretty good at it. He got angry, so we broke up. I bought my own set, which turned out to be very good. They were tuneables. I cut my teeth on bongos.

> This was in the late 1950s. I was told that I couldn't play bongos in church. There were two reasons for that: (1) [they said] girls don't play drums, and (2) [playing bongos means] you have something between your legs. The traditional thought was that I should play tambourine.[47]

Another musician, an Afro-Cuban-style drummer formerly with the avant-garde ensemble Living on the Edge, did not pursue music "in an aggressive way" until early adulthood. Jacque Jones spoke about the connection between gender expectations and instrument selection by women: "In my own particular case, the connection between taking on an instrument that has been traditionally viewed as masculine (at least here in the United States) has to do in part with the willingness or a lack of concern about how one is perceived and whether or not one's so-called femininity would be at stake. If you don't have that concern, then it's okay."[48]

Some might read in to Jones's comment a neglect of the space occupied by black lesbian femmes—or straight women, for that matter—whose self-identities might include expressions of femininity along traditional or nontraditional lines.[49] Still, Jones gives voice to a sentiment to which at least some can relate: "The connection between choice of instrument and how you self-identify can be fairly strong, so there was a willingness for a lot of women who identify as lesbian to go ahead and play those instruments they were attracted to because they weren't afraid of being seen as nonfeminine." In the end, the question arises as to why drumming and not another form of communal instrumental music making? According to Jones, the reasons are related to accessibility and skill:

> For a lot of us, the appeal of the drum is you can participate with other drummers in an ongoing way and not necessarily be well trained or a virtuoso—you don't necessarily have to have studied a long time to at least play for a little while with a group of people . . . And you can buy a cheap drum and get a halfway decent sound from it much more easily than, for example, you can buy a cheap horn. There is a certain level of access with the drum that doesn't happen with other kinds of instruments, so my guess is that that's part of it.

Added to formulations that posit the drum's connectedness to the earth, its role as a conduit of spirituality, a sense of timelessness associated with the instrument, and other characteristics that emerged then and now, not only as components of cultural feminism but as aspects of a range of cultural practices, and you have another reason that drumming is popular in some lesbian-feminist communities.

In the context of a women's music culture in which the history of each festival is quite specific, it makes sense to address the musical and political influences that anticipated and surrounded black women's collective rather than individual involvement in this music scene. As the musicians' stories of discovering and finding a place in women's music reveal, black women artists have found a "home" in women's music via paths of activism and social networking, but, as Bernice Reagon pointed out more than thirty years ago, this home has not always been a comfortable one—nor do we now expect it to be. In the next chapter, which addresses the aesthetics of women's music as well as the politics of representation in women's music concert rosters, I will suggest some of the reasons this has been the case.

TONI: But you know, that whole evening last night was not women's music.
EILEEN: Why do you say that?
TONI: Think about the three groups: taiko drumming; very mainstream jazz, and then Nell Carter—and the songs they sang were not women's music songs. That was not a women's music evening, right, Eileen?
EILEEN: Don't look to me. I'm trying to figure it out.
—EXCHANGE WITH A WHITE LESBIAN ELDER, WEST COAST WOMEN'S MUSIC AND COMEDY FESTIVAL, 1995

CHAPTER 5

"Ideal Relationships"

WOMEN'S MUSIC AUDIENCES

In an essay about the commensurate value of musics cross-culturally, ethnomusicologist Christopher Small argues that through music making of all types, our versions of "ideal relationships" are enacted.[1] In this chapter, I focus not only on what musicians and audience members find of value musically in women's music but also on the types of relationships that audience members expect to see enacted on the stage. I also examine the vision of sisterhood that festival producers project through various promotional materials and through scheduled films included in festival programs. Finally, in an examination of the statement "Black women don't camp"—frequently heard at women's music festivals—I consider black women's supposed reticence in accepting the "open invitation" of white producers and organizers to attend events, exploring the operations of both social memory and the politics of location in this context.

In addition to Small's admonition, I recall the utility of white musician Sue Fink's suggestion that there is no women's music, only women's music audiences.[2] The theory Fink enunciates functions as the GPS equivalent to a soundscape traversed by many different musical styles. Pointing to issues of reception, Fink's theory prevents the reading of musical performances as though they were transparent texts rather than processes of interaction between musicians and audience members in highly specific settings. Fink's insight is one of the most valuable to emerge from the discourse of women's music in that it differentiates reception issues from the factors that contributed to the genre's containment. Based on the formulations of Fink and Small, this chapter assumes that women's music is productively understood as a qualifier to audiences (as in women's music audiences) and that ideal relationships include who the audience imagines itself to be not only through performances but also in its efforts to build feminist community.

Musical Boundaries

The involvement of black women in women's music necessarily expands the parameters of the genre as defined in earlier writings by scholars.[3] The music that has been heard on the festival circuit includes a plethora of styles, among them rock, folk/rock, "world" hand-drumming styles (including *taiko,* Afro-Cuban, and West African hand drumming), blues, rap, a cappella vocals, jazz, hip-hop, musics of the Caribbean and South American diaspora, gospel, country, and the singer/songwriter acoustic musical styles favored by the founding musicians of women's music.[4] Even within this list there is room for individuation: singer/songwriter Laura Love, daughter of a white mother and African American father, describes her style as Afro-Celtic. The list I offer is a composite of genres that are performed at festivals, and as such it references not only the musical styles of black performers but of all musicians regardless of ethnicity. The range of genres that may be performed in the context of a festival renders less tenable facile equations of genre with musical style—an issue a number of ethnomusicologists have addressed.[5]

More integral to the definition of women's music than musical style is the primacy of women in women's lives. Rae Baskin, a white former board president of Women in the Arts, the Midwest collective that sponsors the annual National Women's Music Festival, puts it this way: "We don't have many of those 'he done her wrong' songs."[6] Though accurate, Baskin's comment does not take into account variables that nuance the definition she offers. The use of gender-specific pronouns ("she") is just one of the affirmations of identity adopted by musicians. Live performance affords possibilities for a wide array of additional rearticulations, including the recontextualization of popular songs, the use of parody, and the use of body language.[7]

Writing earlier, I suggested that the combined recorded repertoire of the black musicians who have performed at women's music festivals can be categorized as follows: (1) songs with lesbian feminist content, including love songs; (2) songs concerning multiple axes of oppression; and (3) songs/compositions reflecting black women's cultural/political heritage. Basing a typology on an artist's recorded repertoire alone, however, is a potential danger to which jazz studies scholars, especially those recovering the involvement of women in various communities of jazz music making, have already alerted us. Nanette de Jong's examination of the involvement of women in the Association for the Advancement of Creative Musicians, one of the black avant garde music collectives to emerge in the 1970s, is a reminder that women did not get, and continue not to receive, opportunities to record as often as men, regardless of ability.[8] That recorded repertoire represents only the partial scope of music played at festivals illustrates that these events foster a performance context in which musicians can exhibit a side of their oeuvre or performance personae that for some may not typically be revealed beyond a women's music context. Women's music festival stages enable seasoned performers to work with colleagues in new combinations and perform material that they might not have recorded. "Hazel Turned Me Out," performed by Judith Casselberry of J.U.C.A. at the 1994 Northampton Lesbian Festival, is an example.[9] Nowhere does this very fun, obviously lesbian-identified song appear on recordings. The nuances of kinesis and mimesis, of innuendo and the suggestiveness of musicians' interactions with one another and with members of the audience, cannot be conveyed adequately through an audio recording only.

From an organizational standpoint, board members and producers must balance the draw of an artist who is familiar to a predominantly lesbian audience and its tacit sense of a shared cultural history with the impetus to integrate new talent into the fold. After all, as African American board member Rae Lewis relates, festivals are not in the business of setting out to *lose* money. Lewis (Wiminfest) addressed the challenges this presents:

> It has been really hard to—you know, the audience is mostly lesbians, and they are as diverse as any other group, and so it's really hard to cover a mixture and get stuff that people know—because that's the expectation now. That's one of the hardest things. It's not enough to have good live music—it has to be recognizable—like people can buy cds, and they've heard it on their MP3 players and on the Web. So there is kind of a pressure to have all different types of music that people like—so some of the women's folk music, as well as different types: punk, rock, and then, in terms of artists and comediennes, the big thing is bringing women that audience members recognize, whether it's in the larger community or in the somewhat smaller lesbian community. It's more accessible now, so that's what people expect. They expect name recognition instead of just the girl with the guitar who they discover is really good.[10]

Embedded in Lewis's comments is the supposition that because of the need for the audience to recognize the artist, it is difficult for a musician totally new to women's music to break in, even if she is talented. In that sense, women's music festivals are akin to closed systems. It is unlikely that an aspiring fifty-year-old musician would seek experience and validation through women's music and become a star, even within the small community that women's music festivals represent. Even if she does achieve popularity, she will by necessity be responding to a set of different political, ideological, and musical circumstances than did the founders of women's music.

Appeals to the diversity of musical styles in women's music oversimplify and obscure the contestation over the inclusion of certain musical acts at women's music events. In the festival environment, the issue of musical diversity and its consequences emerges as important not only to concert producers but also to audience members. Music reception, never a process involving one-to-one correspondences, is a multilayered phenomenon involving many elements. When asked, consumers can not help but articulate a notion of "what women's music is" and what it "should do," even if the definition of the genre has not been codified. The exchange I had with a white lesbian elder, cited in the epigraph to this chapter, begins to illustrate the process of unraveling these interpretive threads. Scholars have already demonstrated that the effective performance of gender and sexual identity emerges as important to audience members at festival concerts.[11] White women consumers seemed to adopt one or more of the following perspectives about a black musician's performance: the performance could speak to blackness or it could speak to lesbian identity; interestingly, at the predominantly white festivals, African American attendees thought it was enough that the performer was a black woman.[12]

As the rigidities of cultural feminism gave way following the early years of the women's music scene, many of the essentialist formulations about music were ostensibly set aside and replaced by a discourse of celebratory multiculturalism. Yet, tacit assumptions concerning the subject of lesbian feminism remained an issue in terms of women's music festival concert rosters.

Multiculturalism and the Stories We Tell Ourselves

In terms of programming, women's music festival producers have been caught between a rock and a hard place. On the one hand, it has made sense that producers would want to adopt an inclusive framework both out of their own political commitments and in light of early charges of racism within the festival circuit.[13] Conversely, it has sometimes appeared that the infusion of multiculturalism within festival programs is designed, as bell hooks said many years ago, to assuage or disrupt white sensibilities.[14]

A festival discourse that celebrates multiculturalism speaks more loudly than it did in years past, and by my reckoning, this is a good thing. A celebration of diversity in these contexts, however, still begs the questions of "what type?" and "to what end?" Class, for example, is "invariably named, but rarely theorized or developed in the multiculturalist mantra," which includes race, gender, and sexuality.[15] While working-class codes—if not aspects of working-class culture—are deployed at some festivals, it is more difficult to imagine the strategic celebration of the culture of owning-class women. (The narratives of rich white lesbians are instructive, but they do not figure in the invented lesbian culture of women's music festivals.[16]) In fact, a number of scholars have suggested that feminism's preoccupation with identity politics since the mid-1980s corresponded with the movement's inability to grapple with the issue of class writ large.[17] In abandoning that effort, activists representing a variety of "non-class" identities focused on identity politics even as they set aside a "critique of capitalism and of bourgeois cultural and economic values."[18]

Part of what is lost in the overdetermination of multiculturalism is a sense of the "trench work" that Asian American musician June Millington says was necessary in order to keep women's music going.[19] The desire to include many constituencies under the tent of women's music at times pales against contrasting narratives of musicians and festigoers for whom negotiating conflict—even regular, everyday feminist conflict—loomed significantly in their festival experience and, if this is not too much of a stretch, in the stories they tell themselves and others about their own histories as lesbians and lesbian feminists.[20]

For musicians of color, part of the everyday feminist conflict included confronting "dead" audiences—in other words, concert attendees who experienced an inability to relate to the music. An Asian American rock guitarist and prominent women's music veteran expressed the sense of cultural isolation that musicians of color experienced in the early years: "I used to hate playing for all-white audiences. There was no response . . . no movement or soul. It was very, very hard to get an all-white audience going unless you could play to their culture. Of course, then they aren't really moving; they're just going wild."

Fast-forward three decades from the period that Millington discusses, and tropes of diversity function to varied effect in women's music festival culture. I will address programming issues first. The permeable boundaries of women's music are exhibited through the programming of, broadly speaking, three different types of festival acts. As suggested by Toni Armstrong Jr., the programming for the night stage performances at the Michigan festival, for example, is conceived in three slots: (1) an obviously lesbian feminist act (assumed to be white), (2) an "ethnic" act, and (3) a comedy act.[21]

One ramification of the three-slot paradigm is that sometimes the act signed to fill the "ethnic" slot may or may not self-identify with the diverse attachments traveling under feminism's name. An example is a performance of the Bulgarian State Radio Women's Chorus (marketed as Les Mystiere de Vox Bulgares). The ensemble, which won a Grammy Award in 1990, was a women's choral ensemble that specialized in "post-peasant" styles of singing with traditional text. Even though the ensemble was not feminist from a western perspective, in the festival context the musicians were seen as transversing or transgressing traditional gender boundaries in their home cultures. Ethnomusicologist Mark Slobin points to an interesting and related irony: the 1990 western ideoscape of Eastern Europe as an ever more democratic and free-market corner of the world completely contradicted the philosophy of the creators of the women's chorus—state control of the national heritage.[22]

In an attempt to demonstrate the diversity of festival programming, some scholars have sought to quantify the acts by women of color.[23] The resulting statistics can be misleading in that they do not reflect the actual numbers of nonwhite festival attendees. Often rhetorical gestures fall short of identifying the significance of numbers while attesting to their validity. While appreciating the public relations challenges inherent in festival organization, we are right to inquire into the operations of statistics and to address more deeply their interpretation.

Eventually, women's music festivals began to incorporate the visual arts, dance, comedy, and film into their programming. Kay Weaver and Martha Wheelock's *One Fine Day* is shown each year on the opening night of the National Women's Music Festival.[24] The six-minute film is a retrospective of women's history that includes still photos of feminist precursors and icons such as Sojourner Truth, Eleanor Roosevelt, Shirley Chisholm, Angela Davis, Gloria Steinem, Bella Abzug, Betty Friedan, and Geraldine Ferraro. The film's annual showing functions as a type of ritual for festival attendees, reaffirming their pride in U.S. women's history. Nonetheless, I have experienced an ambivalent reaction to both the film and its reception in this predominantly white lesbian setting. The self-conscious appeal to diversity in the narrative effaces the "hidden transcripts" of history, by which is meant the nonpublic responses, resistances, and actions by those whose public face must remain a façade of acquiescence.[25] Celebratory films like *One Fine Day* do not account for the unequal hierarchies of power that women of different backgrounds experienced both historically and today. As such, the divisions within different factions of the women's movement, or, relationships between "different feminist movements" do not come across in the film.[26] Ironically, the film reinforces notions of a universal sisterhood in a way that runs counter to the festival's attempt to engage difference across gender and sexuality in other aspects of festival life.

The trope of diversity appears as both overrepresented and underrepresented on festival Web sites. Over time, some of these sites have presented a white event as more multicultural than it really is. In contrast, some past Web sites for the Houston Women's Music Festival, for example, have featured no photos that are indicative of the ethnic diversity we have come to expect of these events.

Earlier Web sites of the MWMF, for instance, showed an array of performers in terms of age and ethnicity. In addition to white performers and festival attendees, the Web site for the 2007 festival depicted a photo of elder Ruth Ellis (1899–2000) and a thirty-something light-brown woman of indeterminable ethnicity with a baby.[27] The story of Ellis's early upbringing and the development of her same-gender-loving identity is told in Yvonne Welbon's film *Living with Pride: Ruth C. Ellis @ 100*.[28] The film depicts the role of black lesbian feminist scholar Ekua Omosupe and some of her white lesbian allies in facilitating Ellis's rise to celebrity within black gay and lesbian circles. Eventually she became the grand dame of the Michigan Womyn's Music Festival, holding court, if you will, and sharing her stories and good humor with those who sought her out.[29] She quickly became known as "Miss Ruth" in women's music festival contexts and her face began to appear prominently in films recovering black gay and lesbian history.

With that said, it is unfortunate that Ellis's photo appeared uncredited on the Web site for the Michigan festival. In the photo, her pose mirrored that of Audre Lorde, arms outstretched and over her head, in the well-known photograph by Jean Weisinger.[30] Although the inclusion of the late Ruth Ellis's photo added a much-needed dimension to the MWMF Web site—that of a black lesbian elder—I cannot help but question the rationale for the omission of her name.

From some festival Web sites, which are undoubtedly an improvement over those of earlier years, one might infer that feminism's ideal has been realized when in fact this is not the case. Rather, these Web sites project a proliferation of ethnicities, leaving it to savvy readers to know what these signifiers mean. The phenomenon I outline is a double-edged sword for predominantly white organizations of all kinds that have been accused of racism and strive to be inclusive. The challenge for these organizations is to engage a discourse of multiculturalism in an era in which signifiers of identity are regularly co-opted.

Black Women Don't Camp and Other Myths

Given that celebrations of multiculturalism that stop short of critiquing power relations are problematic, if white festival organizers' celebration of multiculturalism through festival programming strikes a rather hollow note, could it be because black women have failed to respond to organizers' open invitation to attend women's music festivals in the numbers that organizers would like? The question is worth asking, but its framing transfers to black women the failure of white feminism to attract women of color.[31]

"Black women don't camp" was a phrase I often heard African American women voice in jest, even as they pitched their tents on festival grounds. An extension of the attitude reverberates in the recurring statement that "black women aren't feminists" or that "black women don't swim." One of the more illuminating race-exclusive incarnations suggestive of an attributed "black lack," circulated on the Internet in the aftermath of September 11, 2001, was the statement that "black people don't hijack planes."

I return to the quip about camping not for lack of a better topic to consider. To be fair, several women's music festivals build a modicum of indoor comforts into the event: Wiminfest attendees, for example, were housed in the beautifully renovated, grand La Posada Hotel in downtown Albuquerque, a site that was affordable for most, but not all, of the participants. As it had been in earlier years, the NWMF 2007 was held on the campus of Illinois State University in Bloomington–Normal, and attendees were housed in its dormitories. Still, while indoor accommodations such as these are sometimes available, camping, as a mode of experience, looms large in the women's music festival imaginary for previously discussed reasons, including its affordability, the privacy it offers, and the freedom it gives festival attendees to be themselves or whomever they would like to be, at least for a limited period. In a book that theorizes black women's experiences at women's music festivals, many of which are residential and held outdoors, it seems reasonable to contemplate the relationship between black women's agency and this particular outdoor activity. Over the years, white festigoers and festival organizers related their repeated attempts, but uneven effectiveness, at reaching out to black women so that they, too, would attend women's music festivals. Their good intentions, expressed in terms that veteran activists and new social movement theorists alike might advise against, were put this way: "Why don't black women join us out here in the woods?" Questions like these are indicative of what Benita Roth calls playing "the numbers game"; a phenomenon that is manifest in the disproportionate focus on why black women have not been eager to join (white) women's organizations or to identify as feminists.[32]

When I spoke with black women, straight and lesbian, who were unfamiliar with women's music festivals, I mentioned that in many cases camping outdoors characterizes the experience, as does fulfilling a workshift assignment. Neither admission inspired these women to set aside their projects and join me "in the woods." What other modes of thinking can help shed light on this situation?

Throughout history, black collective memory of racialized terror in wide open spaces has often rendered rural locations geographies of danger rather than those of peace and reassurance.[33] Hence, an activity like camping, which many white middle-class women anticipate with joy, or at least equanimity, is viewed with suspicion by some African American women who are more secure with the geographical and architectural familiarity afforded by the city or suburbs in which they live. This phenomenon circulates in black folk discourse as "The devil you know is safer than the devil you don't." The shock of the 1998 death by dragging of James Byrd Jr. at the hands of three white men in Jasper County, Texas, is a more recent reminder that rural spaces are not always safe ones for African Americans.[34] This explanation must be nuanced, of course, to account for personal preferences and generation. There are many white women, especially elders, who associate camping with their youthful and arguably more agile years and therefore attend festivals in recreational vehicles. And beloved black lesbian comic Karen Williams offers still a different take, one infused with working-class sensibility, when she says: "Where I come from, living outdoors is called *homeless*."[35] In response to the prospect of volunteering for a workshift assignment, many black women said they would be uninterested in spending their time away from work *working*. After all, Witold Rybczynski's book about the emergence of the two-day weekend from the nineteenth century to the present is titled *Waiting for the Weekend*, not *Waiting to Work on the Weekend*.[36] Rybczynski argues that leisure activities might fulfill some unmet needs of work, but this point seems to have been lost on most "civilian" interlocutors with whom I spoke.

On the other hand, in light of the "volunteer vacation" trend that affords participants the experience of building a house, helping scientists in Africa track endangered wildlife, or maintaining nature trails, some potential festival attendees might find the prospect of a workshift or two appealing.[37] The festival workshift was part of the overall ethos of lesbian feminist community building; in the 1970s, festival organizers attempted to expand the community by providing easy access for disabled women and sliding scale fees "so that the poor would not be excluded."[38] Still, within this framework, conflicts were and are inevitable, and the different class-related sensibilities that African American women bring to the festival experience emerge in the types of critiques they make of decisions by festival producers. Marietta Beamer, a black lesbian attendee, related her efforts to help organize the Women of Color tent, a responsibility that contributed to making the Northampton Lesbian Festival a "positive experience" for her that year.[39] Her comment brings into focus the politics of place and of class: "Last year, the festival was expensive to attend; plus it was held in the mountains. There was no public transportation to the site. It [the festival] completely catered to women who have money. The women of color tried to point out that if they [the organizers] were trying to be inclusive, they had to think about the needs of poorer women."[40]

The critique that Beamer offers is not new to feminist organizations. Later, she said: "You would not believe where they placed the tent for women of color—behind the kitchen door, like the [proverbial] manor house. There was lots of talk about how to make the festival more welcoming, more inclusive. We all know that racism is in the larger community, so that you can't expect your subculture, the lesbian community, to be any different. You've got to make an effort." In the incident Beamer recounts, the festival's decision to assign the women of color tent to a position behind the kitchen door evoked powerful collective memories of a racialized and gendered social history in which African American women experienced subordination within white homes.[41]

The residue of women's music festival history includes several other injurious incidents in which racism or the perception of racism is implicated. Ranking high on that list is an incident that occurred at the West Coast Women's Music and Comedy Festival (WCWMCF), produced by comedian Robin Tyler.[42] In the following account, Tyler shares how the dynamics of racism came to affect both her and the second annual West Coast festival, held in 1981:

> However, at the beginning of it—and this is still painful for me to talk about—a small group of women of color came to me and said that I had to give one-third of the festival to women of color, as I was a rich Jew, and Jews were responsible for slavery. I couldn't believe what I was hearing! I immediately said that I was from Canada, but they said that it didn't matter, that I had hired "all black women" in the kitchen. Actually, I hadn't. We had hired two African American coordinators, and they had hired all their friends because the kitchen was the best-paid position on the land—$500. But they said that I was just a rich Jew trying to get rich off the backs of the women's community. They told me I had to give them one-third of the business or they would organize a march against the festival. And I said no, that I wouldn't give in to this form of extortion.

Tyler, who, as the festival producer, took to the stage that night as emcee, recounts that more than two hundred women "marched on" her while she was onstage: "A group of women even came with torches . . . and they threatened to burn down the cabin I was in." Reflecting on instances of unexamined anti-Semitism in women's culture and in the women's movement, Tyler continues: "The Michigan festival, with many more attendees, was not attacked for living off the backs of women. But I was called a rich Jew. At the time, no one was discussing the split between people of color and the Jewish community—the anti-Semitism was rampant. Women held meetings in which I was 'put on trial' for being a racist; of course, I was not allowed at these 'trials,' never allowed to defend myself, and the [women's] press carried their stories." Tyler recalls that Barbara "Boo" Price, then producer of the Michigan Womyn's Music Festival, accompanied her to "the only community meeting where some women admitted they had lied" about her: "But by that time I was condemned in the gay press, and not one of them carried the story of that community meeting that absolved me of my 'crimes.' I believe to this day that my only crime was that I was Jewish." This incident had a powerful effect on Tyler both personally and professionally. She concludes by stating that she "did not write another line of comedy for 12 years," and because she was boycotted, she "performed very little for the next five years." She went on to found the Southern Women's Music and Comedy Festival in 1983.[43]

Among other things, the incident that Tyler recounts demonstrates the interplay of fact, rumor, good intentions, and misunderstanding in women's music festival culture. Stories such these are often painful for everyone involved, and many participants would wish to move on. Indeed, perhaps it was incidents such as these that Judy Dlugacz referred to when she said that she understood why women did not want to talk about the bad "good ole days" (see chapter 3). The exigencies of racism, anti-Semitism, and homophobia beat back the tide of a more optimistic claim for women's unity based on shared gender experience—a perfect storm that would come to haunt lesbian feminist movement.[44]

Given the skirmishes in the multicultural wars I have outlined and their connection to the notion of "ideal relationships," would an all-black women's music festival present a tension-free alternative?[45] In the next chapter I discuss two contemporary black lesbian events that are within the purview of this study. The allusion to black futurism conjured by the next chapter recalls the work of speculative fiction writer Octavia Butler, as well as the spirit behind a collection of photographs of prominent African American women, *I Dream a World*.[46]

> Many women have thanked me for having outdoor events. They have said, "We're always in these cramped little clubs. We're never in the sunshine. We're never gay outdoors."—MARQUITA THOMAS, FOUNDER, OUT AND ABOUT

CHAPTER 6

Redistricting

GAY AND BLACK OUTDOORS

This chapter illustrates the type of conceptual realignment described in chapter 1 as "redistricting." Given the persistence of a yearning on the part of many African American women for a majority-black lesbian music festival, this chapter refigures all-black events as sites for the emergence of an ideal relationship that departs from that described in the previous chapter. The focus is two events that are similar in ethos to the other lesbian music festivals discussed in this book. Organized into three parts, the chapter includes an interview with the founder of a one-day music festival for women of color; an interview with a musician who performed at that event; and field notes from Sistahfest, a black lesbian retreat founded in 1991.

Tenderfoot: A New Festival

In 2005 a new women's music festival was founded that did an end run around the thorny question of how to encourage women of color to attend predominantly white women's music festivals: Marquita Thomas organized Serafemme: Women of Color Music Festival—or, as it was called in advertising on white lesbian/gay Listservs, "A Queer Women of Color Music Festival."[1] The difference in nomenclature reflects the selective use of the term "queer" in African American communities.

Serafemme was billed as the only women-centered event of At the Beach, the celebration of Black Pride held annually in Los Angeles. Held in the parking lot of the National Gay and Lesbian Archives, the festival was open to everyone. The one-day event (with an "after party" following the program) attracted black women attendees, mostly lesbian, from eighteen to at least one woman in her seventies. Here, it would be disingenuous and dishonest to modify "black women" with "predominantly," as is often done when an event takes place in a white context. With the exception of a few Asian American and Latina performers, this was a black event. I noticed only one white man (about sixty years of age) and one young African American boy (about nine), who for a while occupied a chair beside me. No adult black men were present.

In contrast to some other women's music festivals held outdoors, attendees sat under the hot sun in the metal chairs provided by Serafemme; there was little shade. Most of the acts were by black women who performed on the main stage—the only stage. In the festival's first year, standout acts included Hanifah Walidah, Vanessa James, Jessica Knox, and Korean American spoken-word artist Skim. Latina comics infused humor into the event; the musical lineup included black women singing original jazz tunes, soul, and acoustic folk, with house-inspired music reserved for the event's conclusion. Pronouns of songs originally addressed to the heterosexual mainstream (Oleta Adams's "Get Here If You Can," sung by Miss Money, for example) were not changed for the audience. With the exception of singers accompanied by either guitar or hand drums, the instrumental accompaniment was prerecorded. Serafemme joins a very small number of music festivals for lesbians of color. Although it is intellectually shortsighted to make broad claims about grassroots phenomena that are difficult to document, to my knowledge there have been few events in the past two decades comparable to the festival that Thomas produced.[2]

Marquita Thomas is the executive director of Out and About, a special events planning company designed to meet the needs of lesbians of color in Southern California. Her activist trajectory is noteworthy for two reasons. First, the founding of Serafemme took place in a political environment that differed dramatically from that which early (white) women's music festival founders encountered from the early 1970s to the mid-1980s. Not only did Thomas have an all-women-of-color audience in mind, but she has been influenced by and is influential in coalitions of black lesbian and gay activists, a phenomenon an earlier generation of black lesbian feminist activists did not experience in the same way. Second, through her discussion of her own activist history, it becomes clear that the festival materialized independent of a conscious framework of feminist organizing, with its implications of coalition work, which was an important value of radical feminism of the 1970s and 1980s. Thomas, in her late twenties, describes the circumstances in which Serafemme was founded:

> I was recently "out," and I was very frustrated because there wasn't anywhere to go to network and to meet people outside of typical clubs and the Internet. I didn't find any support groups, mixers, hip clubs—I wanted to fill that void, so I started throwing dance parties, because everybody likes to party, and I thought it would be a good way to get my name out there and meet people and get my name out. I've done everything from horseback riding—outdoor activities like that—some mixers, panel discussions. I've worked with various lesbian conferences—a little bit of everything.[3]

Although she had never before attended a women's music festival and, indeed, told me that she had never heard of the Michigan Womyn's Music Festival until 2004, Thomas frames her narrative in terms of the white-majority festivals not meeting her needs:

> I wanted to go to a queer women of color music festival, and I looked online and I didn't see anything like that, and I have a lot of powerful queer women of color friends . . . Most women's music festivals have a people of color section, but it's still very segregated, and they are kind of peppered with women of color, and I wanted women of color to be celebrated, so I spoke with my friend Hanifah Walidah, and she was very excited about the idea.[4] I started putting it in motion in about February. I found a location by the end of March, and that left me with ninety days to completely execute the festival, which was a feat in and of itself. It got done, and people loved it, and they are already looking forward to next year.

Thomas envisioned an all-day event that was outdoors and at the same time a "little secluded" so that a modicum of privacy could be maintained. Holding the event on the property of the National Gay and Lesbian Archives, also one of the sponsors of the festival, was strategic for that reason. The festival was purposefully scheduled to coincide with At the Beach.

> MT: I wanted there to be a definitive women's event. Of course, there are women's parties, but I wanted there to be a women's event to coincide with the weekend's events.
>
> EH: Hmm. A lot of lesbians have found that gay and lesbian pride marches around the country have been pretty male-centered. Have you experienced any of that?
>
> MT: That was part of my reasoning for doing it during the gay Pride event.

> I wanted to have one more event just for the girls—well, not just for the girls—men could come, too. But it was an event that was produced by women, executed by women, for women, it featured women—every aspect of it was female, so I definitely wanted to have that.

Recognizing Thomas's go-getter spirit, and thinking of music festival founder Robin Tyler,[5] I suggested that she was indeed an entrepreneur. She replied:

> I don't know if I've always been an entrepreneur. Actually Out and About, for me, is so not about money. It was more about community. For sure, I'm a person of action . . . When I came out, I faced such a void that once I was established in who I was, I decided that I wanted to fill that void. I don't get paid for Out and About events . . . so many women have thanked me for having outdoor events such as horseback riding and potluck barbeques. They have said, "We're always in these cramped little clubs. We're never in the sunshine. We're never gay outdoors."

Thomas's comment dovetailed with those of other black women with whom I spoke—women who valued club life but sought alternatives for socializing and those whose needs for socializing were no longer fulfilled by club life, and it resonates with issues I raised in chapter 5 under the heading "Black Women Don't Camp." The inaugural launching of Serafemme and successive events that Thomas produced demonstrate her commitment to keeping the field of black lesbian networking and outdoor pursuits wide open.

Thomas, who had no prior experience organizing a musical event with live musicians, experienced a steep learning curve as she secured the location, gave herself a crash course in sound equalizers and PA systems, and took charge of securing festival sponsorship.[6] In addition to in-kind and cash gifts from nonprofit organizations, the musicians donated their performances and paid for their own travel. "Everyone just really wanted to be a part of it," Thomas said. "I didn't get any rejections from anyone. There were numerous in-kind donations. I expect that in a couple years we'll be able to pay the artists. There is nothing like this [a queer women of color music festival] out there."

Marquita Thomas's is a strong voice in terms of advocacy for black lesbian and gay rights. In addition to organizing Serafemme, she spoke at Dyke March 2005 in Los Angeles.[7] Given her developing confidence as an activist, and Out and About's focus on social networking for lesbians of color, I asked Thomas if she identifies as a feminist. Her response reveals her understanding of feminism as a mode of thinking that celebrates women.

> MT: I am a feminist, I guess. Not "I guess." I'm very quick to recognize when women are not celebrated the way they should be, but I'm not part of any feminist organization. I wouldn't *not* say that I'm a feminist.

EH: Okay. Is there a reluctance there?

MT: No, there's not a reluctance. I think it's kind of a movement that I'm not as familiar with. I mean, aside from knowing that women should be celebrated, adored, and all that other great stuff—celebrating us as women and in our energy—I don't really know what being a feminist is entirely. You know what I mean? As silly as that may sound. Then again, I'm not really part of a feminist organization. I don't know what the big issues are facing us as feminists. I don't feel I can speak intelligently on the whole feminist movement, and that's what makes me reluctant. I don't organize around women's issues, I organize around gay issues, and minority gay issues in particular . . . I want particularly black lesbians to feel empowered, to know what the issues are for us, to bridge the gap between older and younger women, to have a safe network, to have everything that they deserve. Then, yeah—I'm a feminist, too. (laughs)

Again, Thomas's can-do spirit emerges. Rather than frame her activism in terms of feminist politics, coalition or otherwise, she offers a more pragmatic line of reasoning:

> I tend to just think "We need this in our community" and I do it. I don't really think about what that means or even if it needs to be celebrated. If a house needs to be built, you build it, and you don't worry about if that makes you a contractor. And I think that more of us need to do that instead of worrying about the accolades or worrying, period. Because there is always something to worry about—you know what I mean? I worry all the time.
>
> When I first did Out and About, I didn't want to put my name on anything. I didn't want any spotlight. I didn't want anyone to know who was behind it. And I learned that in this area that's not possible. People want to know who you are . . . As I do interviews, I find myself worrying about things that I say—"Is that politically correct?" I worry—and I feel that there is a lot of worry in our community. "Am I going to lose my job? Is someone going to find out I'm gay? Am I gay enough?" I organized a panel discussion last year, and several people said they were worried they were going to lose their job, that they were going to lose their families, [and asked] "How can I do this?" You just have to set up a Mazer Archive [meaning, take a risk] and not be afraid to fall on your face, and I'm talking about myself as well. I mean, I told you I was worried around Serafemme.

Although Thomas's "come hell or high water" attitude is to be appreciated, the work of numerous black gay and lesbian scholars, as well as my own research, suggests that many black gays and lesbians do not feel they can afford to be "out" on their jobs, let alone with their families. A Latina feminist and longtime organizer of Wiminfest reported being a member of the board for more than two decades even though she was out neither to her family nor to her coworkers. When I asked Thomas to elaborate further, she spoke about appearing on a panel (in a conference format) and related that people reacted strongly to her suggestion that more black lesbian and gays should be out:

> First of all, if you're a meter maid, you're going to be okay . . . People [at the forum] were saying, "Who are you to tell me that I should be out?" Okay, you don't have to be out, but at the same time, there are only so many of us who do activism in the community, and if you don't fight for equal protection under the law, then when we do a press conference or hold a rally, it doesn't look good for there to only be twenty of us. Do you see what I mean? And it's because people worry about being seen on television and "what will the neighbors think?" I can't worry about that.

Later, Thomas compared her activism on behalf of African Americans to her advocacy on behalf of black gays and lesbians.

> MT: I'm a lot more passive in my black activism. I write about those issues. I've noticed in the past couple years that I'm physically present in gay activism more often than I am at black activist events. I went to the anti-inaugural [of George W. Bush] rally in Westwood, and I went to other events, but I guess since I know that my presence is so needed on gay issues because there are so few of us, I will lend my support more through my words (writing an op-ed), but my presence is a definite at the gay events.
>
> EH: Do you see black gay and lesbian activism as a subset of black activism? Are they two different things?
>
> MT: I think I'm a black gay activist before I'm a black activist. I'm trying to think. I'm trying to think of the issues that have been before me. When the whole Rodney King [incident] broke out, I worked everywhere. I don't know. If anything ever went down, I'd lend my support. As a collective, are black gay activists black activists first? That I don't know. I know that if there were two incidents—one involving a black gay and another involving a black straight—and I had to choose between the protests, I think I might go to the gay event. I might think that the straights have it covered, people-wise.

Thomas's activist spirit, political outlook, and entrepreneurial skills coalesce in her work in the black lesbian and gay community and in her organization of the one-day music festival. Her reflections about Serafemme foreshadow issues that arose in conversations with black festigoers who have carved out and sustained programmatic spaces for women of color in predominantly white festival organizations. The work of festival founders and volunteers reveals that a variety of approaches was necessary to mind the gap between potential festival attendees of various backgrounds and the vision of a women-identified solidarity, whether the festival was predominantly white or black. Because black lesbian history is refracted through numerous locations, it would be incorrect to assume that the event Thomas produced was the first music festival for lesbians of color. Recoveries of similar historical events are reminders that scholars as well as queer community archivists should exercise caution when making definitive pronouncements that might inadvertently foreclose on and invisibilize earlier manifestations of black lesbian feminist expressive culture.

A Study in Contradictions: Miss Money

Miss Money (aka Mona Bailey) was one of about twenty women of color who performed at the Serafemme festival in 2005. Her rendition of Oleta Adams's "Get Here If You Can" was well received at the festival.[8] Like Adams, Miss Money is also the daughter of a minister. Her charming and demure onstage persona belied the breadth of her experience, however, as a hip-hop artist and deejay.

For Miss Money, dubbed "the gay Missy Elliott" by her friends, the comparison was a compliment. Wearing a fade (a haircut typically associated with African American men), the artist was quick to add, however, "But I can't be Missy. I can only be Money." While a title such as "the gay Missy Elliott" sounds like a tribute (and a reversal of the familiar practice of a black person being evaluated in relation to a white celebrity), it might figure as only a half compliment. Some might remember that in years past, Elliott, because of her heavier weight and dark skin, did not figure into the hip-hop mainstream either—that is, if women can be figured as members of the industry's center at all. For some, Elliott was the "other" of hip-hop's other: black women. Following a professional makeover in terms of appearance and musical output, however, Elliott assumed a place that was more in hip-hop's mainstream, at least for a while.

Miss Money and I spent a good deal of time talking about appearance. A number of her views will strike casual observers of black popular culture as counterintuitive, especially with regard to hip-hop. In one of our exchanges she counterposed the standards of beauty imposed by the R&B and gospel music industries (think Beyoncé and Yolanda Adams or the gospel duo Mary Mary, respectively) to hip-hop's relative openness to women whose physical appearance falls outside of traditional norms:

> MM: Hip-hop is a genre that you can kind of get in and blend in, because there is so much going on. You know I couldn't really get into gospel and R&B because of the image, so I went into hip-hop with everybody else who looked like me and kind of have branched back into R&B and gospel.
>
> EH: Can you elaborate on that?

MM: I think that in gospel and R&B there is an idea that women are to look and conduct themselves in certain ways in order to be commercially successful and to be marketable by the labels. And so when I first began, I couldn't get any interest from anybody in those genres. No one wanted to support me. I sang gospel as a child, but I also had a different image. I was living with my parents. There was no way I could walk around with a [high-top] fade in the "Reverend's house"—you've got to be kidding me. As soon as I got out, then everything changed. So I had to go over to the hip-hop world, where there are so many things going on. I mean there's everything—drug abuse, you know what I'm saying, violence—there's some positivity, but with so much chaos, you can just settle in, and you're bound to find somebody that will accept you. That's kind of what has happened to me. I got over there, and people just began accepting me.[9]

Miss Money relates that even the history of her name is not unrelated to the music industry's preoccupation with appearance:

> I got the name from a friend of mine. When I first got into hip-hop, I was "Money, the B-girl Wonder," because I was doing hip-hop and I was living the B-girl look: the baggy jeans—it was a really, really hip-hop look. I would sing, and the audience didn't know if I was a man or a woman, so the emcee at a local show I did, one day she pulled me over and said, "Look, we've got to add something before the 'Money.' We just have to. Let's add 'Miss.'" And I've been Miss Money ever since.

I mentioned to Money that many, in a "post–early MC Lyte age," would be surprised at her appraisal of hip-hop as a world accepting of a woman whose appearance did not conform to standards of neo–soul diva glamour. She agreed:

> Right. And I think that the misconception is that hip-hop will not accept gay people or gay women. But for me, I'm not finding that at all. Every once in a while I find that, but I'm finding that people just want to get to know you as an artist, and any extracurricular things that are going on in your life that they might not agree with, well, you might not want to speak on these all the time. I choose not to bring it into my music a lot. I know at Serafemme there were some very queer-friendly artists—you know what I mean—and I applaud that. I think it's great. But for me, I haven't really used it as openly as some of the artists I saw.

The "it" to which Miss Money refers are her identities as both a black woman and a lesbian. With her reference to "extracurricular things," Money downplays the sexual aspect of her sexual identity, a familiar strategy invoked by black lesbians in their narratives and black (straight) feminist critics in their writings or critiques of writing by black lesbians.[10] In contrast to this silence, black lesbian writer Jewelle Gomez offers an appreciation of Audre Lorde's explicit depiction of sexuality in her biomythography, *Zami: A New Spelling of My Name*, suggesting, "She also is able to acknowledge and describe her political perspectives on race, gender, and sexuality without relinquishing the specifics of her sexuality as a Black woman and as a lesbian."[11] Miss Money's reference to her sexual identity as "extracurricular" undergirds the suggestion that instantiations of outness vary, whether the primary context for one's coming out is black lesbian literature, ethnographic studies, or one's day job as a performer.

In spite of the acceptance Miss Money found in the hip-hop world, she was mindful of non-counterhegemonic attitudes within the music industry toward the inclusion of B-girls, or young women whose participation in hip-hop is often characterized, narrowly, as revolving around breakdancing. Therefore, she eased into including images of herself in promotional materials. Money demonstrates that her plan was well thought out:

> Now I had a strategy. I did everything gradually and slowly. I didn't put my picture on my first four mix tapes—they were all illustrations, and they were just my name and my voice. You know what I'm saying—my production. And on the fifth mix tape (*Whoa, Man!* dropped in January), that was the first time that anybody in hip-hop had seen my face, and I thought it was going to be a problem. There was a little bit of chaos at first, because they were like, "This is the image behind that voice? You've got to be kidding me." And then it all died down. And now I'm busier than ever singing with all kinds of rappers, really.

Still, Money admitted that although she found acceptance in hip-hop as a behind-the-scenes artist, her mobility as a singer was circumscribed by reactions to her physical appearance: "I wasn't convinced that I could have a career as a singer based on what people in the industry were telling me based on my image, so I was mixing hip-hop and doing a little bit of singing. Now I tend to be making contributions to hip-hop behind the scenes, like producing and maybe singing the hooks, and my personal stuff is coming down to doing more singing."

Later, Miss Money spoke of the humiliation she has experienced in the music industry as a by-product of confounding its gender expectations:

> MM: People are surprised at how easy I am to work with, but why wouldn't I be? Maybe it's my Louisiana down-home raising. I've been humiliated in the industry. Being humiliated teaches you humility. It works. In the first couple years—I called myself the laughing stock of the industry. People were really getting a kick out of the fact that I was trying to come into the industry wearing a fade, wearing the starched-down pants—they were really trippin' on that. I remember the reactions I got, and I can never become this person who was humiliated. I know what it's like to be at the bottom. I know what

it's like to be ridiculed, criticized, made fun of . . . I never get egotistical with the Miss Money thing.

EH: Right. Was some of that ridicule sexism because you didn't meet that image that they had of performers?

MM: Yes, most of it was. It's not even about the gay thing. It really is about the look. Because if I didn't look that way, people may or may not know that I was gay. People just assume that I am, because of my look, but people are just programmed. They know about Trina and Eve and Beyoncé and Ashanti—they see what all these women are doing, and if you don't come out looking like that, they pull away and say, "Okay, what's going on?"[12]

I continued to pursue the thread about sexism in hip-hop by commenting on Miss Money's prolific career as a writer. She responded:

> Men especially have a hard time accepting the fact that I'm more busy now than before. They'll say, "You're a sister and you're goin' where? You're doing the Budweiser Blues Festival and you don't have my beats yet?" No, bro, I've got other things lined up. I know you're not used to hearing this from your sisters in the industry. You're used to us makin' it in the backseat of your jeep. You're used to us maybe being backstage or on the front row, pulling our panties up there. I'm not the one. (laughs) You know what I mean? I'm not that sister, boo—I can't help you! . . . It feels good to tell brothers, "I know I used to sing your hooks, but you gonna have to wait a little while. I have other things that I'm doing now; I don't just sing hooks anymore." It kinda feels good to say that to my brothers—I ain't gonna lie! (laughs)

Money's mention of hooks was reminiscent of the character Nola in director Craig Brewer's film *Hustle and Flow.* Taryn Maning plays the girlfriend of a Memphis pimp-cum-wannabe-rapper played by actor Terrence Howard. Like Money, Nola, too, grows weary of singing hooks, the repeated and catchy instrumental or vocal riff of a song, and dreams of being bigger.[13]

Unlike some performers who played at Serafemme, Miss Money was not new to the world of women's music festivals; she had performed at the Houston Women's Festival in 2001.[14] Like many of the festivals of size and longevity, the Houston event had a main stage (higher prestige) and a local acts stage, which Miss Money headlined. She contrasts her reception at the Houston festival with her reception in other music venues in her southwestern hometown:

> Houston is very, very segregated. When I lived in LA, it was interesting to see the diversity. In Houston, blacks live with blacks, whites with whites. Being invited to the Houston Women's Festival was the highlight of my career, because I did run into so much racism when I started performing around Houston. They're not used to seeing black women with careers. How ridiculous is that? That's

absurd—I mean, on the independent level. Of course they know the Whitney Houstons, and the Beyoncés and stuff . . . But I mean a young black woman out here hustling deejay tapes and hustling screw tapes and with a radio show—they just can't believe it.

Revealed in Miss Money's statement is the idea that the Houston Women's Festival was a reprieve, a site of relief from the racism she experienced in the Houston music scene—and not a perpetuator of it. Here she reflects further on her experiences in the Houston music community: "People are just shocked—they can't believe first of all that I'm a black woman attempting to do things, and they can't believe I'm a gay woman attempting to do things. I can see it in their eyes. It's kind of like, 'What are you doing here?' I have the same perseverance that my parents taught me—the same tenacity. I apply it to everything: sexism, homophobia, and racism." I picked up on the low expectations Miss Money was describing. She elaborated:

Yeah, I think they do have low expectations . . . their expectation is that you have a low expectation of yourself because of the color your skin, which is absolutely ridiculous—you know what I mean? A lot of it, I think, is just perception. It's because they see the way our brothers treat us in hip-hop. They see how we act in videos. They see the representation of our bodies, they see the way black women are treated by black people. If that's what the white people are seeing—the way our black brothers are treating us—I mean, of course they aren't going to treat us any better . . . I don't really know who to blame—artists like Lil' Kim, or do you blame the labels? I don't know, but I believe that hip-hop has a lot to do with the degradation of black women's image in society.

Miss Money addresses aspects of a much-circulated discourse about misogynistic images of black women perpetuated in hip-hop tracks and videos. In doing so, she echoes the view of many, including hip-hop feminists such as Joan Morgan and Eisa Davis, as well as numerous parents, black feminist theorists, activists, scholars, critics of black popular culture, and young women "round the way." At the same time, she tacitly implicates not only artists such as Lil' Kim (Kimberly Denise Jones), who has fashioned herself into a black woman hip-hop superhero, but also many black women video dancers who, it is often thought, perpetuate derogatory images of black women through their line of employment.[15] Singling out individual video dancers neither addresses nor resolves the real problem, of course. Hip-hop music and related products in which black women are routinely disrespected is a multibillion-dollar business.

It soon became apparent that Miss Money has thought out every aspect of her career development. Part of that meant planning the transition from her role as a deejay and producer to singer. Deciding to host a radio show (on Houston's Radio 713) in July 2004 was a part of that strategy. Given the circumstances, she said, it was something she had to do in order to accrue more credibility as a singer. She explained:

> I didn't feel that I would make it as just a rapper or producer. I felt I needed to get a radio show. I think artists don't know how much helping other artists helps your own career. I've never heard an artist have a hard time talking about themselves. I thought, "What better way to meet artists?" I started it in hopes of meeting more people . . . It helps people hear that I'm human: [they think,] "Yeah, she's a woman, she's gay, but she knows her hip-hop." These are grown black men coming into the studio talking to a sistah. There's no homophobia; we're getting along like two normal people.

"Normalcy"—if not respectability—is a recurrent trope in some gay and lesbian discourses, especially in earlier African American gay and lesbian ones. Miss Money mentions explicitly the context in which an emphasis on normalcy develops: the stigma attached to being both lesbian and black. Following along these lines, I asked if a women of color music festival might be in Houston's future. She answered: "It would be something good to try. With the stigma attached—that it is just for gay women—it might take a couple of years for it to grow in Houston, but it should be tried. Los Angeles is probably a little more open. Houston is more close-minded. This is the South. We're a little behind."

Throughout our conversation, Miss Money referred to herself as a "gay black female," as did a number of women I met at the Serafemme festival. I asked if she had a preference for the term "gay" over "lesbian."

> I don't know if I have a preference. Being gay to me is inconsequential. To me there's no consequence to me being gay, because I don't let there be a consequence. I'm not afraid of being gay. Being black is very consequential. Gay people are an oppressed people, but you don't see it on our faces. You don't see it in our society. We party everywhere we go. Black people are an oppressed people, and we wear it well. We wear our oppression. It's two different inner emotions. I'm very proud to be gay, and I'm very proud to be black, but being black, I'm reminded of it every day. Being gay—people can look at me crazy all day, and that's it. It's kind of a look of curiosity. It's not a look of "We want you out of our store." "She's gonna steal my bag." Or "We're going to pull you over for no reason." It's nonthreatening. It doesn't make me feel any less of a person than I already am. Being black is just something that you cannot escape in this country.

Money, while bypassing my initial question about her preference for "gay" over "lesbian," makes a complex statement that warrants unpacking: first is the suggestion that black identity is foundational in a way that sexual identity is not. This comes across in her statement that "Being black is very consequential . . . Black people are an oppressed people, and we wear it well . . . being black, I'm reminded of it every day." While some might consider this an example of essentialism, I disagree. In highlighting the phenomenon of "surveillance" that blacks of all class backgrounds may experience in the public sphere, Money gives voice to a topic widely discussed by scholars and critics. Patricia Collins suggests that surveillance, which, I might add, ignores gender boundaries, highlights individuality by making the individual hypervisible and on display. The examples Money offers—"She's gonna steal my bag" and "driving while black"—are two of many that have been documented over the past decade.[16] According to Collins, surveillance is one of the effects of the "new politics of containment" that African American women experience in the post–civil rights period.

Implicit in Money's statement also is that sexual identity often passes unmarked and therefore functions differently from visible markers of racial identity and their ramifications ("People can look at me crazy all day, and that's it. It's kind of a look of curiosity").[17] Here our respective opinions diverge. If events reported in the news are any indication, being a black lesbian in the public sphere can indeed have negative consequences. Instances in which a black lesbian firefighter files a sexual harassment suit against the Los Angeles Fire Department and wins or, on a less hopeful note, the "targeted incarceration" of four young adult black lesbians in New Jersey make it difficult to say categorically that the combination of race, gender, and sexual identity is inconsequential.[18]

In the hope of contributing to a wider conversation on both third-wave and hip-hop feminism, both of which reveal inattention to perspectives of black lesbians, I asked Money about her activist history and whether she identified either as a feminist or womanist. She answered:

> MM: No, I've never gotten the activist bug, you know what I'm saying? I'm more of the artist's artist. I don't need to be on TV, we don't need to have no press conference, I'm not doing any parades—you know what I'm saying? We're not going to put no pink triangles on the CD covers. I'm not going to do that. I'm not that kind of artist, but I am grateful that there are artists out there. I don't consider Ellen DeGeneres an activist, but I think that a lot of people do. I don't think that she would consider herself an activist, but there are a lot of people who really think that she is on a mission to help bring exposure to the lesbian entertainer, white or black, but I don't see that when I see Ellen. I just see an extraordinary entertainer who is just having fun. She just wants to be treated like everyone else. It's always the audience that puts that expectation on you. I can't do that. I don't want that expectation. I don't want people thinking that I'm here to be the spokesman for "Studs That

Sing." I'm not going to be the spokesmen for the singing studs committee—you know what I mean—find somebody else. I don't want to do that. That's not my purpose. I don't feel that the Lord put me here for that. So I'm going to have to pass on that one.

EH: You are a comedian.

MM: You know, there was a lot of comedy in that show [the Serafemme festival]. And I thought it was really interesting to see these women clowning—I've never seen anyone pull a dead chicken out on stage [referring to a performance piece by an artist called Sphear].

EH: That was wild.

MM: I've never been to a Houston Women's Festival and have heard women speak openly about their love for other women—you know what I mean. Some were doing it romantically, some were doing it in a vulgar manner—I've never heard that. It's almost as though the women at the Houston festival were creatively frustrated. Why shouldn't you be able to pull a dead chicken out on the stage? Why shouldn't you be able to express your love for another woman? So I've never seen a show like that, personally. Yeah, I had fun at that festival. It was so worth it.

Like some other women of her political generation, Miss Money associates activism with traditional technologies; in this subset, she includes ostensibly gay parades (although the extent to which contemporary gay parades as opposed to marches are "political" in the same way they were in the early 1980s is debatable), press conferences, and pink triangles affixed to cd covers. She also referenced the then-thirty-nine-year-old comedian Ellen DeGeneres ("TV's first leading lesbian"), who played bookstore owner Ellen Morgan on the weekly ABC television sitcom *Ellen*. Her character's unintended announcement of her gay identity over the live public address system of the airport preceded the actor's "carefully orchestrated" announcement of her gay identity in real life.[19] Many in the gay and lesbian community felt that her announcement was a long time coming. Lastly, Money references the fact that women performers at Serafemme spoke openly (in song lyrics and poetry) of their love for women, adding that "some were doing it in a vulgar manner." I did not explore Miss Money's observation about the "vulgar" material, although I assumed it was a reference to some of the black lesbian erotic poetry that was recited. Within the black lesbian community, as is the case with many communities, there is a wide range of opinion about the appropriateness of performing sexually explicit material in public.

Miss Money represents a voice not heard from previously in the scholarship on hip-hop and feminism. The forthrightness with which she discusses not only aspects of her experience in the music industry but also the expressiveness of the language in which her insights are embedded make her interview an important addition to the literature. Although I would like to write that we will hear more from this artist in the future, such certitude and individual talent have fallen short as predictors of longevity in the field. This is as true for women performers in hip-hop as it is for black performers in women's music. While Serafemme was the brainchild of a single entrepreneur, the all-black lesbian retreat Sistahfest emerged from a meeting of lesbian feminist activists. This has a bearing on the difference in mission and approach of the respective organizations as well as how internal tensions are resolved.

Look Homeward, Sistahfest

It might have been predicted that a volume that began with an ethnographic account of the Michigan Womyn's Music Festival would include a visit to Sistahfest, the all-black lesbian cultural, musical, and political retreat founded in 1991 by United Lesbians of African Heritage.[20] That ULOAH emerged in Los Angeles almost two decades after comparable organizations for white lesbians does not interrupt narrative frameworks containing the implicit suggestion that the white women's liberation branch of second-wave feminism was a template that African American feminists later used for their feminist politics. Sociologist Benita Roth dubs this approach an example of "model-making." Critical to an understanding of the emergence of black feminism—and, by association, black lesbian feminism in the contemporary period—is the intellectual framework in which the emergence of black feminist organizations is interpreted. By misunderstanding the timing of black feminist emergence and playing the numbers game—that is, worrying why black feminists did not join mainstream feminist groups—scholars have missed the chance to map out the different challenges of movement loyalty and movement repression that black feminists faced.[21]

Therefore, brief attention to the history of activism by lesbian feminists of color in Los Angeles is important to placing the emergence of ULOAH in context. A number of lesbians of color organizations emerged in the 1970s: Lesbianas LatinasAmericanas began in 1974; out of debates at the founding convention of the National Lesbian Feminist Organization came a group called Lesbians of Color (LOC) of Los Angeles. LOC held many community workshops on racism and organized the National Lesbians of Color Conference held in Malibu in 1983.[22] Other lesbians of color groups from this time period include Debretas, Lesbianas Unidas (organized in 1984), and Asian/Pacific Lesbians (organized in 1985). Interestingly, but not surprisingly, Lesbianas Unidas, Asian/Pacific Lesbians, and ULOAH emerged from what historian Yvonne Retter calls "co-sexual" organizations, or groups for women and men. ULOAH was born during a meeting of the Black and Gay Leadership Forum, founded in 1988.[23] Two longtime black lesbian-feminist activists, Rachel Rahman and Delores Goddard, elaborated on the gender politics that led to the spin-off of ULOAH. Rahman begins:

> That was during the height of the HIV-AIDS epidemic. So the conference [leadership forum] was primarily (a) male and (b) within that context, primarily focused on AIDS and AIDS education—and rightfully so—but within that process, our needs and issues and concerns were not addressed. By that I mean black lesbian concerns. Another woman [whose name Rahman could not remember] called together a caucus for women who were interested in having a black lesbian conference. Sunday night at the conference—I'll never forget it—several women came from out of town to attend. From that meeting came a convicted core group of local women who continued to meet monthly for a year, and it was from that that ULOAH was formed—"spawned," I always like to say. We determined that in the course of forming ULOAH, we would have a black lesbian conference or retreat—Sistahfest. We would also become more of a service organization—service to youth, the elders, to couples—and we are still striving to do that. Some of it we've done; some of it we're striving to do.[24]

Cofounder Delores Goddard described the organization's founding this way:

> ULOAH was formed out of a need to create a safe environment, [a] safe structure for black lesbian-identified women to find personal empowerment, political empowerment, and self-acceptance . . . Black feminism was the cornerstone of ULOAH. It is the hallmark on which our guiding principles were developed. *Home Girls* is actually one of the "bibles" that we used in terms of some of the earlier writings.[25] Also, Audre Lorde, one of our eminent black lesbian literary visionaries, Barbara Smith, Barbara Christian—also Alice Walker (more black-women-identified than lesbian-identified), Toni Morrison—so we drew from all of those areas.[26]

Goddard reflected on the process through which the retreat derived its identity:

> DG: In the beginning, we didn't know what Sistahfest was going to be. All we wanted was to have a shared experience and to validate and affirm who we are. In doing that, ours was a grassroots effort. We communicated by word of mouth. We went to private meetings in black lesbians' homes, we went to local black gay and lesbian clubs trying to spread the information. We used the resources of the [LA] Gay and Lesbian Center—they were kind enough to

advertise and publicize the festival. We also used the Black [and Gay] Leadership Forum to spread the word.

Just coming up with the name "Sistahfest" was a challenge in itself, and we were using the LA Women's Festival that was put on by Robin Tyler [as a model].[27] Then there is the Michigan Womyn's Music Festival—so using those two festivals as kind of models for Sistahfest, we wanted to give it our own flavor, so for us, we thought we'd have a Sistah festival with a unique spelling of "sister" that would connect us to the African/African American identity.

EH: Like Robin Tyler's West Coast Women's Music and Comedy Festival, did you ever consider making Sistahfest centered on music primarily?

DG: We had many discussions about that. Because of the wide and various needs of black lesbians, it was very difficult to just make it a women's [music] festival, so we thought we would turn it into a cultural, art, and personal development as well as political festival so that we can focus in all of those areas and be consistent with our mission statement as well.

The fact that music, particularly women's music, is not privileged at Sistahfest does not contradict the argument I am making with a discussion of the event in this chapter.[28] In fact, in later years, other women's music festivals—notably, the Northampton Lesbian Festival and Wiminfest—attempted to downplay the women's music aspect of their events in favor of an emphasis in publicity materials on women and music, an instructive distinction, and the contributions of women to the arts. Regardless, Sistahfest is organized along the lines of a residential women's music festival and distinguishes itself from the NIA Collective, the longer-standing retreat for black lesbians, based in the Bay Area and founded in 1987.[29]

Emblematic of its engagement with feminist ritual, Sistahfest typically offers an opening festival workshop, which all participants are encouraged to attend. During the two- to three-hour workshop at the 2005 event, the 250 festigoers met in dyads, small groups of four, and larger groups of twenty to address a wide range of issues. The intergenerational atmosphere inspired discussion of butch/femme identities, a topic that at one point many white lesbian writers maintained was passé in lesbian feminism.[30] For an interpretive gaffe of this sort, observers had to impute to all lesbian cultures what was true about some white, middle-class ones. Goddard added that other areas of discussion included internalized homophobia, sexism, and interracial dating, and that visibility is a very important issue:

> In terms of gender role dynamics—that is a huge discussion when you are talking about visibility—and can you make the choice to be out or be androgynous and flow in between the straight and the lesbian and gay community . . . If we're going to build tolerance in the African American community and in the larger

community, there needs to be a visibility. We need to be comfortable with our identity, be it butch, femme, or androgynous. We need to challenge the heterosexual presumptions, and I think that's the message that was trying to get across.[31]

Like other events held annually, the participant base of the retreat is ever fluctuating. Goddard expressed frustration that because the festival includes a consciousness-raising component, it is seldom possible to pursue issues in depth in the opening workshop:

> Actually, we have [had fascinating discussions], but unfortunately, we haven't been able to take those discussions to a higher level. Each year, Sistahfest brings to it new women who are in certain stages in terms of their developmental growth, and so we tend to cover a lot of the same ground, because we are trying to get us all at the same level of consciousness, and I think that that is very difficult to do if you are getting new people every year. I think it's a little easier if you are getting the same group each year. If you can get us all coming consistently, then we can kind of get on the same page, and we can take the next steps in terms of our growth. I think we need to look at that in the upcoming months in terms of how we can get to that next level.

Not only were issues of butch and femme discussed, but also relationships between generations of black lesbians. Goddard credited Lisa Powell, the former executive director of ULOAH, for her work to initiate YES!, a program designed to address the needs of teen and young adult black lesbians. She explained:

> We're making an effort to connect with that younger group to mentor them, to be there for them, and help them have a smoother entrée into their lesbian identities, and to be a support system to them, and to help their families come to terms with the sexual orientation of their young loved ones. So there is a concerted effort to do that. We've also received some grant funding to do some outreach as well. ULOAH has made great strides in a committed effort to attract a younger lesbian so we can all come together as a community: younger lesbians, older lesbians. Also, keep in mind that we were younger when we founded ULOAH.

Goddard's reminder that she and the other founders were once younger brought to mind the conversation I had with Naya'Hri Suhalia, a spoken-word poet, at Serafemme. Suhalia attests that her life and outlook have been deeply affected by ULOAH's youth-centered programming. Reflecting on intergenerational politics between black elder and younger lesbians, Suhalia raised the significance of YES! (Young Empowered Sisters):

> The executive director heard us when we said that we needed something for us . . . This is the only program of its kind in the entire United States, and we're doing

it right here. I'm happy to be a part of that; it's so major and profound. It's great, and I love her. What I love about my peers is that we're actually responding and we're taking advantage of it. It could be the start of something really, really, *really* big. In the end, youth and elders—especially as black lesbians—we have no one but each other, so can we please just get it together?[32]

Suhalia's entreaty for the black lesbian community to come together across generations—"we have no one but each other"—foreshadows issues that will be raised in chapter 9, in that it is at once a statement of in-group solidarity and an enunciation of "us" versus "them." Implicated in her comment is a longing for home, which, with its concomitant implications of family, was a theme that clearly permeated Sistahfest. The "home" that attendees create or find at an event like Sistahfest may differ radically from the homeplaces of attendees not only in their formative years but in the present as well. This understanding has relevance not only if "homeplace" is understood as a physical shelter but also if it is acknowledged as a site of spiritual recovery, comfort, or understanding. Writer Ursula K. Le Guin's observation that "one can return home after realizing that home is a place never before seen" reminds us that the "generative processes of constituting home" are worthy of attention.[33] Sistahfest is an example of an evolving feminist project in which participants negotiate tensions arising from an engagement of multiple axes of oppression and positionalities, thereby imbuing "*home girls*" with new meaning.

Sistahfest Journal

The trip from south central Los Angeles, where I was living for the summer, to Malibu, California, the site of the three-day Sistahfest, was about an hour's drive up the Pacific Coast. Held the third weekend in September, the fifteenth annual Sistahfest took over Camp Hess Kramer, a Jewish retreat within walking distance of the Pacific Ocean.[34] The grounds ("120 private wooded acres") were lushly forested. Drivers received a warm welcome upon entering the campground. Some cars carried one person; others held two or more. Everyone was black—"black black black." This must be the Afrolesbotopia that fans of the late Octavia Butler, the renowned black speculative fiction writer, wish she had written about.[35] I would say that all hues of skin color were represented, but, mindful of the way the politics of skin color are often played out in African American communities, in point of fact there were more brown- and darker-skinned women than there were lighter ones.

As though to anticipate my concerns about accommodations, the festival brochure stated: "And for women who are definitely not campers, take our word for it—at Sistahfest, in no time you'll feel right at home. Sistahfest offers a range of comfortable lodging and support, including SistahShuttle golf carts to assist you." Upon arrival, I hung around the tiny registration room a bit, participating in a phenomenon I had never experienced at a women's music festival. On its surface, the room, jam-packed and small in its dimensions, exemplified the diversity within sameness that musician Melanie DeMore mentioned in an earlier interview. To be sure, there are numerous events that attract all-black, mostly lesbian participants, but this particular type of gathering was rare in the women's music festival world.

ONE HEART OR TWO?

Women staffing the registration table asked us to identify whether we were "single," "member of a couple," or "attending the festival with our partner." These statuses were designated with small red-and-white stickers in the shape of hearts, which we were asked to affix to our lapels. The semiotics of the one I chose was "single but not looking." Our workshop folders included a postcard advertising an upcoming Sweet Honey in the Rock concert in Los Angeles, workshop descriptions, and bios of presenters.

WHAT'S THE WORD FROM MICHIGAN?

As I stood to the side taking in the scene, a short and stocky middle-aged woman entered the room. Later, I learned she had been active in the early years of ULOAH. As though we were in the early days of the telegraph—if not the Pony Express—she greeted the woman standing before her and said in a voice that all could hear, "What's the word from Michigan?" That she was talking about the Michigan Womyn's Music Festival, held a month earlier, was understood by everyone in hearing range of the pair. Ears leaned forward because they, too, wanted to know. "Ah, man, it was the bomb!" the other woman said. The scene set into relief the extent to which the festival culture is and is not actually a network, especially now that the women's music industry has shut down. With fewer institutional vehicles for the transmission of information, women find out about festivals through the Internet and, arguably equally important, through social networks.[36] Yet it was gaps and discontinuities in social networks and the inattention to subaltern voices that inspired me to conduct research for this book.

The woman's asking for news of Michigan reminded me of stories that blacks, enslaved in the Lone Star state, did not learn of the Emancipation Proclamation for up to two years after Lincoln issued his presidential order on January 1, 1863. I could not help but think of Juneteenth (June 19, 1865) and its symbolic significance for African Americans—especially residents of Texas. It always struck me as ironic that Juneteenth was accorded national holiday status by countless numbers of African Americans, even though word of the emancipation reached other areas in the country—particularly those that had a major Union Army presence—in a timelier manner.[37]

PLACE NAMES

Next I caught a lift on a golf cart to my cabin (the one designated "early lights-out"). I would be with some other women past forty years of age, but two women in their twenties joined us, too. After claiming my bunk, I explored the area and tried to establish an orientation to the grounds. For the weekend, the rooms and outdoor areas the festival used for activities were renamed for important figures in black women's history—women who are often claimed by black lesbians as "one of our own": the Bessie Smith Amphitheater was named after the vaudeville blues singer of the 1920s, while the Barbara Jordan Center was named for the Texas congresswoman who rose to national prominence during the Watergate hearings. Less widely known black women figures were acknowledged as well: the Ruth Ellis Playground, in honor of the recovered black lesbian icon whose life is explored in Yvonne Welbon's film *Living with Pride;* the Synthia St. James Craft Center, after the painter and architectural designer; and the Kim Perrot (basketball) Court, in memory of the point guard for the Houston Comets who died of cancer in 1999 at the age of thirty-two. In a clever pun, the pool was renamed after Ruth Waters, a visual artist and black gay and lesbian rights activist from California. These earmarks of past and place are linked by memory. Similar to the way a good song doesn't lead people only to those memories bounded by the release date of the album, the social act of reminiscing extends beyond a nostalgia for a personal past to a deeply felt sense of historical connectedness.[38] It was clear that the choice of place names reflected the organizers' attempt to reconfigure an architectural frame that would allow participants to reinforce claims to a black lesbian feminist history.

HOME

A memorable moment was the opening ceremony in the Bessie Smith Amphitheater, titled "Welcome Home." The evening's host asked each woman to introduce herself and to add something about what "being home" meant to her in the context of a group of black women, most of whom were lesbians. There were few platitudes—well, maybe some. For the most part, however, women seemed moved simply by responding to the questions and listening to others. Since it was just the first night of the festival, there wasn't the huddling together that would be evidenced on future evenings—a scene reminiscent of the summer camp of one's youth.

Though the first part of the assignment was easy, I experienced the request to define "home" as more difficult. Delivered years ago, Bernice Johnson

Reagon's speech on the challenges wrought by coalition politics inspired many to abandon the search for a universal home for women in the political sphere—that is, if home is marked by an absence of conflict, strategizing, and long hours of building sweat equity.[39] The history of contemporary black feminist organizations had already demonstrated that this type of homework was applicable even in all-black lesbian contexts. When it came time for my turn, I said that "home" means knowing I am not alone in the fight for black women's equality. Is that corny or what?

FOOD AND DEMOGRAPHICS

Meals were served buffet style in the dining hall; the food was of high quality. Other than being asked to clean out our cabins and workshop spaces at the conclusion of the weekend, festigoers did not participate in chores. According to the organizer, about three hundred women were in attendance that year. The festival was for women only, although some young white men were members of the kitchen staff. When I asked about the inclusion of transgendered persons at the festival, the response from one woman was, "Do you see any here? It's not as though the brothas are breaking down the doors to be with some lesbians." Continuing in a more serious mode, she explained that the designation of Sistahfest as an all-black event had been a source of contention in the past, since some women have or have had white partners. In written promotional material, however, it was stated diplomatically that the festival was for black women only. This was in contrast to the women's festivals, mostly white and lesbian, that were open to women of all backgrounds but whose participants regularly debated the efficacy of the inclusion of people who were differently gendered as well as, perhaps, sexed.

YES I AM!

There was a lively crew of young women, ages sixteen to twenty-four, most of whom were associated with ULOAH's program for young lesbians called YES! The seemingly tight crew provided a welcomed energy and, yes, entertainment, for the middle-aged attendees just by being themselves in that environment.[40] The opening workshop also made evident that Sistahfest had made a strong effort to reach out to young women.

PROGRAMMING

As is the case with many festivals, there were often two or three workshops scheduled concurrently—at least before dinner. Workshops covered various topics, including building wealth, relationships, face masks, "breast healing," sacred staff making, flirting 101, writing Sistahfest classifieds ("personal ads"), quick dates, creating spoken-word poetry, and the interests of singles fifty-five and over. Organized activities included the ULOAH ten-minute challenge walk; the "Sistah Idol" competition, inspired by the popular FOX television series *American Idol;* a drumming class (type nonspecified); a traditional West African drumming class; flag football; a swimming competition and relay races; a midnight swim; a "hell hike"; the ULOAH stroll; and the Nu Afrakan traditional dance class. Interactive presentations or discussions included an array of topics: the Chicago Gay Games 2006, environmental justice/racism, homophobia and the black church, a discussion for butches and studs, images of black lesbians in the media (sponsored by GLAAD media), and a Sistahfest SexSeries by a trio of women calling themselves SexplorUs.[41] The three workshops they offered were "The Beauty and Power of Loving a Woman"; "Joys of Spankin,' Bitin,' and Bindin'"; and "The Sexual Myths of Femmes and Butches."

FLAG FOOTBALL

After lunch I returned to the cabin to take some quick notes. Apple, a young woman in her early twenties, was tying her shoelaces. "Are you coming out to play football with us?" she said. I felt a "No, honey" rising in my throat but swallowed it, and said, "Thanks but no, my football days are over." That was a lie, but no one will ever know—I mean, since when does "flag football" mean "knock the other guy down—and hard"? I told Apple I would cheer her on from the sidelines, and we walked to the field. Soon I learned that the self-designated butches and butch wannabees of a wide age range hardly needed my support. Waving invisible pom-poms, about six women, all of whom looked to be under thirty, represented for femme black lesbians everywhere. Their cheers—somewhere between a takeoff on the hyper-femme "Ashley" character on the *Fresh Prince* and the stereotype of the white, upper-middle-class and vacuous valley girl—were worth their weight in gold. The usual gender troubles aside, I couldn't tell which was the original and which was the copy. Apple made the winning touchdown, but the game was two shows in one.

I AM NOT MY HAIR

At breakfast the next morning, I wished singer India.Arie had appeared at Sistahfest and sung her well-known 2005 single "I Am Not My Hair."[42] What transpired illustrated the conflation of politics that matter with the politics of hair in African American communities. I was chomping down the last of my oatmeal, and a woman who had come from Bristol, England, said, "I don't mind that you're straight—although I wouldn't want too many of you here. My problem is with your straight hair." "Are you kidding?" I thought. "Three hundred years of oppression, and black feminism has come to this?" I kept silent on that point. The reason? Well, as an earlier generation of upright black folks would have said, I have "good home training." Instead, I asked the festigoer if she had noticed the number of weaves, Nu-locks, braids, relaxed, straightened hairstyles, and dreads observable in the crowd. "Yes," she replied. "All right, then," I said, "You're crazier than I thought." The international visitor laughed.

MISS CELIE'S BLUES

We were in the Bessie Smith Amphitheater for the final show on Saturday night. The headliner, a woman from St. Louis with musical sensibilities in keeping with the town's legacy, sang "Miss Celie's Blues." Most people remember it as "Sisters" from the soundtrack to *The Color Purple*.[43] The song's rendition and its associations drew everyone to their feet; women swayed from side to side and raised their hands as though to "testify," transforming the event into a religious experience. Many sang along, either on pitch or several notes off. The song recalled the relationship depicted between Celie, the film's abused but eventually defiant protagonist, and the blues singer Shug Avery, who encouraged the women around her to stand up for their rights. Their moments together infused Alice Walker's novel with explicit lesbian content, a point that was missed neither by readers at the time of the book's publication nor by those in the amphitheater.[44]

The musician—on the young side of middle-aged—played keyboard and sang without artifice or attention to its concealment. That night was the closest I had ever felt to the singer of the 1920s; Bessie Smith's record sales saved the race music industry, at least for a while, financially. In this context, "Miss Celie's Blues"—a contemporary song made to sound "old school"—functioned like an anthem of black lesbian collectivity.[45] Over and over, women expressed appreciation for the evening. In a way that black folks talk when they are among themselves, women were of one accord about the singer's performance: *she had a voice on her*. Hearing a song can often open a pathway that "can transport the listener to other places," and, sometimes, to homes one never knew.[46]

JUST LIKE AT GIRL SCOUT CAMP

Before the festival was over, I had exchanged business cards with several campers, including my cabin mates. In a demonstration of typical summer camp–like behavior, we swapped phone numbers and promised to write. I had met a wide range of women: a suave FedEx driver who carried my bags to the car; an African American women's history scholar, who excelled at football; a performance arts consultant; a Zen Buddhist priest; a representative of the Gay Games; a Pentecostal woman who held fast to her religion even as its tenets held her in spite; a couple celebrating more than thirty years of life together; a "sage"; a fine-wine sales representative; and an African American literature professor. Just hanging out with my cabin mates was funnier and more enjoyable than watching BET's *Comedy Jam*.[47] Our collective presence was proof positive that the jelly beans at the bottom of the jar were not only black, but that they rocked in ways that were arguably as compelling as the Afroed black lesbian feminist revolutionary stereotype implies. Was I able to pinpoint an Afrolesbotopia moment at Sistahfest or anywhere else along my women's music festival journey? It would be shortsighted to perpetuate an ideal that exists in the imagination of many but that will require an organized and committed effort to sustain. As with all the great utopian projects, the realization of the Sistahfest ideal is in the future.

While I'm not ready to step aside, I do have to allow for the generations of younger musicians who are emerging—women, in this instance, who have different ideas about how they want to make music and how they want to perform it. Just as I was at 22 and 23 years old, finding my way, these young folks have to do the same.—LINDA TILLERY, QUOTED IN *EDEN BUILT BY EVES*

My performance of "Amazon" a parody? Absolutely not. I meant it as a tribute entirely.
—NEDRA JOHNSON, MUSICIAN

CHAPTER 7

Legacy

MUSICIANS OF THE NEXT GENERATION

(for June Millington)

The reflections that open this chapter are voiced by members of two different generations of black women in women's music. Tillery's statement that she is not ready to step aside points to the longevity of some musicians in women's music, as well as to the vibrancy of a generation of middle-aged women in popular music, from rock to soul to jazz, who are dubbed legends by a new generation.[1] The words of the veteran are counterposed to a comment by singer/songwriter Nedra Johnson, who, as ascendancies go, has risen fast in women's music; after more than fifteen years in the music business, she is one of the newest of the "overnight successes." Johnson's version of Maxine Feldman's "Amazon Women Rise"—credited by many as the first "out" lesbian song—appears as a bonus track on her 2005 album, *Nedra*.[2] As an instantiation of feminist ritual, the opening ceremonies of the Michigan festival feature a rendition of the song each year.[3] Johnson's citation speaks to a familiar compositional practice of hip-hop, although her musical style could more accurately be described as a genre-busting range of funk, fused folk, and R&B. The context for citation can be indicting as well as complimentary; in the case of Johnson's recording, it figures as tribute.

The dedication of this chapter to rock musician June Millington signals the guitarist's important role in women's music, the encouragement she has given to younger artists, and the high esteem with which she is held in the women's music community. In 1969 June Millington and her sister, Jean, founded Fanny, the first all-women rock band to be signed by a major label. In *Radical Harmonies,* the documentary by Boden Sandstrom and Dee Mosbacher, Millington recounts her subsequent move away from the mainstream rock music industry and into the more underground realm of women's music during the early 1970s.[4] I interviewed Millington at the Institute for Musical Arts, the center for women's music making that she and Ann Hackler founded in 1986, which has been the site of numerous concerts, production sessions, rehearsals, and reunions of musicians.[5] The organization sponsors ongoing rock camps for girls wishing to hone their skills in music. As I was driving Millington from San Francisco International Airport to her home before the interview, she commented, "It is all too easy for members of a younger generation to forget the work it took, in the trenches, to keep it [women's music] going."[6] Millington's remark is suggestive, but perhaps I caught her on a dark day psychologically, for the interviews I conducted with musicians who figure as the next generation in women's music suggest that, like the "demise" of the American writer Mark Twain, declarations that the trench work carried out by first-generation musicians has been forgotten are "greatly exaggerated." For confirmation, one has only to consider the conceptual space forged in women's music by Linda Tillery, Mary Watkins, and others so that Malika, a black musician based in Atlanta, can describe herself as having grown up "going to women's music festivals." At times paying tribute to an earlier generation while carving out new directions, the artists interviewed for this chapter—Nedra Johnson, Malika, Pamela Means, and Naya'Hri Suhalia—are not unappreciative of the work it took in political activism, women's community building, black feminist activism, or in the alternative music industry, in Millington's words, to keep it (women's music) going.[7]

Instead of offering profiles of individual musicians, which is the approach invoked in most studies of women's music, this chapter is organized along the lines of successive themes. I focus, in turn, on introducing each performer and her start in women's music, exploring her perspectives on feminist and lesbian/gay politics, and engaging her on her relationship to feminism's legacy. This discussion—less about the artists themselves than an elucidation of the critical social theory they articulate and perform—contributes to the literature on music, feminist, and post–queer nation politics. With all the contradictions that an engagement of music, race, and intergenerational struggle entails, this chapter is offered as a collective "talk back" to feminist rocker June Millington.

Four Artists of the Second Generation

Members of the "second generation"—Nedra Johnson, Pamela Means, Malika, and Naya'Hri Suhalia—run the gamut from singer/songwriter to spoken-word artist. Johnson, Means, and Malika record on their own labels, a practice consistent with a fast-changing business climate for musicians and evolving consumption patterns. Independent labels are symptomatic of advances in digital technology, and forays into home recording studio construction. In an era in which radio airplay is difficult to come by, savvy promotional tools such as blogs, social networking sites, and online newsletters make sound business sense, and these artists appear to be expert in all. Although all four regard themselves as activists, a question might arise whether the performers interviewed for this chapter know one another or perform on the same circuit. In fact, they do not. Johnson and Means are popular on the predominantly white women's music festival circuit, while Malika, less known to second-wave festigoers, has performed at Ladyfest events. Suhalia was a favorite at Serafemme: A Women of Color Music Festival (see chapter 6).

Singer/songwriter and tuba player extraordinaire Nedra Johnson got her start on the women's music festival circuit in 1992. She has performed at women's music festivals held throughout the Midwest; at Wiminfest; at (predominantly white) Gay Pride marches in Philadelphia, San Francisco, and Baltimore; at Black Pride events (South of Soul Sisters in Harlem); and in various European countries. Johnson recalls that Toshi Reagon was looking for a bass player for her band and, in the process, gave her an early gig at the Michigan festival. (This was prior to the emergence of Reagon's current band, Big Lovely.) Johnson, who had heard of the Michigan festival but had not attended it, recalls her lack of experience at the time: "There was so much I learned about getting over my fears and insecurities about my playing. So when we were doing the sound check, they were like, 'How is that in your monitor?' I was like, 'Okay.' I didn't know I was supposed to sit and listen to the balance. I look back on that, and it is really interesting; I just didn't know what to do then. A lot has changed since that time."

While Johnson cites the influence of her father, bandleader Howard Johnson, in terms of music, singer/songwriter Malika cites her mother's influence on her musicianship and feminist understandings. I met the singer in the mid-1980s; she was six years old at the time: we were walking with her mother to the neighborhood Slurpee shop near the campus of a midwestern university. Suddenly she came out: "I'm a lesbian," she said. "Right on," I replied. I did not know what to say next, so I said, "What kind of Slurpee do you want?" Her mother, a lesbian and a television and film scholar, smiled at my benevolent clumsiness; I prayed that the small child would not feel harmed for life by my enthusiastic but socially awkward reaction. Fast-forwarding twenty years, Malika is one of the next generation of black women musicians making their way in women's music circles. She has played at Ladyfest South 2004 in Atlanta and Ladyfest Philly in 2003; she has also performed twice at the Southern Women's Festival.[8]

Pamela Means, who grew up in the "hyper-segregated town of Milwaukee," did not become politicized until she moved to Boston, the "center of the acoustic singer/songwriter folk world." At the time of our conversation, I wondered how the segregation of Milwaukee differed from that of Boston, where Means was then living, but I left this question unasked.[9] Like other musicians of the second generation, Means performs in diverse venues, including folk festivals, women's music festivals, Ladyfest events, and Pride festivals in Europe and the United States. Frequently, she has toured with white spoken-word artist Alix Olson. Means remembers playing the acoustic showcase at the Michigan festival in 2002.

Poet Naya'Hri Suhalia, twenty-five ("Some women get defensive 'bout the whole age thing," she told me), was one of the few spoken-word artists who took the stage at Serafemme. Suhalia, a journalist who writes for a number of black lesbian and gay publications, including the online magazine *Sapience,* eschews the term "spoken word," with its connotations of recency, stating that "before there were spoken-word artists per se, there were poets."

As Suhalia's exactitude foreshadows, the use of language in compositional and performance practice is a topic that is relevant to the musicians discussed in this chapter. Nedra credits the Michigan festival for giving her the license to find and be true to herself as an artist:

> In a way, going to festival at that time [in the early 1990s] made me start writing more, because I didn't know what I wanted to do, how it would be received, or where it would be received. Michigan let me know that whatever I write, it would be okay—there is going to be an audience for me to be able to say "she" when I mean "she," because I just couldn't fathom not doing that. Then, I also thought, "That's not going to get me anywhere." It is true that it [using same-sex pronouns] doesn't get you far in terms of the mainstream. Not being ambiguous is not really a great career move. But it is soul-satisfying.

Clearly, Johnson's oeuvre exhibits a sense of humor; the track "Michfest Blues" is testimony to that. Although the idea is worn by now, halfway through the cut, the singer sounds on the familiar trope of (arguably white) dykes eating granola and wearing Birkenstocks. I asked Johnson if, with all the double entendre her work exhibits, she had been influenced by the black blueswomen of the past. She confirmed the suggestion.

It might seem ironic that a lesbian artist who would defend her use of same-sex pronouns and suggestively title her record label Big Mouth Girl Records would experience difficulty writing song lyrics containing sexual innuendo or blatant sexuality, yet this was the case for Johnson when she composed "The World Could Stop Turning," a song scored for drums, bass, and keyboard.[10] On this track, Nedra sings "I'm ready to take you down into the fire" as a Barry White–type rap is spoken over the instrumental ostinato. Johnson reflects on how difficult the sex talk was to write:

> I held on to the song for years knowing that it needed some talkin' shit kind of thing, and I don't really write like that. So I put it out to everybody I know—just to a bunch of different poets. Finally, Sossity Chiricuzio wrote that part. She actually wrote something first that she sent to me as her work, and I thought she would be good for this, so she just changed what she sent me originally, and then I just put myself into it. I can be cool and present in a way that doesn't sound insincere at all, but could never find the language to say, "Why did you drink that wine like it was my fingers?"[11]

But that's not all. Johnson also related that on occasion, she has performed "The World Could Stop Turning," probably the "funkiest, low-down, let's get jiggy with it" track on the whole album, with her father's band.[12] Could you do that? "Drinking that wine like it was my fingers" is only the beginning; the song can make you wonder how you are going to keep from wetting your pants listening to it—unless you are captivated by its inventiveness. Johnson's song is testimony that black lesbian erotica in print form does not necessarily trump its counterpart in music.

Johnson has won numerous awards, some of them from gay/lesbian-identified organizations, such as OutMusic, a network founded in 1990, of lesbian, gay, bisexual, and transgender musicians and their supporters. Johnson submitted "Any Way You Need Her" to OutMusic for entry in its Out Song of the Year competition. A satire, the song is reminiscent of 1950s "old-timey gospel" at the same time that it signifies on elements of feminist spirituality that emerged in the 1970s. Furthermore, the musician's use of double entendre locates the singer in the discontinuous line from the vaudeville blueswomen of the 1920s to the present. Johnson, whose work is already intertextual, infuses sexual innuendo into a song that might otherwise be sung in a religious context—though it would have to be a particular type of religious setting. With a quick change-out of musical style (granted, a big caveat), some of the worship services of churches founded in black gay and lesbian communities come to mind; the Unity Fellowship Church, based on a neo-Pentecostal model, is an example.[13] Minus the double entendre, Johnson's text resonates with the responsive reading recited by Unity's predominantly black congregants every Sunday morning: "God is a lesbian, god is a gay man, god is bisexual, god is a transgender. Amen."

The sense of inclusiveness that resonates in Johnson's "Any Way You Need Her" contrasts with the often-cited homophobia of some black churches, even as they include same-gender-loving/lesbian/gay/transgendered/men-who-have-sex-with-men (MSM) individuals in their membership.[14] Black culture critics as well as radical theologians have identified this phenomenon as a central contradiction in black church practice—meaning the tendency for some congregations to depend on the labor of an African American gay choir director or other musicians while adhering to a theological interpretation that situates these same individuals as "fallen," or as outside the Christian community.

Means is also the recipient of numerous awards, including OutMusic's 2004 Outstanding New Recording for a female for *Single Bullet Theory*, her fifth album. *Single Bullet Theory* addresses topics as diverse as the USA Patriot Act, racial profiling, and the malfeasances of the second Bush administration. The album is capped off by Means's rendition of "Strange Fruit," the song about lynching written by Lewis Allan and popularized by Billie Holiday. Described as a "folk-politico-rocktress," Means issued her sixth album, *Jazz Project, Vol. 1*, in 2007.[15] Included on the album are "Four Women" (Nina Simone) and "Black and Blue" (Louis Armstrong). Means's goal, she says, is to learn Duke Ellington and "more difficult stuff," like Miles Davis.

Music and Politics

By now it is perhaps evident that the collective repertoire of these artists exhibits a mix of self-consciousness in terms of sexual and racial politics. In the case of Means, black experience emerges as a textual theme; as the years have passed, she has delved more and more into performing standards in the African American music canon. "Maybe You Should," appearing on *Cobblestones* (Wirl Records, 1998), is about hair and rage, something Means's protagonist and, to adjudge by both popular and scholarly writings on the subject, many black women have in common. The contrast between the mild-tempered real-life persona of the New York–based artist, at least performed before an interviewer, and the virtuosic acoustic guitar–playing and angry persona Means projects vocally on some of her tracks is worthy of note. The opening of "Maybe You Should" finds the protagonist riding on either the bus or the subway "on the South side," seated by "some greasy white guy," who asks, "Whattaya call that kind of hair?" That line alone reverberates a decades-long history of black women and, as one festigoer put it, "the hair wars," going back to when Madam C. J. Walker popularized the hot comb.[16] The biographies of many middle-aged black women reveal similar incidents in which a white girl or boy asks if they can touch the black person's hair or, as writer Reginald McKnight relates, rub the color off their black skin.[17] In response to the interlocutor's question, Means's protagonist responds, "I call it mine." It's an incisive rejoinder in a textual setting that concerns types of intrusion that some women experience every day.

A prominent strand in the nappy roots of Means's musical influence is singer/songwriter Tracy Chapman, who Means cites as a model for women playing their own instruments. Surely Means can be extended the benefit of the doubt for not mentioning a long line of black women instrumentalists, including Elizabeth Cotton, Sister Rosetta Tharpe, Memphis Minnie (Lizzie Douglas), and Willie Mae "Big Mama" Thornton. Citing a cadre of songwriters that includes white artists Shawn Colvin, Ani DiFranco, and the Indigo Girls, all of whom gained a following in the late 1980s and early to mid-1990s, Means lays out a trajectory in which folk music has moved from being unpopular to a time when a city like Boston has a "whole scene of folk singers." Says Means, "I think folk music of the past just meant 'Puff the Magic Dragon'—lightweight kind of stuff from the sixties—very groovy and not very challenging." I did not get the impression that with one broad stroke Means dismissed all of the work of Peter, Paul, and Mary or the contributions of black musicians such as Odetta and Richie Havens, with whom Means has also performed. She has also played concerts with Joan Baez and Holly Near, artists recognized as much for their music as for their progressive politics and associations with leftist causes. According to musician Ani DiFranco, Means has fused a predominantly white folk-music scene with a racialized political consciousness. So as not to naturalize the demographics of any music scene, it is worth reflecting on the combination of structural forces, social networks, and music-listening practices that work to keep the white folk-music scene white and leave individual black musicians, like Means, to carry the burden of providing the racialized awareness it warrants.

In contrast to other performers who might be more vocal, in conversation, about racism, Means allows her perspectives about race to speak through her repertoire, admitting, "I am always delighted if I see reflections of myself in the audience, but that doesn't happen very often." Still, some of Means's songs are inspired by her experiences as a black woman; "Two Halves," a song concerning the targeting of an African American woman by the police, is an example. She explains:

> I used to be a terrible driver, and I would drive really fast, and I got lots of speeding tickets. When I was just out of high school, I was still in the habit of straightening my hair, and I looked pretty white. When I would get pulled over when I looked like that, I always got off. As soon as I started wearing my hair more naturally and I continued with the bad driving, I got pulled over and got a ticket every single time. I had my own firsthand experience: same person, different look, different outcome.

While my interview notes do not reflect an expansion on this point, I interpret her comment to mean that she had her own firsthand experience with the capriciousness of the justice system. Although the scenario Means recounts appears to be a gendered version of "driving while black," it is useful to note that in the familiar scenario recounted by numerous black male critics, scholars, African American politicians, and actors, the black male driver, regardless of class background or appearance, is treated the same. For him and many other black women drivers (who do not benefit from the coupling of beauty and youth), there is no "different outcome." That Means can, under some circumstances, look "pretty white" might lend credence to the idea that race identities (statuses) in the United States are more fluid than they actually are for the majority of African Americans.

Like Means, Malika also records on her own record label, blackgoddessrecords.[18] The artist, whose musical background includes classical voice training and acoustic guitar infuses her cuts with a social consciousness that reflects her reading of African American history, as well as the contradictions of black political culture. Addressing the latter, Malika offers her perspective on the limits of community membership.

> We [black people] really need to get our own stuff together—but then I'm really not [a separatist], because so many of my friends are white, and I think that happens because, as sad as it is to say, our African American culture has become so conservative-minded that a lot of times it is hard as an African American to make other African American friends who you can be yourself with. The whole queer thing is a taboo. It is like a serious taboo. There is so much that is just not openly accepted.

Malika's mention of conservative factions within the African American community—"the whole queer thing is a taboo"—leads to a discussion of black community membership and also the labels these artists use in discussing their activism. Given that Ladyfest participants tend to maintain that the fluidity of gender identities necessitates a revision of the identity politics engaged in by an earlier political generation, it is not surprising that Malika finds that a generational divide also adheres in terms of the use of the word "queer":

I do identify as queer; my mother does not like the word . . . I like the term "queer," because originally it comes from the term "query," to question, to investigate. I was just reading an article today for one of my [master's degree] assignments about breaking down the word "queer" and where it comes from.[19] I like the word "queer" because it is a huge umbrella. I am not exactly comfortable identifying as a lesbian, because it is really confining. Like saying, "This is what I am." I'm not sure how accurate that is for me. I am in a relationship with a woman, and I plan on being in this monogamous relationship for as long as it works, which will hopefully be, you know, forever. If I weren't in this relationship, the odds are I wouldn't date a man, but I wouldn't say that I would never under any circumstances ever be with a man. That's what lesbianism is. For me, once again it is like the word "feminist." I claim lesbianism to get the point across as quickly as possible to less informed people. "Queer" I love, because it is just such a huge umbrella for everybody who is just not straight, straight, straight. If you're not straight, straight, straight, to me you are queer—like there are possibilities.

Whereas Malika addressed her negotiation of identity labels, Suhalia spoke to the relevance, for her, of the term "hip-hop feminist." She could be expected to have a strong opinion about that; at the time of our meeting, she had just finished writing an article on diversity in the LGBT hip-hop movement for a gay hip-hop online publication.

Hip-hop feminist? I'm more of a womanist, because "feminist" usually describes someone who is interested in anything having to do with feminine women per se, and I'm more of a womanist because I'm for women, so I am a womanist. I try not to define myself as too much of anything, but yes, you could say that hip-hop is something I'm passionate about. I am music. Hip-hop grew out of poverty, and now look at it: it's a four-billion-dollar industry, and that's just in the United States . . . I want to keep hip-hop alive. So am I down for hip-hop as a woman? Damn straight. Yeah, you could call me that. [EH: Maybe you'd prefer "hip-hop womanist"?] Sure. Why not? Absolutely.

Interestingly, Suhalia associated the term "feminist" with someone who is femme-identified. Unlike other women I met in the course of preparing this book, she identified as a "womanist," although it was not apparent that her use of the word was related to its deployment by Alice Walker, Clenora Hudson-Weems, or other womanist theorists.[20]

Like Malika, Suhalia claims an activist identity. Here, she expresses both pride in the visibility of the black lesbian and gay community and, at the same time, disappointment in it:

NS: I try to be as active as I can, especially in the black lesbian community, so to speak—I never believed in being gay for gay's sake. I feel like it's important to know my history, to know where I come from, because we stand on the shoulders of people who literally died so that we can be out as we are and have all these organizations, and cruises, and travel agents, and damn—our own section in the West Hollywood (L.A. County Sheriff) police department! I'm like, "Good lawd—that's some good stuff right there." All of that is important to me. Helping people know their history—empowers—enlightens—uplifts my community.

EH: So you definitely identify as an activist.

NS: I guess you can say I wear that and many hats. Apparently, I wear quite a few hats . . . Everyone doesn't have to play the role of activist, but they must stay informed. It may sound corny, but it's true when they say that knowledge is power . . . The more you know, you can turn around and use that as ammunition against any of those who would try to oppress us as a "community."

I use community in quotes, because I'm not really seeing "community" yet. We use the word "community" when we describe black gays and lesbians, because it's kind of a habit. We don't know any other word to use, but I feel that to have a community, there has to be a common unity, and I don't see that too much . . . It's kind of like a circle and clique thing . . . if we can get it together in our own camp first, that would help.

The Difference a Generation Makes

The performers of this chapter have thought deeply about the intersections of African American cultural politics and sexual politics in black communities. At the same time, their remarks reveal continuities and disjunctures with the perspectives of members of an earlier political generation. Malika's activist roots run deep, and women's music plays a central role:

> The political piece definitely came from my mother. Even before I was too young to understand it, I have always classified myself as an activist. When I was in preschool and kindergarten, they asked you what you wanted to be when you grew up, and I wanted to be a freedom fighter—but I didn't know what that meant. I just knew that it sounded cool. So, I was like, "Yeah, I want to be a freedom fighter." Now, with what I am doing with music and spoken word, I am excited because I feel like that's actually what I'm doing. So I feel like I have kind of realized the catchphrase . . . like I walked around with a button that said "I'm a mini-feminist" at the age of six. So I grew up being really empowered in women's space. That is a really corny term, I think, but you know what I mean.
>
> I grew up going to the National Women's Music Festival . . . It was always extremely exciting and a treat to go, because every year I would get a new crystal.[21] I got to see Sweet Honey and the Rock. That is when I met Ysaye [Maria] Barnwell

from Sweet Honey and the Rock . . . Up until now she still remembers me when I see her. She is very warm and—what a musician! . . .

So, yes, I grew up going to women's festivals, and I believe I saw Tracy Chapman before she completely blew up [became famous] on that stage. I remember Casselberry and DuPreé; I saw Holly Near numerous times. The cool thing was that [years later] I got to be her [Near's] chauffeur to the Southern Women's Music Festival. That was really cool, because I was like, "I'm picking up Holly Near, HOLLY NEAR!" and my girlfriend was like, "Who is Holly Near?" My girlfriend had never been to a women's music festival before, so I took her to one. Of course, that is crazy to me, 'cause I'm like, "Who hasn't been?" But of course, I take it for granted.

You know I went to the I Am Your Sister Conference, which was Audre Lorde's last big conference, and I think it's where *A Litany for Survival,* that film, takes place. I am actually in that film for a split second—where she [Lorde] is hugging me, but if you blink, you'll miss it. I was also at her memorial service that was held in Harlem [January 17, 1993]. Of course, during these times, I didn't get it.[22] I'm like, "[It's] 12:13 [P.M.]—it's Christopher Columbus weekend and I want to be with my friends, whatever." Of course, looking back on it, I am like, "I have been in the presence . . ." I'm about to cry just thinking about it, but I have been in the presence of these people, and now that I am old enough to read their works, I'm like, "I have been in the presence of these people!"—like I have heard them speak live. It is just so amazing to be able to say that I breathed the same air as Audre Lorde. That is definitely how I feel about that. I definitely took it for granted. I had fun at women's festivals, though, because I feel they are definitely very child-centered, or at least the ones my mother took me to were.

Malika cites some of the well-known figures in women's music. In retrospect, she regards her preference for her friends over her mother's peers as myopic, but given her relative youth, these leanings were to be expected. Touchstones in black lesbian history also come to the fore in Malika's narration. She mentions the I Am Your Sister Conference held in 1990, as well as Lorde's memorial service, which, though attended by more than five thousand mourners, received scant attention from the mainstream media. Lorde is championed in part because, against the forces that would require her to divide her allegiances in terms of identities, she gave voice to all of them as a "black feminist, lesbian, poet, mother, and person living with cancer."[23]

Malika's comments are a welcome addition to the literature that examines the relationship of young black women to feminism. Her comments reveal regard for the theory generated by members of her mother's generation. She demonstrates that by learning about and finding value in the past, she has cultivated "her mother's gardens"—a phrase inspired by Alice Walker's influential collection of nonfiction essays.[24] Although neither mother nor daughter deny experiencing familiar mother-daughter conflicts over the years, the respect the narrator accords her political forebears is palpable.

Pamela Means and Naya'Hri Suhalia also identify second-wave black feminism as significant to their evolving political consciousness. Means, who characterizes her politics with a formulation that has little currency in academic black feminism, says: "I think that people are still so afraid of the word 'feminist'—that it is bad. I think there has been a campaign to fight the women's rights movement of the 1970s. I think that a *radical* feminist [emphasis mine] is not afraid of that and embraces the feminist ideal and goes forth pronouncing it." Means cites her move from the Midwest to the East Coast as the beginning of a whole new chapter in her life; this includes her exposure to black feminist writers:

> Everything happened with leaving Milwaukee and moving to Boston [with its vibrant folk-music scene]. I had my first real girlfriend. She finally gave me *Sisters of the Yam* [by bell hooks] and *Sister Outsider* [by Audre Lorde], and those books changed my life, and from that moment forward I became an activist. Those books gave me the language to reflect on my own life, and it gave me a way to deal with all the anger that I had from growing up and channel it into something useful—you know, music. I have been influenced by Audre Lorde's writing as well—just to be honest about my experience, about my existence as a biracial queer person.[25]

Returning to my attendance of Serafemme, judging from the applause, I sensed a polite but supportive reaction of the middle-aged crowd. As Suhalia took the stage, she called attention to her long black-and-lavender dress. With her politically self-conscious poetry that cited Barbara Smith and Audre Lorde, Suhalia's performance seemed to touch a responsive chord, regardless of age, with those gathered. I commented that Serafemme had a good representation of older and younger women in the audience. She responded:

> It did . . . that was amazing, fantastic, I had a blast. To me, that was my [gay] Pride festival. We can stand to have some more events like those. Hanifah Walidah [a black actress from New York City who stars in the one-woman play *Sucka for Life*] said it best when she said, "How can you know when you are a part of history when no one is around to define it or claim it?" I say, "That was a historic event." I was one of the pioneer performers. We laid the foundation, laid the groundwork that this could be something that is annual until it gets to the point where it's as big as the Lilith Fair or the Detroit Women's Music Festival or whatever—except that it's just for us. I can see it, because, you know, I like to think big . . . I would love to get involved working behind the scenes, because things like that are so important. It gave youth and elders a chance to come together and socialize with

> one another. Nobody's looking down at the other one or rejecting the other. There was none of that there that I saw, and that's a good thing.

In this exchange, Suhalia voiced a structure of feeling that permeated my talks with performers at the Serafemme festival—that is, a yearning for the future, as though women's music festivals are at the beginning of the arch of radical feminist expressive culture rather than an echo of an earlier reverberation. Suhalia's reference point is, first, Lilith Fair, the multi-city concert tour by women performers that was open to men and women, and, second, to the Michigan Womyn's Music Festival, which here she dubs the "Detroit" festival. The contrast of an 81.55 percent black Detroit with the mostly white MWMF could not be more stark.[26] Suhalia's use of the phrase "or whatever" suggests that in this case her inexactitude does not matter, given that she is focused on the bigger project of a (black) women's music festival for the future.

There were also ways in which these representatives of the second generation expressed views that diverged from those of an earlier generation. Malika, who was the only musician whose experience with women's music festivals dated back to the formative years of her youth, said she would not take her own children, if she had them, to such events:

> Number one, because I think it is adult space. Number two, I had never seen women walking around naked just randomly in the woods or whatever at these festivals. Apparently this is not a strange practice, but I guess it's something my mother kept me sheltered from. So I personally would not take my children, even though I want them to be comfortable with their bodies. I was a little in shock. However, I think it's really cool that people feel comfortable enough, and I understand the power behind it.

Suhalia related nudity to manifestations of a sometimes vacuous politic of the black lesbian and gay activist community:

> If Pride [meaning African American gay Pride celebrations] is us running around on the beach half naked, I'll stay home and read a book. We're on our way to achieving Pride; I don't think we're there yet. I think we're a little bit inaccurate on what that is. But everything serves a purpose—but for once, I would like to see a Pride that is not associated with ridiculous debauchery. Yes, let's celebrate our diversity, that's wonderful; let's bring them all out, let's call them all out. But also with that, let us feed the mind. We're feeding the body and the visual with the eye candy and the "women-ride-a-mile on Harley Davidsons with their ass hanging out of a thong and that's great." I'm not gonna lie. I like to see that, too, and that's wonderful. But after all of that, can I get a little mental stimulation please? Can I learn something? Can I be informed? And I don't see that happening—not at all—not at a Pride festival. I mean, you have the National Black Lesbian

> Conference, you have Fire and Ink, Black Gay Writers Tour. I think that's great! Wonderful! Can we associate that a little bit more with the Pride festival? Now, I think ATB [At the Beach] kind of has it on the ball. They have the literary café, conferences, and what not. But they don't pump it up enough, which is why it usually ends up being poorly attended. But everybody's at that beach party. Whew! They came out in droves!

Suhalia refers to At the Beach, the annual celebration of Black Pride held in Southern California. Throughout the United States and in some other countries, Black Pride observances are held separately from those of the majority culture.[27] Suhalia's recall of the efficacy of the beach party vividly illustrates Judith Butler's discussion of the slide between the gay march as a site of the call for expanded gay rights and the gay parade, which some regard as a site for pageantry and spectatorship.[28] Suhalia's remarks reveal her enthusiastic engagement with the politics of gay Pride as she offers both an appreciation of its celebration of difference and a critique of its emphasis on the display of "debauchery" over "mental stimulation." She went on to express a more hopeful sentiment: "The time for accepting homophobia is coming to an end . . . People in the black community are beginning to be called out on their stuff now. And that's good. The foundation is being set, and as long as we can continue to build on that foundation, that is when we will have truly achieved Pride in every sense of the word, and it won't just be a beach party."

Suhalia and Malika confront and respond to feminist and intergenerational politics in lesbian communities in contrasting ways. Malika addressed similarities and differences between the second-wave festivals discussed in this book and those at which she performs now (Ladyfests), saying that they were on a continuum:

> I do see it as a continuum, which is on the one hand kind of cool, but on the other hand part of the issue there. I was really in shock, because, I didn't know this—but there is racism in the grassroots community! I had a very idealistic idea of what it means to be a lesbian and a feminist and what it means to be grassroots. So I was really surprised to find out that there is racism. I know that there is racism, because some of the performers at these festivals were renowned performers and African Americans, and they were given crappy slots, like completely horrible slots [of time during which to perform]. It has happened to me also. I have also noticed that a lot of times there is a main stage and a little side stage, and I know a lot of the black performers end up on the side stage. I have heard—I guess the word would be "prejudiced" comments at women's festivals. Just the absence of women of color there is disconcerting, but I'm not surprised. Why would you want to go somewhere where you're not going to be treated equally or you're going to have to deal with the same crap that you do in everyday life, when these are

> supposed to be like retreats? The horrible thing is that I think that is also part of the continuum, because after talking about it with my mom, I find out that this is a fight that has been going on for a long time. So, yeah, there is racism within the grassroots community.
>
> The other thing that traumatized me was that there is backbiting within the grassroots community. I really felt like the industry—I was like, "It's grassroots, it's not the major label industry. So it's all about the love of the art." I have found that this is not necessarily true. I think I understand where it comes from, even though it sucks. I think that since I teach full-time and I have a job, that it's not as serious to me. I don't want to say that it's not serious to me, because I love performing, and I hate to lose opportunities, but I'm not about to stomp on somebody else; it [performing] is also not my bread and butter. So I know that for some of these musicians, if they don't get to where they are trying to go, they are not going to eat. So I get it. I don't necessarily condone it, but I think I get it. I think it's a very different issue when you're talking about doing art for a living. And part of me thinks that if you're going to do art for a living, you might have to be a bit of a jerk, but I don't know.

Malika's mention of performers who "do art for a living" segued with her views on live versus recorded performances. She spoke to the downside of making determinations of performance quality based on albums alone:

> The other thing that I have learned on the underground circuit is that the majority of artists sound better than their albums, which I didn't know was possible, because being a hip-hop and R&B artist, usually those people—you don't want to see them live. If you see them live, they are off-key, or you find out they can't really perform or whatever. The first person that I ever saw who was better than her cd was Erykah Badu, and I was blown away. She was amazing, and when I got to the underground circuit, I realized that that was not abnormal. It is not abnormal for . . . I don't want to say "real" performers, for musicians. I think a lot of us make cds that don't really do justice to our music a lot of times, because they are self-produced and because they are self-financed. That makes a big difference.

Although the Ladyfest events, founded in Olympia, Washington, in 2000, are grassroots in nature, Malika distinguished between them and some of the other events at which she performs. The fact that many of the "smaller names" donate their services, for example, speaks to their commitment to the Ladyfest ideal:

> Some of the bigger names get paid. For the most part, the majority of Ladyfest is made up of people like me, jumping in their cars and driving eighteen hours to get to Philadelphia to play this little gig and maybe sell some books. The cool thing about Ladyfest is that they feed your spirit. Ladyfest—there is nothing like it. They feed your spirit even if you don't make money. Because when I went to

Philly, I didn't make any money. Nobody bought my book. Why? Because we were all trading books. We were like, "I'll give you one of mine if you give me yours." As a result, I have a collection of independently produced books and cds that can't be gotten, like, anywhere. It's just such an exciting thing. Yeah, you go to Ladyfest, and it's like it waters your spirit. It's just the coolest experience—being around women and people who support women; going to music and tarot workshops, and belly-dancing classes. It is just a lot of fun. Now, that is a retreat from your day-to-day life.

It is not surprising that Malika's comments and enthusiasm about the Ladyfest events exhibit contours of an excitement expressed by members of an earlier generation over women's music festivals. Yet, in contrast to the increasingly older consumer base of women's music festivals, Ladyfests attract attendees in a younger age range and, not inconsequently, of another political generation.[29]

Naya'Hri Suhalia also shared well-formed opinions about the generation gap in the black lesbian community. In the following passage, she details the marginalization she has experienced in the black lesbian and gay community because of age. Cathy Cohen would say that the experience Suhalia outlines is a manifestation of secondary marginalization—that is, the dominance of one faction of a subordinate group over another.[30] Suhalia elaborates:

When I first came out, I was fourteen years old. I became active in the black gay community not too long after that. When I really started knowing about the ins and outs and places to go, I was nineteen. One of the things I noticed off the bat was that elders are looking at youth like they don't know anything, like their age grants them wisdom automatically. And a lot of the events that were happening—the conferences, retreats, social circles and all of that—were not geared or advertised for us, for young people. Or they were set at a price that is so high that we couldn't afford it. I found a big problem with that. When I would talk with my elders, especially about things pertaining to black lesbian culture, I would happen to know what I was speaking about, and sometimes I would find that they didn't. Then they would turn around and use the last trump card they had, which was to ask, "How old are you?" when I was nineteen, twenty, and twenty-one years old. "Oh, you a baby. What do you know?" . . . Then I would find my peers rejecting their elder counterparts because they felt like, "What's the point?"

I thought that was really wrong, so I started going to a lot of events like the National Black Lesbian Conference, and Sistahfest, and whatnot. And I started saying, "Look, I don't see any young people here. Why is that? They should be here. Why are you not including us? Don't you know that you need us? I hate to be the bearer of bad news, but I'm gonna be real. Y'all gonna be ancestors one day. Y'all will go from elders to ancestors one day. It's inevitable. If you don't

> include us and tell us about our history and ourselves and where we come from, then everything will become ancestral when you're gone, and it will be gone if you don't include us. Just as you had to start somewhere, so do we."

Suhalia's statement contains reverberations of Linda Tillery's comment, cited in this chapter's opening epigraph, that members of her generation need to make room for the emergence of a newer generation of young women musicians, some of whom are in their twenties. Suhalia continues, suggesting that within the black lesbian community, the generational divide is not the only fissure; that many events are cost prohibitive for young adults is also an issue. She observed that sometimes older and more-middle-class black lesbians set prices for events so high that the "undesirable element"—"young black lesbian thugs"—can't attend. She said: "I'm sorry, that's not bringing the black lesbian community together; it's still separating us to a certain extent, because you are being discriminatory. I find it highly offensive." As Kimberly Springer points out, black feminist organizations of the 1970s found that they, too, had failed to predict and subsequently address the range of variance that members brought to their understandings of black feminist identity. Unreconciled class distinctions and members' very different relationships to money figured prominently in the demise, by 1980, of some of these organizations.[31] Highlighting the nexus between a generational and class divide in the black lesbian community, Suhalia remarks: "There is a difference between wisdom and experience and elders, who, instead of having fifty years' experience, have about one year's worth of life experience that they keep repeating fifty times."

The tone of Suhalia's comments resonates with those made by the other artists interviewed for this chapter, all of whom in their own way acknowledge the achievements of an earlier generation of women's music veterans and lesbian feminist theorists, but also chart their own course in music, performance, activism, and politics. My argument for studies of a redistricted women's music festival imaginary supports the inclusion of all of the performers in this chapter. Although it would be hasty to generalize, Nedra Johnson, Malika, Pamela Means, and Naya'Hri Suhalia engage what an ethnomusicologist, in another context, called the "political economy of exuberance."[32]

The weekend; our own, and not our own, it is what we wait for all week long.—WITOLD RYBCZYNSKI, *WAITING FOR THE WEEKEND*

CHAPTER 8

Working for the Weekend

FESTIVAL ORGANIZERS AND WORKERS

Denaturalizing the work involved in the production of women's music festivals, this chapter emanates from my conversations with black lesbians about their experiences in festival organization—in other words, their roles behind the scenes as they work, often for periods as long as a year, in anticipation of the festival. Women play various roles: as program series organizers, as board members of the nonprofit entities that produce the predominantly white women's music festivals, or, as workers who are charged with greater responsibility than the rank-and-file festigoer and who in turn receive a modicum of compensation. Board members, whose roles are more administrative, set policy, suggest musical artists to producers, do grant writing, and establish different workshop series, among other duties. Although many of the voices of women involved in festival organizing and production may never be recovered, these interviews provide a valuable glimpse into the efforts of black lesbians to contribute to the festival scene and to make festivals responsive to the needs and interests of women of color.[1]

This chapter is organized by the themes that emerged during my conversations with those who have assumed greater levels of responsibility within festival organization.[2] Sections concerning the business aspect of festival organization and topics that fall loosely under the category of feminist identity are framed by the organizers' "coming out to women's music" stories, or, in other words, their introductions to the women's music scene. The conversations I relate illuminate different understandings, across political generations, of what women's music is and the relevance of feminism and activism in the lives of the narrators.

Coming Out and In to Women's Music

The coming out story figures centrally in lesbian narratives, yet there are astonishingly few in the nonfiction literature concerning the life cycles of black lesbians and bisexuals.[3] This is remarkable in an era that attends the emergence of a belated but critical examination of gay and lesbian life in African American studies. In this section I use the term *coming out* in relation to narrators' experiences of becoming acquainted with the women's music scene. My focus here responds to the call for further studies of the emergence of black women's feminist consciousness in the contemporary period.

I met Marietta Beamer, forty-one, an artist and single mother of three, at the Northampton Lesbian Music Festival. Beamer credited her initial exposure to Sweet Honey in the Rock to her involvements as a political activist. This led to a brief discussion of her marriage: "That's part of why I married my husband. We thought we were on the same wavelength . . . As it turns out, my husband wasn't sincere about his activism . . . So yes, I've always done something around feminism, though in my twenties I don't think I was calling it that—but working toward the empowerment of women, definitely." Beamer's marriage was far from ideal, and she left the relationship with a new appreciation of Sweet Honey: "My marriage was abusive, and my husband was alert to influences that he felt were dangerous, and music was one of those things that he was sensitive about. He went with me to the Sweet Honey concert. On one level, he enjoyed it; politically, it was threatening . . . Sweet Honey planted seeds that I didn't know they were planting. What it really did was to lead me back to a love of gospel."[4]

Aspects of Beamer's story are familiar. Many black feminists, lesbian and straight, were introduced to SHIR through their work with women's activist organizations. Beamer recalls that she was introduced to the women's music community more broadly through contacts she made in bisexual social networks:

> I was exploring the idea of being bisexual. I was going to bisexual potlucks. One of the women said she was coming [to the Northampton festival], and I told her

I'd go, too. It was a great experience for me. I had no idea of the importance of being at a women's festival. Last year—just seeing thousands of women—different shapes, hairstyles, ethnicities—it occurred to me that I was seeing the range of what it meant to be a woman. By then I was forty years old, but I still had the idea that there was a narrow range of what it meant to be a woman; for instance, masculinity versus femininity, sizes, shapes, and attitudes. If you were outside of that, it was an aberration. I thought that the more masculine females had something wrong with their hormones. I had an idea I had that prejudice . . . I was seeing all of humanity in one spot. It was extremely diverse.

Some might jokingly suggest that Beamer's response reflects at least one vestige of lesbian-feminist-inspired women's culture: the potluck. That she was "exploring the idea" of being bisexual, however, is a rare admission, even in coming out narratives of white women. As Ellen Lewin and William Leap suggest, the inclusion of bisexuals in examinations of gay and lesbian experience is uneven.[5] The festivals also facilitated Beamer's becoming acquainted with a wider range of performers in women's music, both white and black.

EH: When you were married were you familiar with women's music?
MB: Very little. I only knew Holly Near.
EH: Well, all right! How did you become more familiar with the others?
MB: There has been a significant jump in who I know and what I know because of the festivals . . .
EH: Is there anybody you especially like?
MB: Ferron and Suede [both of whom are white] and Sweet Honey in the Rock.

I asked Beamer to detail events that inspired her initial involvement with the Northampton festival. Emphasizing her work as a political activist, she stressed the opportunities the festival creates to build coalitions among diverse constituencies of women: "It was the momentum of all those joys. Building community here has put me in contact with a number of political activism groups. For instance, I belong to a feminist collective, and here in Northampton one of our hot political issues is trying to get a domestic partnership ordinance going. We're fighting against the religious right . . . I'm proud to be a part of this coalition. The community is filled with people of integrity."[6]

In a separate interview, Karla Gee, fifty-two, recalled her introduction to the women's music scene. Gee, who has been involved with NWMF since 1992, became a respected sound engineer on the women's music festival circuit. She recalled: "I was in my middle twenties and had been out for just a couple of years. I started going to the bookstores, the local bookstore. [EH: Meaning feminist bookstores? Women's bookstores? KG: Yes.] I started meeting some people there and heard about the NWMF. The first one I went to was number six, I think. And I had heard about them a year or so before I was actually able to go."[7]

Afterward, Gee explained that the "racial stuff" (tensions) she experienced en route to the festival inspired some initial concern. Still, she ended on a humorous note as she correlated the effects of an aging body with the exigencies of camping outdoors:

> KG: Off I went to Southern Illinois University—I think that's where it was. At that time, the town (I think it was Cairo) was experiencing a lot of racial stuff. In some ways, it was scary to go there, as I recall. Once I got there, I had a blast.
>
> EH: And you went as a regular attendee—not as a crew member?
>
> KG: Yes, I just went. Then I went to MWMF that same year, paid my money, and I slept on the ground that year. Can't do that now—I'm too old.

Narratives of black women interviewed are remarkable also for the signposts of time, place, and music they invoke. Cal Mitchell, thirty-five, a former board member of Women in the Arts (sponsors of NWMF), mentioned a familiar and beloved landmark for feminists in Chicago: "When I lived in Chicago, there was a women's coffeehouse that was a woman-only space where female artists would perform (I can't remember the name). So the women's music scene wasn't foreign to me, but the idea of going to a festival and working there was new. . . . I had plans to attend Michigan, but I never made it. That first festival for me [NWMF] was in 1999."[8]

Mitchell refers to Mountain Moving Coffeehouse, located on Chicago's north side and one of the last of the great non-festival-associated, women-only establishments to call it quits. In 2005, after being in business for thirty-one years, Mountain Moving closed its doors for the final time.[9] The closing of the coffeehouse is a reminder that the women's culture of the 1970s and 1980s fostered opportunities for women to gather in women-only spaces for the performance of music on a more regular and local basis. Social networks emerge as sites of women's discovery of women's music relatively near the period of their coming out. All of these factors are cited by Nancy Whittier in her discussion of radical feminist activity in the 1970s, 1980s, and 1990s.[10]

Members of a newer cohort of festival organizers were also influenced by the women's studies courses they took in college. In the case of Trade Roberts, thirty-five, a seven-year board member of Wiminfest, this extended to her studies in graduate school. In contrast to women who spoke of their festival organizing as part of broader initiatives that contribute to social change, Roberts spoke of her work as enabling "the arts," adding that it provided psychic relief from her efforts to stem domestic violence through working in battered women's shelters, a mainstay of feminist activist experience:[11]

When I was in college during my undergrad years, I worked at the Women's Center, and I was involved in a lot of activities on campus. I got my MS in women's studies. My program was very focused on social action as opposed to theory, at least at the time that I was there from 1994 to 1996. That was a lot of what the students did. I was actually happy to do something in the arts rather than antiviolence work, because it was just a bit lighter than other stuff I had worked on. So I was excited to do something like that—supporting the arts.

Before becoming a board member, Roberts had not been to Wiminfest, but she had attended another festival:

I had just moved to Albuquerque in the summer of 1996. I had been to Campfest [produced by Lee Glanton] in Pennsylvania, the state I'm from originally. And I had just graduated from a women's studies program at Minnesota State at Mancato. I was very familiar with feminist organizations and doing stuff in lesbian- or women-centered activities in the arts.

Toward the end of our interview, Roberts offered what she described as her "original" coming out story, which included a narrative frame:

TR: This is my "introduction to women's music" story. It seems like such a long time ago. I went to school in this little town in Pennsylvania, and I was living with two other black women, and I had started dating this woman who was white. She introduced me to women's music—not so much the folk festival women's music scene but popular folk music that was available—well, like the Indigo Girls, for example. This was the early 1990s, and they were on TV and everything like that. I can't remember if they were out then—but you know, like Sara Hickman and all these different people who had albums out and you could buy them in the store, but I had never heard of them. Even people I didn't identify as lesbian—like Tori Amos and all these different artists who I had never really listened to before.[12]

I mean, I would hear a little bit, and so my roommates and I would always listen. We loved dance music, house music, and hip-hop. So I'd be in my room listening to this music [the "women's music" she has described], and they were like, "What the hell is this?" And I was like, "Oh, this is women's music"—and they would give me the hardest time. They would just tease me mercilessly. They would say, "Why are you listening to this shit?" (laughs) I mean, you know—it was just the first kind of blending of my identities, because I had been introduced to women's music.

EH: That's so great. And then did you pursue this interest on your own?

TR: Oh, yeah. It spoke to me in a certain way, just because at the time I was just getting used to identifying as a lesbian and seeing the value in a woman-centered reality. But I didn't necessarily give up my love of anything I had

> grown up listening to or liked or had identified with. I just added it to my repertoire of other things that I liked.

Roberts's comments point to the permeable borders between the very specific women's music scene that is the topic of this book and a more popular, commercial manifestation of neo-feminist-inspired music by pop artists. The Indigo Girls (Amy Ray and Emily Saliers) received one of their starts in women's music and have since achieved mainstream success while still touching base periodically with their lesbian consumer base at festivals.[13] White pop musician Tori Amos has exerted a chameleon-like presence in pop music as a feminist-portender, while white folk rocker Sara Hickman also rode the wave of the feminist presence in pop in the early 1990s. Given their ambivalent embrace of an avowed and consistent lesbian or feminist identity, these musicians can be added to what white lesbian culture critic Arlene Stein refers to as the "new breed" of pop women.[14] Roberts refers to all three of these acts as "women's music," even though Tori Amos has demonstrated an ambivalent and opportunistic claiming of feminist identity and it is not clear that Sara Hickman has performed in women's music festival venues. These artists are close in age to the women of Roberts's generation, so it makes sense that she would claim them as representative of women's music.

Roberts's coming out story posits the "first kind of blending" of her identities. She implies that the blending occurred in the nexus between music genres. On the one hand, her African American friends with whom she listened to dance music, house, and hip-hop (all black- and urban-associated musical genres) derided her even as they celebrated their friendship. On the other hand, Roberts enjoyed the music of white folk erstwhile feminist rockers, to which she also listened. Noteworthy is that Roberts added women's music to her existing listening repertoire as opposed to supplanting her other musical preferences with women's music—a phenomenon that holds true for the black women of this book, regardless of generation. Although she is representative of a more recent generation of organizers, Roberts's expansive musical palette is par for the course. "I listen to pop, rap, hip-hop," she says, adding that she also likes folk music, jazz, and country music. In fact, I encountered no black woman veteran musician or festival attendee who suggested that "back in the day" she restricted her listening choices only to the music of black performers affiliated with the women's music circuit. During the heady days of women's music, lesbian consumers listened to both chart music and to the music of lesbian-identified performers.[15]

African American festigoers affirm the significance of all-black musical acts and performers to festivals. Exchanges with festigoers over the years confirm that black women performers are critical to festigoers' evaluations of the festival experience. Both SHIR and, as one woman put it, "Linda Tillery either alone or with a group," present larger-than-life onstage personae. Although Tillery only rarely reprises hits from her lesbian-identified 1985 album, *Secrets,* her longevity in the women's music festival scene and commitment to lesbians—and, indeed, all women—is well known by members of the community.[16] Both Tillery and Sweet Honey in the Rock have performed their commitment to lesbians and black women respectively; in some cases, of course, these categories are not mutually exclusive. This is most important to the women with whom I spoke. In an interview conducted more than a decade ago, Tillery commented on the transgressive nature of women's music in the era in which it emerged and what she herself expects to see on the stage:

> Saying "I love a woman" as a woman isn't the most popular thing to do in life, but it had to be spoken, because there were people who needed to hear it and who needed to be affirmed—people who needed to see themselves reflected in that larger-than-life way—you know, the way artists have of doing that from the stage . . . People who go to concerts, they choose the people they choose because they see certain parts of themselves in those performers. So it is really a part of themselves that is standing on stage and becomes as big as the room and becomes awesome and powerful . . . You know, when I have gone to hear Aretha Franklin, for example, I feel magnified ten times. I know that if I go to hear this woman, I will find some parts of myself there.[17]

Middle-aged black cultural insiders also demonstrate familiarity with and appreciate the role of women's music founders, including white musicians such as Holly Near, Alix Dobkin, Cris Williamson, Margie Adam, and Meg Christian, as well as Asian American musician June Millington. The music of both white and black musicians figured prominently during the period when black women became acquainted with the women's music scene. Like Trade Roberts, Cal Mitchell encountered opposition when she attempted to introduce her other black (lesbian) friends to women's music later on:

> CM: And when I think about Ubaka Hill—my friends say, "Who is Ubaka Hill?" or "Who is Linda Tillery? I don't listen to her music"—you know, they don't care for the music. Like when I think of SHIR—I'm not saying that they play at women's music festivals, but to me, they fit into this whole women's music genre. When I think of SHIR and the political statements they make with their music—and I like their sound—that's cool for me. But my friends are like, "Girl—whatever." They are much more into mainstream music. [To them,] it's not important to support women's music in that way. There are people in my head who I can remember seeing at [the

NWMF] festival, and my friends are like, "I don't like this music. I don't like this style . . ."

EH: I was thinking of people like Casselberry/DuPreé, Deidre McÇalla.

CM: Yeah, and like I said, I was so excited to see Ubaka Hill. "Oh my gosh! Oh my gosh!" And my friends were like, "Who?" At the pitch-ins [potluck suppers she would hold for her circle of black lesbian friends], I would try to have Linda Tillery's music, or Ubaka's or one of Deidre McCalla's CDs—just for them to hear—and their reaction was "Nah."

As the conversation progressed, I suggested that given the fact that her friends appreciate urban music genres such as hip-hop, they might have a greater tolerance for sexism in lyrical content.

CM: I think so. Okay—you asked me earlier if I was an activist and I said "no," but you know what? I am, because I think we are walking around asleep. We have been lulled to sleep, and I say to my friends all the time, "You need to wake up and see what's going on. Are you listening to [the music and] what is being said about you and about your daughter?" Yeah, okay. So I'm an activist, maybe. (laughs)

EH: I think it's *more* than an activist, maybe! (laughs)

In retrospect, Mitchell's comments made me wish I had followed up to ask if her friends appreciated progressive musical expressions of any sort and from any era: OutKast, Nina Simone, or India.Arie. If read too quickly, the exchange in which Mitchell's friends figure as politically unconscious aficionados of black popular music situates them as unknowing in contrast to her more enlightened sensibility. As music consumers and scholars can attest, the phenomenon of listeners jamming to compelling instrumental grooves laced with derogatory lyrics is not unusual.[18]

Later, Mitchell raised the phenomenon of independent label artists who cross over to the mainstream charts:

EH: And so your friends and others who came to Women in the Arts came for the social aspect and not as much for the music?

CM: Most of the artists that my friends like cross over really quickly. A person who comes to mind is Me'shell Ndegéocello.[19] She crossed over. Like Lizz Wright . . . she crossed over, too.

Mitchell's mention of jazz vocalist Lizz Wright in the context of a conversation about women's music is of interest. Here, she seems to conflate an understanding of women's music as a musicking phenomenon rooted in a historicized lesbian feminism with the subject position of "black lesbian musician" in general. This illustrates that for some women, the sexual identity of the artist is not necessarily commensurate with intimations of a particular political identity. Asking consumers directly about their musical preferences is a preliminary guide to their musicking practice, although it is not always a reliable indicator of their actual practice. I am reminded that often my undergraduate students claim to appreciate a wide range of musics only to contradict themselves through their disdain for particular genres, examples of which I play in class—early country music, for instance.

That so many of the women I interviewed mentioned the importance of black artists in the women's music scene suggests that the music of these artists provided affirmation, and even sustenance, to black women who found themselves in predominantly white lesbian settings during a certain period. Just as Linda Tillery describes, the music of African American performers seems to have resonated for each in a special way. Even now, when, as Joy James argues, a "radical feminist" voice has been co-opted, if not supplanted, in mainstream culture, the performances of these musicians carry messages—subliminally, kinetically, and textually—of justice and the love of women for women, although in ways that can be complex.[20]

The coming out stories that festival workers shared concerning their introduction to women's music were diverse, as well as revealing of some generational differences. Whereas some of the earlier organizers came into contact with women's music through their activism and through women's networks that developed alongside institutions such as women's bookstores and coffeeshops, a next-generation organizer spoke of the influence of college classes and of the contemporary folk music scene in bringing her into the festival community. What all of the women shared was a desire to transform women's music festival space into a welcoming site for women of color.

Maybe the "Only" but Not the "First": The Business of Festival Organizing

African American women who had followed in the footsteps of others in festival organizations readily admitted that they did not have to do the groundwork in terms of heightening an awareness of race in an environment of predominantly white board members. Trade Roberts appreciated that other women of color had walked that path before her, recalling that at the time she joined Women in Movement in New Mexico in 1996 (she was twenty-six), there was only one other black woman on the board:

> By the time I got on the board, it had usually been about half women of color and half white women. It had been pretty diverse in terms of trying to represent

people from different backgrounds. One of the things they struggled with was having women of different ages. You know, we all kept getting older anyway . . . By the time I became a member of the board, it was half women of color. We could talk about things. I didn't feel like a token black woman or a token young black woman. People had done a little bit of homework to challenge themselves in terms of being accepting. It was just the way they set things up. It wasn't going to be all white women with one black woman who is supposed to speak for everyone. So that was good.

A member of the same generation as Roberts, Cal Mitchell recalled meeting the longtime festival producer Mary Byrne at a social function.[21] Byrne recruited her to work at the festival, which in turn led to her joining the board. Mitchell served on the board for a year; being a new mother and board member at the same time was a challenge. She intimated also that cliques were noticeable in the group and attributed her subsequent feeling of "outsiderness" to that compounded set of circumstances:

CM: It was more difficult than I bargained for. One of the things that was difficult was that I am in a circle of [black] lesbians who have children. Most of the women on the board did not. I also host a lesbian social event called a pitch-in. Women bring their children. My partner and I had split up, so essentially I was a single parent. My daughter was three or four, but she was used to being places with me and being quiet. But the other board members didn't have children, or if they did, they didn't bring them, and I felt it was cultural. She goes where I go. The other piece was that since WIA [Women in the Arts] had financial hardship, things were strained, since I was not in a position to give money and I didn't run in circles where I came into contact with people who could give money. Tempers would flare. It was a unique learning experience for me.

EH: Did tempers flare because everyone wasn't able to give the same amount of money?

CM: Yes, but also there was an attitude of "this is how we've always done it." I was new, and many of them had been friends and acquaintances for twenty years. Some of the old garbage from past disagreements carried over, and I was amazed by that . . . All these talented women with a diverse set of skills, and we couldn't stay in the present.

According to Mitchell, the predominantly white board encountered the challenges she described even as it strived for inclusivity. The women who organized the festival's Women of Color series also encountered challenges; just one of them was encouraging members of the various constituencies represented by the label "women of color" to identify with the term, a challenge that career activists might recognize. Outside of its use by academic feminists and feminist activists, or its indiscriminate use and manipulation by corporate profit centers, members of these groups (African Americans, Asian Americans, Native Americans, Latinos) across economic statuses, age, and region identify with the term on an uneven basis, if at all.[22] The situation Mitchell describes is one that has a long history at NWMF:

> There were only two of us [black women], and one didn't live in town [Indianapolis]. One thing I appreciate about the board is that they were very aware that there was not a lot of participation by women of color and that in the Midwest, "women of color" is a euphemism for black, when it truly is a diverse set of women. In the three years I participated, we were never able to move past "women of color" meaning black. We even tried changing the name, and that didn't help. We even said "open to all women," but nothing worked. I spoke to Latino women who didn't come to the multicultural dinner because, they said, "we're not black."

Mitchell's observations have been critical for organizations advocating for women across race, age, class, and region to bear in mind. While one would think that the interactions of race and gender are significant in the lives of Latina, Asian American, black, and Native American women, the combination of variables is not equally significant to members of those different constituencies.[23] While it can be argued that Asian American women also experience the effects of racism, they experience these effects differently from the vast majority of African American women (and the focus is collectives, not individuals). The lesson to be gleaned from this varied response to the term "women of color" is that each constituency brings to the project of "liberation" a different political history at both the macro and meso levels.[24] Collins elaborates on this to useful effect in her discussion of intersectional approaches as they pertain to the social locations of different groups of women. The lessons raised by Mitchell's experiences are worth remembering. Although it is outside the scope of this book, an investigation into the many women's communities in Indianapolis and other cities would highlight local knowledge concerning the degree to which nonblack constituencies—and different cohorts of black women, too (elders, disabled, those who are not politically active)—identify under the rubric of women of color.

Other black women, like Jay Howard, who preceded Mitchell on the board of Women in the Arts, stressed that their organizational expertise was a determining factor in their being asked to join the organization. Howard, who has been involved with the festival since 1983, joined the board in the 1990s. She remembers: "One year there was an infrastructure struggle, and because of my management skills, organizing and mobilizing skills, it was time [for me] to get involved. I immediately got involved on the board of directors and became chair of the administrative committee responsible for setting up policy, infrastructure related to the task force, organizational structure, and how it operated internally and externally."[25]

Unlike Mitchell, who employed her expertise as a clinical social worker in contributing to the mental health workshop series, Howard brought her experience as a grant writer to the organization. She helped to initiate the Women of Color series, but the board had an even wider target market in mind: "If you look at the membership of the organization at that time—both on the board and off—it was very much white women over forty who made over fifty thousand dollars a year, and because of that, the board implemented some strategic initiatives to help undergird and actively recruit communities of color to be involved . . . our goal was to increase not only the numbers of people of color but to conduct research in terms of age difference, younger and older women."

In my interviews with festival organizers, it became evident that the incorporation of a workshop program series designed to meet the interests of women of color was the result of a process of negotiation over time. Parsing together the history of the women of color tents or programs at various festivals was beyond the scope of this book, but a number of organizers' names emerge in addition to those referenced in this chapter.

Feminism and Its Camps

While all of the women I interviewed for this chapter participate in activities that many outsiders would probably identify as feminist, the differences in their approaches to the women's music scene suggest the possibility of differences in their politics and in their definitions of feminism itself. In this section, exchanges with festival volunteers move away from discussion of the business of organizing to a cluster of issues falling under the heading of feminist identity: nudity at festivals and its relation to radical politics, the claiming of feminist identities, and butch/femme. Humor, as I have mentioned, figured into many of my interactions with black festigoers; a friend suggested that maybe I was the target of the jokes and just didn't get it.

Topics such as nudity were treated seriously by some and signified on by others. My interview with Karla Gee (NWMF) is a prime example of the performative quality of black orality. In the following exchange, Gee, who, with her long brownish/blackish/graying dreads, cuts a handsome and almost sartorial visage, shared her reflections about the nudity the Michigan festival affords. This conversation followed my asking what she liked best about the Michigan event:

KG: The fact that I can be naked.

EH: Okay (laughing), and what is it about nudity that you like?

KG: It's just a very freeing and liberating thing. You know—I never do full nudity, because I'm not about having bugs up my ass. When I want to sit down, I want to sit down, but it's very liberating and freeing not to have to wear a shirt.

EH: If Michigan were not a women-only festival, would you feel as free to do that?

KG: Oh, hell no. [EH laughs] It's bad enough to try to talk to guys and have them look you in the face. . . . But in this society? Where women have implants and become 55DDDs [EH laughs] so they can dance on poles? No, no, no. Boys just couldn't handle it.

EH: Hmm.

KG: Straight boys couldn't handle it, and the gay boys would be puking all the time.

EH: (laughs) Okay, right on, so we've got nudity and what else?

KG: That's pretty much it.[26]

While the juxtaposition of Gee's sardonic quips to my straight man could be part of an amateur comedy hour, other women expressed their views on nudity in a more serious mode. Jay Howard said that NWMF appeals to her more than the Michigan festival because it's indoors. She explained: "It is not dictated by the weather. It is more mainstream, meaning that you don't have the radical activities that you would see at Michigan such as bathing outside or walking around nude—those kind of things." Given that festival veterans and socially conscious younger women alike have decried the decreasing political relevance of festival workshops, if not the festivals themselves, and insistence of political theorists that "radicality" be clearly defined, I queried Howard further on her characterization of the Michigan festival.

EH: Do you mean that Michigan's politics are radical, or do you differentiate between the nudity and something else? Do you think of the nudity as separate from the politics of the festival?

JH: I don't know if I label it as political. I believe that because it is female-owned space, they can choose, like any business, to dictate how they set things up and how they allow things to occur on their property. As a result of that . . . it's not uncommon for lesbians to have male children, and by design, the way Michigan is set up, it is only a space that women-born women are allowed to be on. So it creates a whole other set of issues for women who have kids that are male [and over the age of eleven]—that they can't be involved and can't participate. The other piece is that anything goes, so it's okay to walk around freely and be naked. While that's freeing for some, it can be offensive for others, but because it's women-owned space, they can dictate what the mandates are or are not for the people who are coming on to that space.

In making her point about the freedoms afforded by women-only space, Howard employs a bit of essentialism in equating gendered ownership of "the land" with opportunities to go nude. To wit, it is entirely possible that if the ownership of a festival such as Michigan were to trade hands and be purchased by a male investor who was sympathetic to the philosophy of the current owner (Lisa Vogel), the festival could continue as a women-only enterprise at the "retail level." Second, Howard's comment that some find nudity offensive is not off the mark, particularity given the conservatism of what Gwaltney referred to as "core" black culture.

Taking a lead from Howard's comment about the "radical activities" of the Michigan festival, I asked board members to share their conceptualization of themselves as feminists. Often, this led to an exchange in which I shared my definition of feminism, a strategy that scholar Tricia Rose used during her interviews with young women rappers.[27] Interacting with research subjects as though they are capable of and willing to take in new information and consider alternative ideas sets Rose's work apart from those whose fieldwork methods do not demonstrate a similar commitment to feminist praxis.

Various perceptions of feminism emerged in my exchanges with organizers. Cal Mitchell revealed that even during the time she was a board member, she did not identify as a feminist:

EH: Did you consider yourself a feminist, or an activist, or a womanist, or anything like that?

CM: No.

EH: Even as time went on and you were a board member?

CM: No.

EH: What about identifying as an activist?

CM: No.

EH: Even though you're very active.

CM: I don't know. I wanted the people who came to the social pitch-in to see the festivals as a good place to go—that it was a good thing. It's not like I was trying to get people to vote or canvass on the corner.

While Mitchell invoked traditional technologies of protest of the 1970s and 1980s women's movement, Karla Gee recalled rallying points of mainstream feminism:

EH: What about feminism—do you think that women attending the festivals still feel the same way about feminism?

KG: I think that would depend upon the age of the participant. And there have been many changes, even though the ERA [Equal Rights Amendment] never passed. I doubt that anyone in this country who is not a white male will ever have full parity with white males, regardless of how much money they make, education they have. Yeah, I think it depends on the participant and where they were in the 1960s and 1970s and what they were doing. I am who I am based on the experiences I have had. I have always done "men's work," so at this point it [feminism and access in the workforce] does not consciously impact me. It may on a very subconscious level, but I am not conscious of it in my daily life. I don't always think about it in terms of consciously making a political statement.

EH: Do you think that's a little different from when you were younger, or the same?

KG: When I was younger, I was more conscious of my actions making a political statement. I attended the various rallies for the ERA. Would I do some of those things today? Probably not—not because I have better things to do, but because there are things that are more important to me, like the work that I use to feed myself.

The critical theory Gee outlines is instructive on a number of levels. Particularly insightful is her suggestion that those who are not white males will not have full parity with them, regardless of how much money they make or education they have. Gee's formulation illustrates an idea put forth by political theorist Wendy Brown, and that is that blacks, women, gays, and lesbians have based their claims to injury and exclusion on the "white, masculine middle-class ideal."[28] This practice on the part of nonclass identity groups is not to be faulted, but these groups face consequences for using this ideal as the standard "against which to pitch their claims." Adhering to a "phantasmic middle class" ideal not only "preserves capitalism from critique, but sustains the invisibility and inarticulateness of class—not accidentally, but endemically."[29]

Contrasting with Gee's reference to the ERA, an initiative identified with liberal feminism, Trade Roberts discussed her negotiation of labels that emerged in connection with radical feminism.

EH: Do you think of yourself as a feminist or as a black feminist, or does it matter? Is it circumstantial as to which one you'll use?

TR: I guess I think of myself as a black feminist. If someone asked if I were a feminist, I would say yes. If they asked if I were a lot of things, I would say yes. If they asked me if I were a lesbian, I would say yes. If they asked if I were a mother, I would say yes. I don't feel that I have to pick one or the other—a black feminist or feminist. I feel like I'm both of those things.

Some of the organizers I spoke with felt comfortable identifying as feminists, while others, like Mitchell, did not, although they were clearly doing what others would regard as feminist organizing. Although Mitchell shied away from the term "feminist," she was more adamant about the role of butch/femme subject positions in the black lesbian community. Mitchell's experience contradicts some lesbian feminist literature of the early 1990s that maintains that butch/femme divisions in lesbian communities no longer hold sway.[30] In contrast to lesbian culture critics who characterized women who inhabited butch/femme subject positions as out of step, Tracy Morgan writes, "For many dykes, butch-femme has never gone away."[31] From my participant observation at women's music festivals, I knew that these distinctions were significant to some black women. In our exchange, Mitchell linked her locked hair to butch/femme identity construction. It soon became clear that Mitchell identifies as femme: when I asked "How do you feel about butch/femme?" she replied, "We have our own culture! My hair is locked and it's long." This exchange was followed by an extended discussion of her former relationship, which, she stated, was modeled on a traditional heterosexual relationship:

CM: I didn't cut the grass or take out the trash or put oil in my car—none of that stuff.
EH: Oh, you mean you had a traditional relationship from the 1950s.
CM: (laughs) No. I do those things now.
EH: Before you were in that relationship, did you do those things?
CM: No.
EH: You mean your mama never made you take out the trash?
CM: No, my dad did [it]. I grew up in a traditional household, I told you . . . I've come a long way.

I suggested to Mitchell that outsiders to the black community might identify a woman as butch when in fact she is working-class. Although my own observations suggest that this is indeed the case, Mitchell refuted the idea that butch/femme attribution was in some ways and under some circumstances relational, and that some people do not "look like what they are":[32]

CM: Nah, sister, you know there's a radar.[33] You know the difference between a hardworking heterosexual woman and a hardworking stud. It's just a totally different energy that comes with that. (laughs) Let me clarify that and say, I know it's different in the Midwest; I don't know where you are from.
EH: I'm from Maryland.
CM: Okay. Indy [Indianapolis] is a very unique culture. This is the place where the butch/femme thing is the most rigid, because even in the South it's not as rigid as it is here.

Although I could neither confirm nor dispute Mitchell's perspective, her comments are a strong caution that as academic feminism diverges from lived experience, as scholars we must remain humble in our claims.

This same caution emerges, too, perhaps, from the interviews with organizers discussed in this chapter more generally. The women I spoke to were far from uniform in their views, but this chapter is but a sampling and partial representation of the women who helped make festivals potential sites of feminist praxis for black lesbians and other women of color over the years. And although I agree that it is wise not to confuse "the experience of empowerment" with "an actual capacity to shape the terms of political, social, or economic life," these organizers found in women's music an empowering vision of community that they worked hard to create and sustain.[34] The narrators offer an array of perspectives about women's music, their negotiation of feminist labels, and their contributions to women's music festival organizations.

It seems to me that there are some very obvious spaces in which gender difference simply does not work right now. . . . From drag kings to spies with gadgets, from butch bodies to FTM [female-to-male] bodies, gender and sexuality and their technologies are already excessively strange. It is simply a matter of keeping them that way.
—JUDITH HALBERSTAM, *FEMALE MASCULINITY*

Rest at pale evening . . .
A tall slim tree . . .
Night coming tenderly
Black like me.
—LANGSTON HUGHES, "DREAM VARIATION"

CHAPTER 9

Guys like Us

COMMUNITY MEMBERSHIP REVISITED

In recent years, drag kinging—the opposite of drag queening in that it constitutes a performance of masculinity by women—has become a source of entertainment and debate on the women's music festival circuit. This chapter unites an exploration of drag kinging with an analysis of the Michigan festival's women-born women admission policy and its ramifications. In 2006 the Michigan festival changed its policy of admitting only "womyn-born womyn" and, in response to pressure by transgender activists and allies, began openly admitting male-to-female (MtF) transgenders. This action brought to a close a controversy of nearly two decades over the admittance of MtF transgenders at the festival.[1] Though the performances of drag kings at women's music festivals and the exclusion of MtF transgenders from these same festivals are admittedly two different phenomena, I unite them here in order to consider what they reveal about the women's music community, its definitions of what it means to be a woman and a feminist, and its understanding (or lack thereof) of the expression of identities that do not fit neatly into a heterosexual or "lesbigay" framework.

More to the point, I use this chapter to explore black pathways into the subjects of drag kinging and transgender identity and notions of community membership. Prior to Michigan's change in policy, the women-born women issue animated the women's music festival circuit in a way that is difficult for non-festival attendees to appreciate. Although a great deal of discussion was engendered within women's music festival environments, scholars writing about these issues neglected to consider the perspectives of black women musicians and festigoers. This chapter constitutes my response to a hypothetical but typical footnote in feminist texts that characterizes the experiences of African American women as outside the scope of this study.

As I was preparing this book, two women's music festivals included drag king troupes on their performance rosters.[2] At the time I saw these troupes perform, each ensemble had one black woman member. The phenomenon of black women being "the only one" in women's music festival contexts, then, is not limited to the experience of being a festival attendee or musician; that I saw only a very small number of black women drag kings perform at festivals over the course of my research suggests that African American women have figured only around the edges of drag king performance and reception in the context of the festivals. Likewise, I address the issue of transgender inclusion at women's music festivals even though during the course of my research I met no black MtF transgenders who were interested in attending these events.[3] As Judith Halberstam argues, however, female masculinities may also fall under the rubric of transgender subjectivities. Therefore, I address the ways that issues affecting black FtMs (females-to-males) are dealt with in festival culture. While I use the festival community's preoccupation with the women-born women policy as an entrée to explore the role of boundaries in both African American (predominantly heterosexual) and (white) lesbian community formation, I use the performances of black drag kings at festivals as a heuristic device to illuminate pathways of thought in regard to black racial identity and the politics of spectatorship.

I begin with an introduction to contemporary drag king performance, followed by an interview I conducted with a black drag king performer at Wiminfest in Albuquerque, New Mexico, and a conversation I had with a white woman spectator after a performance and workshop featuring a different black drag king at NWMF.[4] I then shift to the subject of the women-born women admission policy, summarizing the received history of transgender activism at the Michigan festival and drawing attention to the role of boundaries in (white) lesbian feminist community formation. Next I report on exchanges I had with black women festigoers about the Michigan admission policy and examine the salience of black transgender collectivity to notions of African American community membership.[5] Finally I offer an analysis of *The Aggressives,* a film about black female masculinities that has been shown at the predominantly white women's music festivals.[6] Here I continue my probe into the operations of multiculturalism against a backdrop of white spectatorship.

Droppin' Drag King Science

"Droppin' science," meaning "to educate or inform," is a phrase with which those acquainted with the hip-hop lexicon of the past decades will be familiar. I use the term to introduce the phenomenon of drag kinging, a topic that is part and parcel of the "breakdown of gender" referenced, in the first epigraph to this chapter, by white queer cultural critic Judith Halberstam.[7] Halberstam and her collaborator, photographer Del LaGrace Volcano, define the term *drag king* as "a performer who pinpoints and exploits the (often obscured) theatricality of masculinity." They elaborate:

> The drag king can be male or female; she can be transgendered; she can be butch or femme. The drag king might make no distinction between her off-stage and on-stage persona or she may make an absolute distinction; she may say that on- and off-stage personae bleed into each other in unpredictable and even uncontrollable ways. The drag king may be extremely self-conscious about her performance and may have elaborate justifications and theories about what she is doing, or she may just think of her act as "having fun" and make no further claims for it.[8]

That black women perform a range of masculinities in a theatrical context harks back to the acts of performers such as blues singer Gladys Bentley and, later, Stormé DeLarverie of the Jewel Box Revue.[9] The performances of these artists thwart the expectations of those who have equated constructions of masculinity with the black male body. Tropes of black masculinity typically are defined against the "construction of an ideal of white masculinity as a paradigm of civilized humanity."[10] Freeing concepts of masculinity from the male body can facilitate examinations of racialized female masculinities in performance.

The small but growing drag king circuit has been abetted not only by performance workshops given by actors such as Diane Torr and others but also by conference-type events referred to as "drag king extravaganzas."[11] The first International Drag King Extravaganza (IDKE) was credited for bringing together performers, fans, scholars, filmmakers, novices, and others for an inclusive, cooperative gathering of the burgeoning drag king network. Held on the campus of Ohio State University in Columbus, Ohio, the weekend event consisted of performances, a conference, and a "Science Fair" at which attendees were exposed to some of the technologies of drag king performance. According to written descriptions, the latter provided participants with opportunities to receive instruction in performative gestures such as walking or opening doors "like a man." Conference attendees were taught how to don chest binders and "apply facial hair gel, condoms and so on."[12] The Science Fair did not include any vocal training. Scholar Kim Surkan suggests this is indicative of the fair's emphasis on the stage context of the drag kings, as opposed to the workshop participants' attempts to pass in real life.[13] Donna Troka, one of the event organizers, described the first extravaganza this way: "There were leather numbers, boy band numbers, several interpretations of Prince, punk rock, hip hop and maybe even a little country." The performance showcase included twenty-five members from sixteen states and two Canadian provinces.[14]

The significance of IDKE events warrants mention in this context because they have played an integral role in the small but growing drag king movement. Since the first four IDKEs held in Columbus, successive conventions have been held in Minneapolis (2003), Chicago (2004), and Winnipeg (2005). The 2006 conference, held in multiple locales in Austin, Texas, featured guest speaker Leslie Feinberg, author of *Stone Butch Blues* and a frequent presenter at women's music festivals.[15] Advertised events included an open mic drag night, cabaret-style brunch, gender-bashing party, and an academic conference and film festival. Reflecting and gaining momentum from several sources, the drag king movement is now complemented by a rich and engaging literature on drag king performance.[16] Halberstam's *Female Masculinity* played an important role in ushering in a new fluorescence of writing about the performance of female masculinities.

The (Drag) King and I

Drag kinging infuses new meaning into the title of Oscar Hammerstein's 1956 film adaptation of his 1951 Broadway musical, *The King and I*. For drag king Kory Chandler performing can be big fun. Chandler, an African American woman, is a member of the Albuquerque Kings Club (AKC), an ensemble that has made repeat appearances at Wiminfest in New Mexico.[17] "Kinging" often emanates from a network of friends that develop their king personae together, sometimes in duos.[18] Chandler's kinging career began in this way; in fact, she cofounded the group in 2001 and functions as an ensemble member rather than as a featured performer. In contrast to Chandler's experiences, black performers are given cursory attention in the drag king literature and are represented as members of troupes rather than as troupe founders.

I asked Chandler, thirty-six, how she started drag kinging. She replied that a coworker (whose stage name is Seymore Johnson) asked if she wanted to give kinging a try and, with a bit of hesitancy, Chandler agreed: "A gal moved in town from South Carolina and we decided we wanted to do something together. Then Toma, whose stage name is Sterling Maxwell, went and got some connections with local club owners. Then we got a regular gig [at the Pulse Nightclub] for the first Friday of the month, and then we just started raising money for different organizations and tried to get people to come look at us."[19]

Although Chandler was the only black king to perform on the night of the ensemble's appearance at Wiminfest, she is not the only black woman in the group: "We got another guy named 'Sharp' so that's nice. I mean, for Albuquerque, having two black drag kings is pretty incredible. So it's pretty great. You know, Sharp is a great performer, and it's great to have that kind of camaraderie."[20]

When they perform, members of the Albuquerque Kings Club, like many drag kings, lip-sync to recordings. The AKC works with outside choreographers, although some groups do their own choreography. Chandler noted her favorite stage roles: "Sam Cooke, Sammy Davis Jr., once in a while Stevie Wonder, Rick James—I kind of go old-school, you know? I let the younger guys do all the new stuff." By "new stuff" I understood the artist to mean more recent musical genres that are typically considered black or black-influenced, such as rap, house, and hip-hop. Chandler's choice of repertoire dovetails with the music choices of Dréd and Shon, the drag king performers Halberstam interviewed in New York City.[21] Halberstam writes that the pair "manage to pull off close replications of the performers they imitate, and in many of their shows parody gives way to homage."[22] Chandler's depiction of black music icons is likewise a matter of respect.[23] Addressing ways her offstage persona compares with that of her character, Mac D, Chandler related: "I wouldn't say that Kory is Mac. Mac is cockier, a little more outgoing, a little more flirty; Kory is more reserved . . . but Sharp—she carries her character with her pretty much of the time. My performance onstage is a little hammier than I let myself be in real life." Chandler's admission that her stage performance of masculinity differs from how she lets herself be in real life is noteworthy. Like some, but not all, drag kings, Chandler does not attempt to pass as a man offstage.[24]

Since the AKC's performance took place at a women's music festival, I asked Chandler to address audience expectations for a feminist performance. She laughed: "That's really interesting. Sharp and I were just having a talk about this." Riffing on the politics of venue that I mentioned earlier, Chandler admitted that the Albuquerque Kings tame their shows down for the Wiminfest crowd, adding that they "want to make sure that everybody's happy." To illustrate why the AKC deems it necessary to offer a tamer show at Wiminfest, Chandler related what she called the "flap about the mud flap," an incident the AKC experienced several years ago. "One of the guys" in the AKC made a logo to go on the mud guard for the truck that was often used by members of the organization. Laughing, she said: "He put the mud flap [a sketch of scantily clad girls or women] on the club's logo." Apparently, the design created for the polymer splash guard was controversial with some of the local feminists, who, Chandler added with emphasis, "do come to the shows and enjoy it very much." Reflecting on the "flap" that followed, Chandler continued: "'You know,'" I said, "'Why are we doing this? Are we just doing this so that we can have arguments?'" The tensions Chandler points to reveal a familiar fault line in lesbian feminist communities. Fuelling the discord over the mud flap logo was the incorporation of an iconic image that second-wave feminists had regularly decried as sexist. Now it was being appropriated, if not celebrated. Women I spoke with related that over the years, a similar level of cognitive dissonance has registered in the reactions of some festigoers to the inclusion of drag king performances at festivals.

Chandler's admission that the AKC tones down their performances for the festival crowd speaks to the real or perceived boundaries of gender, sex, feminist politics (or perceptions thereof), and generation. Simply put, Chandler's admission underscores that in the case of drag king performances, venues matter. Indeed, the suggestion that "the venue makes all the difference" mirrors my experience as an observer. Scholar Tara Pauliny deftly elaborates:

> The audience's recognition of and (dis) identification with codes occurs because a drag king's performance relies as much upon context as it does upon discourse. It is, therefore, not only relevant what subject positions are engaged by the performance, but it is also pertinent where the performance takes place, in front of whom, by whom, and for what purpose. These "real" or immediate contexts are important because they also affect the arguments being made and the persuasive quality of those arguments. It matters whether the show takes place in a gay club or at a university function, whether it is performed in front of a crowd familiar with drag king culture who might be politically and socially aware of gender issues, or in front of people largely unaware of these issues. The actual onlookers, setting, and performers work in concert with performance to create meaning; they are not separate from it.[25]

Although current and past board members of Women in Movement in New Mexico reiterated that Wiminfest welcomes and encourages drag king performances, individual women have expressed their discomfort with the practice. The discomfiture some festigoers have felt in regard to drag kinging cannot be dismissed with a condescending nod to their antisex attitudes or neo-Puritan values. Rather, the attitudes of audience members reveal, in part, their conceptualizations of feminism if not the period in which they came of political age. At issue for many is whether drag king performance represents an avowal of female identities or, contrastingly, a type of male identification. Cultural critics have outlined the contours of the tension experienced by those who have historically felt uncomfortable with drag king performances, regardless of venue: "The practice of appropriating, seen momentarily and with some irony, a masculine subject position . . . gives kings a very uncertain ground within feminism. While the queen's performance of 'femininity' is often seen as misogynist, the king's is conversely misinterpreted as an idealization of masculine attributes and patriarchal values."[26] It might seem ironic that for some, objections to the programming of drag kinging at women's music festivals contrasts with the incorporation of performances by butch, lesbian-identified performers at those same festivals. Through talking with older white festigoers informally, it became clear that for some women the lines of distinction between drag king performers (who might identify as lesbians, as heterosexuals, or as transgender, as Halberstam makes clear) and those who identify as FtMs, and are held to deny their femaleness, were sometimes blurred. For these spectators, drag king performance was seen as a repudiation of the femaleness upon which their conceptions of feminism is or was based. The performance of the AKC at Wiminfest revealed a conservatism, or a caution, that is difficult to quantify.

Gender Breaks Down; Race Runs as Usual

At the National Women's Music Festival, I attended an afternoon workshop and evening performance by H.I.S. Kings, a white drag king troupe that has one black king member. Few black women festigoers attended either the workshop or the performance, and as a result I conducted an interview with a white woman festival attendee after the show. Consistent with a project that problematizes flygirl demographics, my concern for the ramifications of conducting research with black women in a predominantly white lesbian social field is reflected in my field notes.

> I attend an afternoon workshop led by Si'le Singleton and the H.I.S. Kings, a drag king troupe from Columbus, Ohio. The workshop, titled "If Not Here, Where? Trans-Identities and 'Womyn's Space,' Part II," is described as designed to seize upon the interest generated in women's music festival communities around transgender identities and notions of community membership in ostensibly women-only spaces. An African American woman who looks to be in her early thirties, Singleton is one of the founders of the troupe. Later, I learn that the troupe's name should be interpolated as a possessive, as in "his kings."[27] The session follows an earlier screening of filmmaker Robin Deisher's *XY:DRAG,* a documentary about the burgeoning drag king subculture. H.I.S. Kings are featured.[28] A promotional blurb in the festival booklet promises "a provocative and passionate discussion about this often community-dividing topic."[29]

As I wait for the workshop to begin, along with about fifteen white women between twenty-something and middle age, I wonder silently why there aren't more women of color in attendance. Singleton and I are the only African American women present until well into the workshop, when another black woman joins the group. Carlos Las Vegas, a popular Asian American performer on the drag king circuit, is the only other person of color on the panel. The relative youth of panel members (although I believe one king said he was thirty-two) does not go by unnoticed. Is it too personal an admission to admit that by this time even thirty-two seems akin to a continuation of youth? The drag king performers are slightly built and project the appearance of flat-chestedness; I do not know if this is because they actually are or because they have bound their chests. Their rather waiflike appearances contrast with the more ample proportions of one troupe member, a young woman who performs as a (female) drag queen. A number of the kings voice their desire to transition to men rather than to identify as butch lesbians or, for that matter, heterosexual, butch-identified women. Several of them seemed invested in rather rigid and static notions of feminine and masculine. In spite of attempts by theorists to separate notions of gender from physical embodiment, the kings seem to hold less-current notions about the mapping of these qualities onto each other. Feminist theories align in an uneasy tension with lived experience.

Eleven P.M. The H.I.S. King's Club puts on a late-night show that follows the main stage concert. Throughout the performance, I look for more sistahs to come into the large auditorium, yet the H.I.S. Kings performance drew a similarly low turnout of black women. Possible conflicts of interest could be three events scheduled concurrently: a drum jam with Wahru Cleveland, an African American drummer; an evening of women's erotic films; and a "goddess jam coffeehouse" that provides performance opportunities for women who have been selected in the open mic series.[30] Another militating factor could be that the performance is filmed under the auspices of the Discovery Channel and Alliance Atlantis for use in Drag Kings on Tour, directed by Sonia Slutsky.

After the show that evening, which lasted into the early hours of the next morning, I could not identify any other black women attending the H.I.S. Kings performance, so I took the opportunity to talk with Kelly Marshall about the show. Marshall is a middle-aged white lesbian attendee who, I later learned, is a longtime feminist who had thought deeply about these issues.[31] Marshall asked for my feedback on the afternoon workshop, which she was not able to attend. I related that some of the drag kings' descriptions of their genders reinforced gender stereotypes more than they resonated with philosopher Judith Butler's productive notion of performativity.[32] A memorable aspect of Butler's discussion is her reminder that sexual identity (lesbian, gay, straight, bisexual) could, for example, be separated from butch/femme identities, making it possible to describe a straight woman as a "heterosexual femme" or "straight butch" with as much ease as it is to attribute butch/femme identities to lesbians. Although I shared my enthusiasm for the workshop's inclusion in the program, I lamented that the subject position of the butch lesbian had been evacuated and that many of the young women seemed intent on making the "full" transition from female to male, aided by hormones and possibly surgery. Marshall replied:

> There's kind of an irony here—that people who are transitioning are teaching us something and they are also (and how do I want to say this?)—they are invested in these stereotypes. They are invested in femininity staying one way and in masculinity being a certain way. I'm sure that there are people who transition so that they can get what to them has always been this holy grail. But then the culture is going to change and they are not going to fit anymore, and they are going to have done big things to themselves [meaning, to their bodies through the use of hormones or surgery] that I hope they can find peace with. I mean, already we're seeing that a lot of the early MtFs, at least who I know of, like Kate Bornstein and Riki Wilchins, are saying—and I think Les Feinberg is saying this also—"I'm not a man, but I'm not really a woman either."[33] And at least the people who are writing are saying, "What I've really discovered from this whole journey is that the space in between is really what is interesting. And let's look at that and let's look at that gray area and let's celebrate it and explore that."

Marshall mentions three transgender activists and theorists who by now have been accorded celebrity status in parts of the women's music festival community. Both Bornstein and Feinberg have given invited keynote addresses at women's music festivals. Feinberg, author of a number of important books on transgender-related issues, gave the keynote at Wiminfest in 2005.[34] These writers point repeatedly to the idea that many transgendered persons identify as neither male nor female, a phenomenon encapsulated by the subtitle of Kate Bornstein's *Gender Outlaw: On Men, Women, and the Rest of Us.*[35] H.I.S. Kings panelists, however, did not give voice to thinking along those lines during the workshop. Instead, the impression I got was that they regarded sex reassignment as the promised land of a static subjectivity.

Marshall and I discussed how, as middle-aged feminists, we seemed to be caught in a time warp. We both remembered that as young women, in preparation for and during women's music festivals, we anxiously and deliberately attempted to grow beards—or facsimiles thereof—as indications of our liberated womanhood. I mentioned that the facial hair I so willfully grew years ago has now, in my perimenopausal years, returned with a recalcitrant vengeance. No amount of queer, black, or black feminist power can stem the tide of that. Not to underestimate the commitment that the decision to take hormones or to undergo sex reassignment surgery necessitates, I asked Marshall to register her views. She responded:

> You know, I worry about that really, because I think that in the greater culture, I think it's a bit of a fad. I mean, high school kids are taking hormones or steroids to bulk up. I think that stuff is really awful for your body. What I'm really curious about in terms of these kinds of issues is—and I guess a central question for me in the whole transitioning process is—What's the difference between stretching conceptions about what being a woman can mean, and at what point do you have to change your body physically? At what point do you not just change your performance? I can understand changing your behavior, I can understand acting out in performance, but what makes it imperative that you change your body? And take a risk. It's a huge risk. I don't think anyone can give you a clear answer about what is going to happen. I can see why you would want to get rid of your [menstrual] period—but not really. I can see wanting to have facial hair, but enough to risk your health when you are fifty, sixty, forty?

My discussion with Marshall foreshadowed exchanges I had three years later with singer/songwriter Nedra Johnson, then forty-two, about what appears to be a growing trend among young white women in particular for FtM transitioning. I asked Johnson about the use of her song "Uh Huh" as background music during an episode of *The L Word,* a popular television program that orignated on Showtime and includes FtM transitioning ("Moira" becomes "Max") in one of its story lines. Johnson spoke to the phenomenon of transitioning:

> In a sense, as someone who has a butch nature, I understand a lot of the same things that Max had to go through—just because of that. Like, I hear young folks repeating . . . like people used to say things like "Girls can't climb trees," and I'd say, "Well, I'm up a tree, so obviously they can." I define what a girl can do; it's not defined by anything else. Now they say, "Girls can't climb trees, so you must be a boy." That is a simplification of it. It's shocking to me how many people I know are transitioning. It's irresponsible of me not to say something. Finally, Kit—Pam Grier's character—finally says something.[36]

Later, Johnson elaborated on her sense of, not "lesbian chic" but of what, even in my own experience teaching at a public university, bespeaks of "white transgender chic," especially FtM, on college campuses.[37]

My conversation with Kelly Marshall touches on real-life ramifications when identities constructed through female masculinities are held to extend offstage as well as on. Marshall also raised points that serve as signposts for thinking about the subversive potential of drag king performance and the way that the exoticization of drag king performers limits or cuts short this potential. Indeed, the racial othering of drag kings is part of what must be taken into account in discussions of whether or to what extent the "breakdown of gender" and its mechanisms is productively regarded as transgressive or subversive. Although I am thinking here of the mobilization of racialized fantasies that performances such as these may invoke, the issue of whether an art form that is presumed to be inherently transgressive actually is or not is one that scholars have addressed across genres.[38] For example, what emerges from some studies of clothing as an "unstable marker of identity" is that, far from being unquestionably transgressive, gender crossings "could be carried out successfully and without disturbing the basic normative boundaries of gender."[39] Judith Butler emphasizes that there is "no necessary relation between drag and subversion, and . . . drag may well be used in the service of both the denaturalization and reidealization of hyperbolic heterosexual gender norms."[40] Gender-bending practices are often tied to the mobility of other types of identity, including those of class and race. Carole-Anne Tyler suggests that what is going on here is that "differences other than that of gender have a phallic significance," noting that class and racial differences figure regularly in the fantasies of audience members (spectators). Moreover, as Tyler observes, "the fantasy of the 'other' as phallic Other is not necessarily radical since s/he may be phallic in exactly those terms a sexist, racist, and classist symbolic legitimates."[41]

These issues came to the fore during my exchange with Marshall about the role that the exoticization of race played in the evening's performance:

> It was starting to make me feel really uncomfortable, because it was like, "Oh, and how is this different? Here are these 'black' men, who are here for our sexual enjoyment. This is not revolutionary or transgressive at all. This is the same old thing in that here I am, as a white person sitting in the audience, and these people are going to offer up their bodies . . . You know—be exotic, be interesting, be 'other' in some kind of way for my consumption. . . . And I felt really uncomfortable with that. And then when I saw that the troupe itself was more balanced, that evaporated a little bit for me. But I guess that in the performances, it was the darkest people who I thought were the hottest.

Indeed, if applause is any indication, it seemed that the predominantly white audience found performances by the kings of color hotter than those of the white kings.

It might be argued that acts such as these are unwittingly designed to corroborate—or in other cases, as bell hooks writes, to interrupt—"white sensibilities." In this regard, the heightened visibility of a performance by a black drag king such as Si'le Singleton at NWMF results in an act that is perhaps less counter-hegemonic than some might claim. This should not come as a surprise; the idea that "the other" also participates in othering practices is not new. Only if one forgets or ignores that women's music festivals are situated not outside but within discourses inflected by racism, anti-Semitism, and other differentials could this phenomenon be considered ironic. As Tara Pauliny states: "Parodic and potentially disruptive in its play, the work of the drag king can encourage both complicit and critical readings of discourses of desire."[42]

Several issues emerged from my attendance at drag king events held at two women's music festivals. First, it became apparent that in the course of everyday conversation at the festival, festigoers often conflate matters pertaining to drag kinging with transgender issues. As transgender theorists have suggested, while there may be common threads, these modes are not coterminous. Still, the topics raised during the afternoon workshop in fact suggested a slippage between drag king performance and transgender experience. I think once again of the comment by Judith Halberstam that appears in the first epigraph to this chapter. I am intrigued by her suggestion that the "breakdown of gender" might "hasten the proliferation of alternate gender regimes in other locations." In light of the intransigence of certain types of structural inequalities and the lasting effects of the racialized imagination, let alone segregation and disproportionate opportunity, I am inspired to ask, And what type of difference will that gender breakdown make? Although drag king performers enjoy popularity in the drag king performance circuit as well as in lesbian cabarets, their appearances are less frequent in the women's music festival scene. In the acts in which they do appear, black women performers comprise an obvious minority. This racial distribution is in stark contrast to the intensity and frequency of debates about the appropriateness of drag king performances in women's music festival culture.

The Michigan Admission Controversy and Issues of Community Membership

In August 2006 the Michigan festival officially began admitting transgender persons to the event. Few, if any, other women's cultural institutions had attempted to emulate the model of the Michigan festival's women-born women policy.[43] As Lisa Vogel, the festival's cofounder and producer, said in a *Bitch* magazine roundtable: "What womyn-born womyn means to us is women who were born as women, who have lived their entire experience as women, and who identify as women."[44] Vogel's wish to exclude all but women-born women (and their young male children) from the festival was in contrast to those of transgender activists who advocated for the inclusion of any person who self-identified as a woman.

Debates over the issue were carried out in postings to online sites, letters to editors of lesbian newsletters and magazines, in festival workshops devoted to the topic, and in writings by feminist critics. Prior to August 2006, newer festivals to emerge on the scene, such as the multi-locale Ladyfest events, touted their relatedness to and distance from festivals such as Michigan in terms of their admission policies. For example, the Web site for Ladyfest South 2007 read: "Volunteer-driven and organized by women, Ladyfest South welcomes everyone—of all ages, genders, backgrounds and communities—to attend and participate."[45] Because most festivals are held on public property, moreover, the dictum of Ladyfest South would be the de facto policy regardless.

Details of the origins of the controversy vary, but a basic outline of events emerges. Although the presence of transexual women in women-only spaces was an issue of dispute periodically during the 1970s, especially with the publication of Janice Raymond's *The Transsexual Empire,* the issue did not explode at MWMF until 1991.[46] At that time, Nancy Jean Burkholder, a white male-to-female transexual, was expelled from the festival after revealing her sex and gender history.[47] Burkholder's expulsion set off a controversy that lasted until August 2006. In 1992 a small group of women (including at least one transexual) set up a literature table at the Michigan festival to provide information about gender issues, led workshops about transexualism and the MWMF policy, raised questions, listened, and passed out buttons reading "Where's Nancy?"[48]

Against the backdrop of a burgeoning queer identity movement, in 1993 four transsexual women (including Burkholder) and non-transexual allies attended the yearly event to "'conduct scheduled Festival workshops and outreach to other attendees,' but they were once again thrown out by the festival security."[49] Protesters camped across from the main gate in the woods—an event that marked the unofficial founding of the alternative encampment thereafter referred to as Camp Trans. The official founding of Camp Trans took place the next year, in 1994. According to the "What We Do" section of the Camp Trans Web site:

> Camp Trans is an annual gathering of transgender people and their allies in Michigan with the intent of:
>
> PROTESTING the exclusion of trans women from women-only spaces, most notably the Michigan Womyn's Music Festival;
> BUILDING a trans-inclusive community that is welcoming and safe for all;
> EMPOWERING the next generation of activists to fight for trans issues locally through organizer trainings, workshops, and leadership development; and
> ADVOCATING for the inclusion of trans issues in progressive, queer, and femi-

nist movements by building coalitions with supportive organizations and bringing attention to local campaigns.[50]

Following the establishment of Camp Trans, a new compromise was reached: producers decided to leave it up to individuals to decide whether they were women-born women. In 1994 a group of protesters entered the festival, and they were not refused admission or asked questions. After a brief hiatus, Camp Trans resumed operation in 1999, and since that time the encampment has had a yearly presence. A statement issued in 2006 stated that even with the changed admission policy, Camp Trans will continue "to be a place for trans people and allies to build community, share ideas, and develop strategies for change."[51]

The history of controversy over the women-born women admission policy exemplifies the "types of negotiation central to the construction of politicized collective identities."[52] Issues of importance to social movements are often framed along identity lines. The admittance policy of the Michigan festival, haunted by the "subject of woman," was no exception. For many years, at issue was the experience of femaleness that counted most to members of the festival community. The disagreement over the policy, however, did not negate the value of the women's community to participants. Community members can exhibit varying opinions on a matter yet still retain a notion of cohesion.[53] The debates surrounding the admittance policy of the Michigan festival reflected the complexities that attend the formation of collective identities in general. At issue were the processes of inclusion and exclusion not in terms of race but in terms of lesbian feminism and its relationship to gender and sex identities. Sociologist Joshua Gamson reminds us that "social movements depend on the active, ongoing construction of collective identity, and that deciding who we are requires deciding who we are not." Thus, all social movements, and identity movements in particular, are in the business, at least sometimes, of exclusion.[54]

The admittance policy debates of the Michigan festival lifted the veil of surface homogeneity of the lesbian feminist community. A focus on what Gamson calls the "muddle" within lesbian feminism revealed various mechanisms at work as lesbian feminist communities renegotiated the meaning of "woman" with those "who might reasonably be considered members or protagonists" of the community. Characterizing the relationship aptly, he writes: "The *us* is solidified not just against an external *them* but also against *thems* inside, as particular subgroups battle to gain or retain legitimate *us* standing."[55]

Internal movement debates over inclusion and exclusion are best understood as public communications, which depend on the nature of the primary audience.[56] Gamson is not alone in suggesting that what was at stake was not a definition of who belongs to the broader queer community or, indeed, who complied with a "rigid version of what womanhood, which comes in many expressions and shapes and colors at the festival, can look like."[57] Indeed, as some transgender activists contended, had they not revealed their transexuality, they might have been allowed to remain at the festival.[58] (Some transgender activists suggest that the spelling of *transexual* with one "s" distinguishes it from medical meanings of the term. I follow this usage throughout the text but maintain the "ss" in quotations by others.) Rather, at issue for the Michigan festival were the symbolic boundaries of what the openly acknowledged inclusion of transexuals communicated to the feminist community members gathered at the event.[59] Suggests Gamson, "The expulsion of transsexuals has been much less about some need to deny participation to transsexuals than about reinforcing the clear difference between women and men in a setting in which women cannot stop making sense."[60]

Although individual festival attendees registered a range of opinions concerning the inclusion of both MtF and FtM transgenders at women's music festivals, the Michigan policy debate revolved around the admission of male-to-female persons only. Some argued that Michigan's policy of allowing transgenders into the festival without either public welcome or acknowledgment had the effect of reinscribing them back into the closet. Gamson addresses and expounds upon this point in his analysis, pointing to the gap between the practice of the festival (which was to admit transexuals quietly after they were officially "expelled") and public discourse about the event.

In light of this, how are we to understand the apparent inconsistency between practice and public discourse? Gamson puts it this way: "As long as the category woman was left loose but intact, allowing both separation (we know who we are) and community (we are diverse), actual participation by the 'excluded' was not disturbing to others."[61] With anxiety removed about the definition of "woman," and with the recognition that "woman" was indeed a "designated category," in August 2006 the festival was opened to all who decided they were women.

Black Women Speak: Civil Rights Revisited and Notions of Linked Fate

Conversations I had with several black women festigoers provide examples of how the MWMF's public communication about the former admittance policy was read by a subgroup of women seldom referenced in discussions of the Michigan event. Although the majority of black women with whom I spoke regarded Michigan's policing of gender as ironic, they fell short of agreeing that the rights of MtF transgenders to attend the festival figured as a civil rights issue comparable to those fought for by blacks from the mid-1950s to the early 1970s.

The first interviewee, a fifty-eight-year-old black lesbian academic named Penny Jameson, described herself as active in the women's music festival community during its golden age. Jameson said she was "broadly sympathetic" with the "plight" of transgenders but drew a few distinctions, one of which was between transexuals and transgenders. The festival veteran suggested that black transexuals who wished to have "sex change" surgery were less likely than whites to be able to afford the procedures involved.[62] Alluding to the workings of class and race, Jameson equated transgender identities with postoperative bodies only. Her opinion was anticipated more than ten years earlier by Riki Anne Wilchins, a well-known white transgender activist, who wrote: "Essentially surgery breaks down for me as a class and race issue. People who are economically empowered and want surgery, get it. Which means, essentially, people who are white and educated and largely middle class."[63] Raising the issue of transgender demographics, Jameson drew parallels between the relevance of transgender inclusion at the Michigan festival and the accessibility of in vitro fertilization to the African American community. She concluded, "The numbers just aren't there"—a comment I took to mean that the relatively low percentage of transgenders (MtFs) in the black community means that "the specificities of transsexual political needs and demands" do not rank high on the list of priorities for black people.[64]

A number of threads from my conversation with Jameson can be teased out further. First, her viewpoint recalls what Cathy Cohen identifies as the notion of "linked fate" among African Americans.[65] With the term "linked fate," Cohen refers to the idea, pervasive in racialist discourse, that blacks share a common destiny based on a shared heritage. The ramification of this notion is that the black community is mobilized politically by what is believed to be a common set of issues. Cohen uses the HIV-AIDS crisis to illustrate her point that in the early years of the epidemic, issues that were specific to black lesbians and gays, not to mention transgenders, did not figure centrally in the discourses about the disease, which was held to affect whites primarily. In light of Cohen's insights, I interpret Jameson's observation that "the numbers aren't there" to mean that the concerns of postoperative black transgenders fall outside the linked fate for African Americans.

Second, by mapping transgender identities onto only those who have undergone sex reassignment surgery, Jameson ignores the suggestion that "transgender describes a gender identity that is at least partially defined by transitivity, but that may well stop short of transsexual surgery."[66] Still, I found that an emphasis on the privileges associated with sex reassignment surgery looms large for some black attendees of women's music festivals. This reflects, at least in part, the sentiments that members of the general public hold toward transgender identity. While most black festigoers with whom I conversed were sympathetic toward, and indeed active in, the gay/lesbian rights movement, they, like Jameson, expressed resentment at white, middle-class preoperative men (male-to-female) who, from their perspective, had most likely benefited from class, gender, and race privilege prior to taking steps to becoming women. Whereas the black women I interviewed about the Michigan policy reported knowing black "queens" or having black gay friends who were "kinda queens," not one stated that their friends or acquaintances had expressed interest in attending the Michigan festival. Likewise, African American festigoers reported that they knew neither blacks who had attended Camp Trans nor black MtF transgenders who wished to attend the Michigan festival in the future.[67]

I have already mentioned that a rhetorical strategy black women employed when they offered criticism or critique was the use of humor, much of which was deployed for my entertainment. Following my observation that NWMF invites everyone to participate as audience members regardless of gender and sexual orientation, longtime festival worker Karla Gee opined: "I don't have issues with transgendered folks. My basic issue is . . . those men who transition from male to female are way too girly and dress badly. They're trapped in the 1950s. I guess that's really my issue. Like, okay. My point is, be a woman in this decade!" She continued, taking full advantage of her audience (me), "You know, they all want to be June Cleaver."[68] Interestingly, with this comment, Gee distanced herself from a subject position her female ancestors, fictive and otherwise, most likely had not occupied.

Lastly, I spoke with a black festigoer at NWMF 1995 who planned to boycott the Michigan festival that year in light of what she called the "civil rights issue." "Yesterday, it was us [blacks] on the outside—we've got to stick together," she told me.[69] I interpreted the festigoer's decision not to attend the Michigan festival because of its admission policy as an indication that she saw the transgender movement as paralleling strongly the black liberatory struggle. I am not sure, however, whether this festigoer made a distinction between the relatively small percentage of transgenders who affiliate with the women's music circuit and the broader transgender movement. Her response, in any case, suggests the difficulties of gauging alignments and affiliations in a social field deeply inflected by identity politics. Posing an equal conundrum, we might ask: How does one measure the numbers of individuals who refuse to attend an event out of protest? How do we trace those histories?

"Black like Me?" Thinking Past the Limit

In this section I invoke Langston Hughes's "Dream Variation" as a heuristic device to examine the extent to which transgender-specific issues are included in the constellation of topics of concern to the black family or body politic. Appeals to the black nation wrapped in the cloak of "family" have been an integral aspect of black political discourse at least since the time of W. E. B. Du Bois.[70] "Thinking past the limit," borrowed from Stuart Hall's essay interrogating the postcolonial, calls to question the logic by which (black) kinship is reckoned.

Despite the fairly frequent representation of black lesbians and gays in fiction, film, and literature, few cultural critics have addressed the cultural production or lived experiences of black transexuals and transgenders.[71] Occasionally, the narratives of blacks identifying as transgenders in real life (as opposed to blacks performing onstage as drag kings or queens) are represented in the sex and gender scholarship or in journalistic accounts. Given that Camp Trans, the activist-oriented encampment outside the Michigan festival proper, was and is held to have a resonance that supersedes the boundaries of the women's music festival community, I decided to explore affinities between transgender-specific issues and the positioning of those same interests in the hierarchy of priorities of black LBGT communities. I became intrigued by the contrast between representations of racialized sexual minorities in the media and the incorporation of members of the same group into the fold of the African American community.[72]

With the matter of my starting point wide open, I canvassed by phone eight black gay and lesbian centers in cities of significant size to inquire about programming designed to meet the needs and interests of the black trans community. Not one of these organizations offered support groups or services directed toward these particular interest groups. To be sure, organizational budgets and size of the LGBT population served could figure as integral criteria affecting programming decisions. Perhaps this is why in several cases I was referred to the larger, predominantly white gay and lesbian center in the same locale.

One response was particularly illustrative of the complicated nature of gender and sex identity posed by my inquiry. A staffer at a black gay/lesbian center on the West Coast offered that "men [meaning MtFs or FtMs?] were certainly welcome to join the black gay men's group." I was struck by this statement and tried to understand what this particular black gay activist meant by it. Did he assume that all transgenders (including FtMs) would feel comfortable in a "men's" group?[73] I wondered if this were an instance of insensitivity by default on the part of the staffer or the organization, or whether I should have followed up on his response with a query specifically about female-to-male transgender persons. Or was it my failure to take heed of Halberstam's observation that perhaps differences between gay and lesbian and transgender subgroups in communities of people of color are not as significant as in white communities?[74]

Ethnographic research conducted by anthropologist David Valentine supports and offers a corrective to my admittedly narrow survey. Valentine reports on his experiences in New York City working with a support group for HIV-positive transgender people. Valentine's point is that none of the feminine-identified but male-bodied members of the group with whom he worked used the category "transgender" in talking about themselves.[75] In fact, the anecdote Valentine provides is that one of the members, born male, states, "I've been gay all my life, been a woman all my life."[76]Although this overlap of identities might strike some as unusual, Valentine suggests that "if gay/lesbian/bisexual people are at root defined by sexuality, then transgender, in this view, is different because it is based on variant expressions of gender."[77] Valentine's argument suggests that his stance might mirror Halberstam's comments about the limits of the term "queer" to mediate the differences between subjectivities described by gay/lesbian on the one hand and transgender on the other.[78] Halberstam writes: "Although one might expect the emergence of transsexual activism to fulfill the promise of a 'queer' alliance between sexual minorities by extending the definition of sexual minority beyond gay and lesbian, in fact there is considerable antipathy between gays and lesbians and transsexuals, and the term 'queer' has not managed to bridge the divide. Whereas transsexuals seem suspicious of a gay and lesbian hegemony under the queer banner, gays and lesbians fear that some forms of transsexualism represent a homophobic restoration of gender normativity."[79] Valentine's study throws into relief the problematics of queer theories that rigidly postulate the separation of gender and sexual identities.

Specific issues of interest to transgenders are often erased symbolically. For example, a Web site devoted to a discussion of domestic violence in transgender communities addresses the erasure of the *T* in LGBT, maintaining that although many LGBT resources and articles relay demographic information about LGBT populations, their statistics may in fact be reflective of only the experiences of lesbians and gay men.[80] Another example of transgender erasure can be found in some writers' adoption of the moniker "lesbigay," a shorthand term that most obviously erases the presence of transexuals and transgenders who may identify instead as "queer" or may prefer another term. As a colleague pointed out to me, however, these writers or speakers are perhaps more up front than other observers about the constituencies they are addressing.

The Camp Trans protests and the subsequent transgender debates illuminate that for some transgender activists and scholars, the admittance policy of the Michigan Womyn's Music Festival is indicative of more than a missed week's vacation at an outdoor retreat. Likewise, the issue is larger than can begin to be understood by contemplating the confusion for some, and fear for others, that attends suggestions of creating unisex bathrooms.[81] Simply put, the range of issues implicated, but yet not addressed, by transgender activists and allies who protested the festival's admission policy is wider than the Michigan protest would lead a relatively new observer to believe.

The National Center for Transgender Equality, based in Washington, DC, is one example of an organization devoted exclusively to transgender advocacy.

It is described as "a national social justice organization devoted to ending discrimination and violence against transgender people through education and advocacy on national issues of importance to transgender people."[82] An article appearing in the fall 2004 newsletter of the Transgender Law Center (TLC) enumerates many of the firm's successes in terms of transgender rights. Operating statewide and based in San Francisco, the center has been in the middle of many victories for transgender rights, including efforts in California to clarify that state law protects transgender employees and tenants from gender identity discrimination. The city of San Francisco successfully passed policies spelling out how transgender people are protected from police harassment and school-based discrimination, and it strengthened regulations protecting transgender people who don't identify as male or female. Since opening its doors, the TLC has "also confronted transgender legal issues affecting employees, tenants, immigrants, shelter residents, youth, and consumers."[83]

My goal in writing this chapter was to follow black pathways through and around an issue that is represented as either white or marked as raceless. Patricia Hill Collins attempts to come to terms with transgender status in black communities; to do this, she uses the lens of "love relationships" among black LGBT persons, which, she admits, remain understudied, although social science research is making progress.[84] Collins's emphasis on relationships as a marker for LGBT identity is problematic in that it oversimplifies a complex phenomenon. Census data is not an accurate indicator of the size of the transgender/transexual community, because many transgenders, like lesbians, gays, and bisexuals (and a smaller percentage of heterosexuals), do not live with their partners, and hence at any given time they might be represented in the census as "single." Although as this book was prepared no question on the census form compelled one to identify one's sexual orientation, according to a conversation I had with a policy analyst at the National Gay and Lesbian Task Force, analysts infer sexual orientation from responses to the long form of the census. This form allows respondents to mark combinations of categories, such as "unmarried partner/same-sex," "unmarried/different sex," "married," and so on.[85] Although Collins is one of the few black sociologists to address black transgender identity at all, I would argue that the standard concerns of black sociology (housing, employment, health and wellness, crime) have not been addressed in terms of black LGBT communities. An emphasis on relationships seems to be part of a trajectory that values so-called normalcy over other valences of social life.[86]

Potentially promising in terms of accessing data concerning black transgender demographics—yet still falling short—are the results of "Say It Loud, I'm Black and I'm Proud: Black Pride Survey 2000."[87] "Say It Loud" is described as a survey of 2,645 African American attendees of the nine regional black gay Pride celebrations.[88] In this survey, named after the signature song of the same name recorded by singer James Brown in 1968, transgendered people comprised 2 percent of the sample.[89] While Collins's interest in this data is that it provides "an important preliminary snapshot of the love relationships of Black LGBT people," I am interested in the self-identifications of black transgenders and the enunciation of issues that are important to them.[90] Again, Valentine's illustrative example that a person born male might identify as gay and as a woman—but not as transgender—is worth bearing in mind. These suggestive findings point to the limits of quantitative research and to the necessity of future study.

To Be Young, Aggressive, and Black: Racialized Female Masculinities and Spectatorship at the Movies

The title of this section recalls singer Nina Simone's "To Be Young, Gifted, and Black" (1972), a song that, based on the poem by Langston Hughes, became a popular sonic signifier of Black Power during the early 1970s. Its recontextualization here serves as a segue to a discussion of David Peddle's *The Aggressives,* one of the few documentary films to address the topic of black female masculinities. This film has a particular bearing on the focus of this chapter not only because of its content but also because it has been shown at women's music festivals, including the National Women's Music Festival. Here, I consider the showing of *The Aggressives* as a "film event." This strategy enables me to pay equal attention to the audience discussion that followed the show I attended.

I have found particular inspiration in the writings of black gay and lesbian film critics, including David van Leer's "Visible Silence: Spectatorship in Black Gay and Lesbian Film."[91] In this essay, Leer critiques the black gay and lesbian presence in white documentaries as well as in films by black gay and lesbian directors. At first viewing, the work of filmmaker Peddle confounds the insistence on characterizing the final product as an instantiation of either "gay filmmaking" or "black filmmaking." The film of the young white male documentarian focuses on a minoritized subculture: young butch-identified lesbians, most of whom are black (African American and Jamaican American), living in New York City.

I saw the film initially as part of OutFest (2005), the Los Angeles gay and lesbian film festival founded in 1982. Cosponsored by ULOAH, the showing was held at the Ed Gould Plaza Village. On the night of the viewing, attorney Lisa Powell, then director of ULOAH, introduced the film to the audience of approximately 150, issuing an invitation to those present—almost all African American lesbians—to support the organization, especially its program for young black lesbians ages fifteen to twenty-six.[92] Powell, who is middle-aged, remarked that there were few venues for black lesbians—especially young butches—when she was young and that she was proud of the programming track YES! that ULOAH had developed to address their needs.[93]

While white lesbian director Jennie Livingston's *Paris Is Burning* received much acclaim, *The Aggressives* has received less critical commentary. Although it is not my intent to discuss both projects here, I would note that *The Aggressives* compares favorably with Livingston's film, which, though frequently cited, was the subject of criticism from numerous commentators.[94] One obvious way that Peddle benefited from appraisals of his former film instructor's documentary concerning a black/Latino drag queen community in New York is that the lives of the narrators in *The Aggressives* are more closely drawn than are those of transgenders in *Paris*. Conversations with subjects' family members are strikingly absent in *Paris*, a feature that complements the observation that the most positive gay figures are often represented as isolated from the rest of the black community.[95] Peddle, on the other hand, takes care to interview the mothers of at least two of the young subjects, as well as the butches' girlfriends.

The word *aggressives* is a term adopted by (primarily working-class) lesbians of color to describe their butch identities. The black narrators of the film include Marquise, Kisha, Rjai, and Octavia. Flo is the only Chinese American interviewed. Made over a five-year period, *The Aggressives* consists of crosscut chronicles of the lives of these women, who range in age from eighteen to approximately twenty-two. Like the technique employed to capture the testimonies of the narrators in *Paris*, the interviewer is off camera and, throughout most of the film, out of sound range.[96] *The Aggressives* provides viewers a valuable glimpse into the workings of race, class, gender, sexual identity, generation, and, in some instances, performance. Given that the women ("butches") are interviewed separate from one another, we are offered no reason to believe they think of themselves as a community, feminist or otherwise. Since there are few representations of black butch lesbians in the social science and cultural studies (nonfiction) literatures, I will focus here on details of their narratives.

Describing herself as a tomboy, Marquise lives her life as a man ("I love lesbian women. I'm a lesbian, I'm just very aggressive. I'm masculine 24/7—that's just me"). From the first, she is seen rapping in a male posture ("A true survivor / bitches can't get no wilder"), playing a male-oriented video game, and, later, playing basketball. Marquise describes the labor involved in attaining and maintaining her young mannish physique: she wears an athletic bra, bites her teeth so as to develop a "strong jawline," mentions how difficult it is for young women to grow facial hair, and, like many FtMs, binds her breasts with bandages.[97] Viewers, introduced to Marquise when she is twenty years old, follow her path as she joins the army, first attending boot camp. Only at the film's conclusion do we learn she went AWOL during the first war in the Persian Gulf.

We are introduced to the second narrator, Rjai, via an excerpt of an episode of the *Ricki Lake Show* titled "Straight women can't resist lesbian studs." In response to the talk show host's query about whether the idea of masculine women is a "new thing," Rjai replies, "Studs have been around. It's not that you're trying to be a man or that you want to be a man. It's just who you are inside." In contrast to those who might assume otherwise, Rjai declares that she feels like a woman every day: "My sexuality has nothing to do with my gender." Rather, according to Rjai, to be aggressive is to be forceful, and she "wears the pants" in her relationship with her girlfriend.

Later, the camera follows Rjai to a ball, a same-sex competition that, in her words, is "a get-together of gay people who act like superstars." Those familiar with vogueing practices such as those depicted in *Paris Is Burning* will recognize that the competitions are modeled on or are similar in conception to those depicted in that film. In its brief attention to the balls, *The Aggressives* enables the viewer to glimpse a butch riff on a black gay appropriation of a runway modeling practice that draws on African American vernacular dance movements.[98] The runway performances of the butches are set in relief by the dancing of a number of young, super-femme black women. Prizes are given for winners in various categories: Construction Worker v. Painter, Pretty Boy v. Thug, Tropical Fantasy, Best Butch of the Year, Pretty Boy in Spring Colors, and Wall Street v. Blue Collar. Rjai has won many of these awards.

Next, we meet Flo, a heavyset Asian American woman. Evoking racialized images of black men, she describes herself as "just like a nigga," meaning, presumably, just like a black man. Peddle's camera focuses in on her preparation of fried chicken, a visual that is offered, perhaps, to cement the latter claim. Flo also considers herself an aggressive butch ("Being a butch is like being a man—you just don't have that between your legs, that's all"). In a narrative strategy that is rare in queer autobiography, Flo expounds on her marginality not in terms of gender but in terms of finances ("Females expect butches to take them out for dinner—what men do—but I can't do that right now").[99] She also recounts a public restroom incident that took place years previously: one day she tried to use the ladies room only to be questioned by a woman who challenged the appropriateness of her presence, since she "was not female." Since that day, Flo says, she has not used a public restroom.

Octavia, age eighteen, describes herself as a "straight-up lesbian," declaring she has no plans to change her sex: "I'm being me; I'm not perpetrating." Octavia's ideal woman is "not too skinny, caramel complexion," and she "has to have some fat" in order to keep her warm. One day Octavia is arrested; upon her release, she gets a job as a security guard.

Kisha, the last "aggressive" profiled, works as a messenger and rides a motorcycle, hence her self-adopted moniker of "Honda rebel." With her light skin color, the tall, thin young woman thwarts the representation of black, butch-identified lesbians as dark-skinned, trading on this detail in her moonlighting work as a model. Kisha is shown preparing for the balls by affixing a fake silver tooth that helps her achieve a hard look. Presumably, this strategy will help detract from what a photographer describes as her natural beauty, facilitated by her high cheekbones and light skin color. Illustrating the confounding of identities associated with postmodern understandings of gender construction, Kisha describes herself as a "butch pretty boy" and as a "femme aggressive." Drawing attention to the meta-frame of aggressive identity, Kisha offers that being aggressive includes "your strength, your courage, [and] your whole aura."

The Aggressives is part of a film oeuvre in which there are relatively few representations of black female masculinities outside of the stereotypical butch lesbian in the prison movie genre. F. Gary Gray's *Set It Off* (1996) with Queen Latifah, Jada Pinkett Smith, Vivica A. Fox, and Kimberly Elise exemplifies the latter; in this often-cited film, Latifah plays Cleo, a butch lesbian and one of four working black women who decide to rob banks in order to get ahead. Their lack of hope in the context of black impoverishment has devastating consequences.[100]

As much as Peddle succeeds in creating a documentary that maintains audience interest in the process of raising complex issues, the film does not expand upon some of the contradictions raised by the subjects' stories. White gay and lesbian filmmakers whose works include black characters are often faulted for the ways that sexuality subsumes race in "well-meaning white narratives." In *The Aggressives* it isn't that sexuality subsumes race; indeed, with the exception of the lone Asian American narrator, all the subjects in the film are black. Even Flo constructs her identity via black (and masculine) codes. Sexuality and age, however, subsume the women's experiences in a racialized economy; the production of working-classness and economic marginality are treated in ways so as to naturalize both their mechanisms and their effects. In order to accept what we are seeing as real, audience members must suspend certain questions about the film's cinematic techniques and, I would add, about the social conditions that shape, as much as mirror, the lives of the narrators. It might be argued that documentary techniques contribute to these interpretations as much as the partial readings of audience members: "minority autobiography," a convention put to effective use in the film, depends largely on the "reproduction of conversation and thought" in achieving its realist effects.[101]

Still, Peddle's film has the opportunity to shed light on some important issues, yet, at times, the viewer is literally and figuratively left in the dark. One such example is that although dark-skinned black women dominate the butch competition in which Rjai participates, the colorism that appears to be an important aspect of black butch identity construction is hinted at but not further explored. Left unexplained as well is the participation of super-femme performers (scantily clad black women with long, straight hair wearing makeup and high heels) whose dance routines complement the runway performances of the butches during the competition. This suggests the relevance of the observation made by many commentators that butch and femme identities are often best seen (or exhibited) in tandem with each other.[102] Likewise, the savvy viewer is left to conclude independently that colorism plays a role in class differentiation in black communities, although this is not explained in the film. Extending the theme of colorism, the film's narrative hints at but does not resolve contradictions inherent in Kisha's desire—and, according to her agent, her potential—to become a top "classic" model. This attempt is undermined by what her agent describes as her "different look and attitude." In the absence of further explanation, I infer that the agent refers to the model's "failure" (meaning her unwillingness or inability?) to present herself in ways that would satisfy the traditional male gaze.

In contrast to a practice familiar to white films, wherein people of color often speak "more narrowly as people of color—as if race were their story," Peddle's film provides a different example.[103] Here, and ironically, young black women speak as though gender identification and sexuality were their story. This would not be a cause for concern except that the documentary does not explore the unintended consequences of a preoccupation with those affiliations. Unelaborated on in the film is the fact that Rjai ends up getting a hysterectomy. She admits that one reason she let her symptoms go for so long without seeking medical attention is that because of her butch identity, she did not feel she was subject to health issues that affected women. A filmmaker with an awareness of black women's collective reproductive history might have, first, situated the physician's suggestion that Rjai get a hysterectomy within the overall reproductive rights history of black women and, second, explored Rjai's admission that she conflated, and indeed confused, a mutable gender (butch) identification with a sex identity (female) that up until this point had proven quite foundational to her existence. The failure to distinguish between the two threatens to have serious consequences for her long-term health. By glossing over this admission, the director misses a valuable opportunity to share information that might ultimately lead to the saving of lives, particularly those of black lesbians, who, as a group, have notoriously low rates of interaction with the medical establishment.

Another instance in which the viewer could benefit from additional information occurs late in the film, when we learn that Octavia has become pregnant and had a child. Her pathway to pregnancy was not artificial insemination. Was she coerced? Raped? Did she decide to identify as bisexual temporarily? By frustrating the viewer's desire for personal revelation, the film reinforces the image of the tough black butch lesbian, compromising her full representation as a vulnerable young person. As in the case of Rjai, one wonders whether Octavia viewed birth control as unnecessary since she identifies as butch. Or did she actually desire to become pregnant? The answers to these intimate questions are never revealed.

Ironically, my questions in this regard speak, perhaps, to a type of voyeuristic desire for more. Our own complicity as spectators is implicated again when we are privy to a conversation between Rjai and her former girlfriend, of whom it appears she has expectations that mirror those of a straw (white) man in a traditional (1950s) marriage. In this case, Rjai "wears the pants in the relationship," telling her girlfriend, "You'll iron my shirts the way I want you to; you need to be more in tune with how I'm feeling." One wonders how the well-intended impetus to allow youth to live and let live affects the viewer's suspension of critical assessment of Rjai's reinscription of gender norms that many would see as less than progressive. The viewer is given enough to pique her interest but denied a glimpse into some of the complex relationships and circumstances depicted in the film. To what extent does the presentation of partial knowledge function as spectacle in an otherwise well-intentioned project? In contemplating future studies of racialized sexualities and performance that make a difference that matters, it is useful to bear in mind Caren Kaplan's warning "against a form of theoretical tourism on the part of the first world critic; where the margin becomes a linguistic or critical vacation, a new poetics of the exotic."[104]

The film's showing was followed by a question-and-answer session with the director. Based on the enthusiastic reaction to the film afterward, the audience was pleased with Peddle's final product. Repeatedly, however, black middle-aged women in the audience asked Peddle to justify his focus on young black butches to the exclusion of older black lesbians who also identify as butch. Interestingly, it appeared to several others and to me that the film director didn't get it, meaning, he did not seem to comprehend that the fetishization of youth throughout the film was its greatest shortcoming. In that I suggest that the intended audience for *The Aggressives* is middle-class (and middle-aged) white gays and lesbians, the primary constituency of gay and lesbian film festivals in the United States, the voyeurism the viewer experiences is not only along lines of race and class, as I have outlined. Youth itself becomes part of the fetishized allure. The audience at this particular showing of *The Aggressives* was predominantly a black lesbian audience, which was more the exception than the norm.

My decision to follow black pathways through drag king performance, reception, and the boundaries of community membership in the women's music festival scene was productive, but in ways I could not predict. Barometers peculiar to flygirl demographics must be borne in mind when contemplating the material presented in this particular chapter. Beyond the festival circuit, black women are involved in drag kinging (as actors) in greater numbers; drag king parties held annually at My Sister's Room in Atlanta or performances held at some women's bars in New York City are examples. In the acts in which they appear on the festival circuit, on the other hand, black drag kings comprise an obvious minority. This racial distribution during the course of my research is in stark contrast to the intensity and frequency of debates about the appropriateness not only of drag king performances in women's music festival culture but also in discussions of community membership. Given the paucity of black lesbian representation in the ethnographic literature, productive research remains to be carried out with festigoers concerning their conceptualizations of community membership, whether gauged by race, sexual identity, embodiment, or politics.

Conclusion

As this book goes to press, I think of the women who contributed to this study and their candor, strategic silences, and activism in music and lesbian-feminist community formation. Black women's involvement in women's music—from Sweet Honey in the Rock to the Varied Voices of Black Women tour, and from the first to the next generation of musicians—comprises an important chapter in the annals of black women's music making and in the history of African American feminist thought. At the same time, this book is not a history of the localized contexts, meaning specific festivals, that are focal points of musical, political, and social activity. The project I have carried out is a theoretical exploration of issues raised by black women's presence in women's music, most productively understood as a site of women's thinking about music, and an example of the type of community building that the meld of music performance, identity politics, and music consumership can facilitate. In this world, audiences are crucial and musicians are naturally a significant part of the equation.

This book eschews a defensive posture justifying the relevance of women's music and, instead, illuminates the ways this realm matters to black women, mostly lesbians. Adopting a variety of narrative strategies, I address what, from their perspectives, is at stake in their involvement. The theoretical infrastructure through which "flygirl in the buttermilk" demographics can be meaningfully interpreted emanates from my desire to bring new vistas of perspective to the general reader and the specialist alike. As for this book's impact on the musicologies, I do not argue that the collective repertoire of musicians highlighted should be added to the canon of African American music; canon formation and strategic maintenance has its usefulness some of the time, but the significance of the worlds described in this book cannot be fully comprehended within the confines of such a narrow goal.

My hope is that this book will be used as a supplementary text in undergraduate classes, because studies that combine communication, music, and speech about music and social movements grounded in the experiences of black women are in short supply—and in the experiences of black lesbians even more so. The literature appropriate for undergraduate-level classes provides few representations of this African American subgroup. In its stead are a plethora of assumptions about black women as a collective. After gleaning a glimpse of the "different world" represented in the book's first chapter—and adding their own imaginative twists—a number of students in my classes have raised questions with which anthropologists who conduct research in gay and lesbian communities are familiar. While some, such as "How is Spillane [my festival compatriot]?" reveal a request for an informational update, others, such as a nervously voiced "Did anyone make a pass at you?" impart their interlocutors' first-time contemplation of what scholars call "the erotic equation in fieldwork." In formulating questions like these, readers share their assumptions about the risks that attend carrying out a study of this type. The answers to these two questions are as follows: "Okay, thanks" and "once or twice, but memory fades." The second question reveals the tendency of those who are unfamiliar with ethnomusicological research in lesbian communities to magnify the risk to the researcher and neglect and minimize the risk that study participants take on in sharing their perspectives. This tendency, which I encountered over and over in discussing my work informally with non–study participants, indicates the need for pedagogical vigilance in music and sexualities studies.

Although my list of regrets is relatively short, one that perseveres is that I was unable to accommodate a study of Sweet Honey in the Rock and the SHIR community into my research design. In important respects it is helpful to disaggregate SHIR from the world of black women on which this study is based. The fact that the celebrity of the ensemble deflects attention away from awareness of the musicians and consumers discussed herein is indicative of a circumscribed black lesbian expressivity, organized around and through music and lesbian feminist politics. SHIR and its gender and race-inclusive consumer base, in other words, is a unique socio-musical institution and as such deserves a monograph devoted completely to it.

I have argued that women's music is an underexamined site for the emergence of black feminist consciousness, and in making the case I incorporated the narratives of a selected number of musicians and consumers who are insiders to this cultural scene. Neither dead nor what it used to be, the changing face of women's music is a barometer of where a movement has been and its ability to reinvent itself in the aftermath. Contemporary women's music festivals remain a vacation destination for many women, affording them opportunities to hear music by some of the best performers in the business. A wide range of women—festival attendees, organizers and workers, and musicians—helped keep black and lavender hope alive in lesbian feminist spaces during a formative period and afterward, a journey that for many was well worth the price of the ticket.

I would go to James Brown's shows when I was younger, and I would scream so loud. I couldn't talk for days, because there was some part of myself that was being fed and affirmed, and that is true for all people. I don't think it's a separate experience. I think lesbians and gay men need that, I think white teenagers need that, black teenagers need that, middle-aged people need that—people need to get that kind of affirmation. Babies need it.

—VETERAN MUSICIAN LINDA TILLERY

Dreamgirls

A STAR-GAZER'S GUIDE TO MUSICIANS

When I called a festigoer acquaintance to review the list of musicians, mostly headliners, included in this section, she replied, "Oh, yeah—those are our dreamgirls." We spoke during the period of acclaim for director Bill Condon's film adaptation of Michael Bennett's play by the same name.[1] This list is an approximation of the black artists whom black star-gazers could have seen or would see in performance at women's music festivals. Biographies and links to the Web sites of these musicians and other key figures can be found at www.blackandlavender.com.

In the comment cited in the epigraph, Linda Tillery, the dean of black musicians in women's music, references the bigger-than-life quality that many of our stars, particularly musicians, seem to embody. James Brown, the godfather of soul, represented bigness in blackness and musical spirit for countless numbers of African Americans during a critical period in American social history. Like Brown, the performers cited within this book responded to—and in some cases, continue to address—the complexities of their time in an arena in which music and cultural politics are held to be inseparable. Embedded in Tillery's remark is a reminder of how important the musicians listed are to the history and persistence of women's music festivals. Of course, participant involvement is also integral to the perpetuation of women's music events, and therefore each festigoer should receive a token of appreciation commensurate with her involvement in these ventures over the years. I would send you autographs of these musicians and other key figures, the highest tribute in this context, but I do not have them myself.

Nurudafina Pili Abena
Lillian Allen
Kim Archer
Joan Ashley
Gwen Avery
Rachel Bagby
Phyllis Bethel
Rhonda Benin
Bernice Brooks
Elouise Burrell
Judith Casselberry
Barbara "Wahru" Cleveland
India Cooke
Emma Jean Foster
Nedra Johnson
Laura Love
Melanie DeMore
Ubaka Hill
In Process . . .
Malika
Deidre McCalla
Debra Kenya McGee
Pamela Means
Miss Money
Faith Nolan
Vicki Randle
Toshi Reagon
Doria Roberts
Sweet Honey in the Rock
Naya' Hari Suhalia
Linda Thomas Jones
Linda Tillery
Edwina Lee Tyler
The Washington Sisters
Mary Watkins
Laura Irene Wayne (visual artist)
Regina Wells
Karen Williams (comedienne)
Women of the Calabash
Urban Bush Women

ACKNOWLEDGMENTS

In researching this book over a period of many years, I benefited from the generosity of the musicians, festival attendees, producers, and others associated with the women's music community. My engagement with this topic has been influenced not only by women too numerous to mention but also by women to whom I am otherwise unknown. I thank musician and producer Linda Tillery, not only for her encouragement to complete this project, but also for serving as a larger-than-life figure for countless numbers of women over the course of a decades-long career. It is no exaggeration to say that Linda Tillery *is* women's music. For sharing their time and insights, I thank Lillian Allen, Rhonda Benin, Judith Casselberry, Melanie DeMore, Emma Jean Foster, Mary Watkins, Ubaka Hill, Deidre McCalla, Regina Wells, Pamela Rogers, India Cooke, Elouise Burrell, Michelle Lancester, Phyllis Bethel, Debra Kenya McGee, Bernice Brooks, Barbara "Wahru" Cleveland, Renaye Brown, Sandra Washington, Sharon Washington, Nedra Johnson, Pamela Means, Sphear, Miss Money, Linda Thomas Jones, Naya'hri Suhalia, Malika Freydberg, and Faith Nolan. Volunteers, festival organizers, and others participating in this project included Marquita Thomas, Lisa Powell, Kory Chandler, Rae Lewis, Donna Jones, Debra Wells, Robbin Brooks, Rae Baskin, Lena McQuade, Yolanda Whitingdon, and Saundra Tignor. Festival attendees completed surveys and granted me interviews, suggested recordings, and shared food and blankets; some invited me to dance. I am also grateful to activists and musicians who played foundational roles in the women's music movement and shared their observations about the network, suggested musicians I should contact, or facilitated introductions early on. These individuals include June Millington, Ann Hackler, Susan Freundlich, Amy Horowitz, Judy Dlugacz, Sandy Stone, Toni Armstrong Jr., and Bonnie Morris.

The joys of learning about music, society, and ways to write about them are cumulative; therefore, my thanks ought to begin with Vera Cooper, my college preparatory piano teacher, and extend to Portia K. Maultsby, Mellonee Burnim, Ruth Stone, and the late Ronald Smith, faculty with whom I attained my master's degree in folklore at Indiana University. My doctoral work at the University of Washington was completed under the supervision of Christopher A. Waterman, Ter Ellingson, H. Lorraine Sakata, Johnnella E. Butler, and Sue-Ellen Jacobs. Chris Waterman, my adviser and dissertation chair, offered insights into the complexities of and contradictions in African American culture that altered fundamentally the manner in which I understand and engage the study of black music. He also introduced me to African American anthropology, and I have strived to reckon the full weight-bearing load of this intellectual legacy ever since.

Colleagues at the University of North Texas offered helpful comments and encouraged me to keep pushing forward. They include Steven Friedson, Margaret Notley, Deanna Bush, and John Murphy. For early identification of my promise as an academic, I thank Lester Brothers; J. Michael Cooper provided exacting and generous mentoring during the early years of my career. Joán Groom, Tyson Gibbs, David Schwarz, Donna Emmanuel, Terri Sundberg, Jacqueline Foertsch, Steven Slottow, Bernardo Illari, and Dawn De Rycke provided companionship and an engagement of critical issues, musical and otherwise. For research support and institutional guidance at various stages of this project, I would like to thank the Dorothy Danforth-Compton Foundation and the University of North Texas's Dean James Scott, College of Music.

A postdoctoral fellowship from the Ford Foundation facilitated my residency in the music department at the University of California, Riverside, in 2004–2005. Deborah Wong pored over successive drafts, urging me to clarify why my subject mattered and what was at stake. The opportunity to engage with a scholar of her integrity has inspired me to reset the bar in terms of my professional stewardship in academia. Paulo Chagas, René T. A. Lysloff, Byron Adams, Walter Clark, Renée Coulombe, Leonora Saavedra, and Jonathan Ritter warmly welcomed me into their department as a visiting postdoctoral fellow.

Portia K. Maultsby and Mellonee V. Burnim, editors of the African American Music in Global Perspective series, provided unfailing belief in this project. Maultsby has mentored more scholars of African American ethnomusicology than either you or I can count; truly, the heart of the subfield resides in her. I thank the staff at the University of Illinois Press, especially Judith McCullough, for identifying the topic as one of interest, and acquisitions editor

Laurie Matheson, for attention to detail and for seeing the book through to its completion.

For their critical feedback on my writings about black women and women's music, I thank Miles White, Brenda Romero, Maria Johnson, Tammy Kernodle, Sherri Tucker, Sarah Schmalenberger, Roxanne Reed, Anthea Kraut, Portia K. Maultsby, Guthrie P. Ramsey Jr., Timothy Cooley, Zoe Sherinian, Kimberly Brown, Amy R. Corin, Suzanne Cusick, Linda F. Williams, Cornelia Fales, Martha Mockus, Mary Fechner, Nicki Cohen, Beverly Davenport, Boden Sandstrom, Robin Lakes, and Stacy Bourns. A coterie of scholars far and wide encouraged my professional advancement, including Timothy Taylor, Timothy Rice, Maureen Mahon, William H. Watkins, Philip Bohlman, Cheryl Keyes, Jacqueline Dje Dje, Nanette De Jong, Miriam Dow, Yolanda Moses, Mark McKnight, Anncristine Fjellman-Wiklund, James Briscoe, Naomi Andre, Sang-Hie Lee, C. Victor Fung, Kristin Wendland, Kathleen Lamkin, Nancy Whittier, Robin Moore, Charles Fuget, Aaron J. Fox, and the late Elizabeth Amelia Hadley. As I was writing this book, Sue-Ellen Jacobs said that my ethical engagement of the issues addressed herein would matter the most: readers will decide. Appreciations to research assistants Pamela Ward and Rian Davis and to members of my graduate seminar in African American music: Eric Jones, Carl Vermilyea, Jeff Hodges, Cynthia Beard, Aaron West, and Jackson Ross Best.

Space does not permit a listing of all those who contributed to my well-being, and hence to the completion of this project, through their friendship and personal support. Although this project has morphed significantly since its beginnings, I should credit those whose companionship and insights provided space for me to ponder initially some of the ideas contained herein: Elizabeth Amelia Hadley, Cynthia Newcomer, Sue Letsinger, Claire Jones, Anne Sheeran, Avis J. Davis, and Juanita McCauley. Likewise, I thank Patricia Bush, Ellen Deacon, Leslie McGovern, David Clemens, Linda Haight, and William Barnes for friendship, love, and generous regard for my welfare. My parents, civil rights activists, are long deceased, yet their commitment to social justice looms large in my memory. The legacy of their lasting influence is that I stand shoulder to shoulder with friends, colleagues, musicians, and festigoers in the quest, no longer straightforward, for justice and representation.

This book is for Elizabeth.

NOTES

INTRODUCTION

1 Obviously, the term *women's music* obfuscates more than it clarifies. At first hearing, it begs for definition in light of its implicit association with notions of the "universal woman" that have long been refuted. I use the term because it has special meaning for participants in this arena.

2 See Nancy Whittier, *Feminist Generations: The Persistence of Radical Feminism* (Philadelphia: Temple University Press, 1995), and Joy James, *Shadowboxing: Representations of Black Feminist Politics* (New York: St. Martin's, 1999).

3 Private communication, Toni Armstrong Jr. See also Toni Armstrong Jr., "An Endangered Species: Women's Music by, for, and about Women," *Hot Wire: The Journal of Women's Music and Culture* 5 (September 1989): 17. *Hot Wire*'s online site can be found at http://www.hotwirejournal.com. An important precursor to *Hot Wire* was *Paid My Dues,* the women's music journal from the 1970s. See Armstrong Jr., "The Great White Folk Music Myth," in *Lesbian Culture: An Anthology,* ed. Julia Penelope and Susan Wolfe (Freedom, Calif.: Crossing Press, 1993). The newsletter "Musica," published by Indra Allen, was a precursor to *Paid My Dues,* which was published by the Women's Soul Collective. See "Women's Music," The Rainbow History Project, http://www.rainbowhistory.org/musica.htm, accessed May 28, 2009.

4 Kath Weston, *Families We Choose: Lesbians, Gay Kinship* (1991; New York: Columbia University Press, 1997), 174.

5 Composer and pioneering musician Maxine Feldman died on August 17, 2007; musician and author Kay Gardner died on August 28, 2002. Ruth Rhiannon Barrett, "Kay Gardner," Pagan Passages: The Circle Dance of Life, http://www.witchvox.com/passages/kaygardner.html, accessed May 19, 2009.

6 Bonnie Morris chronicles a list of twenty-seven festivals, past and present, in her book *Eden Built by Eves: The Culture of Women's Music Festivals* (New York: Alyson Books, 1999). A note of clarification: Over the years, the National Women's Music Festival, founded in 1973, has been held either in Illinois, Indiana, or Ohio. In 2008 it was held in Madison, Wisconsin. Additional sites of festivals include Arizona, Pennsylvania,

New York, Nevada, Maryland, Iowa, New York, Connecticut, Georgia, and Virginia, among others. It would be impossible to keep up with the ever-changing list of events as new ones are founded and others cease operations. The most salient point for my purposes is that few of the festivals inspired directly by second-wave radical feminism are extant.

7 According to some, at ten thousand, the MWMF rivals the Dinah Shore Golf Tournament for its purported lesbian attendance. The alternative spelling of "women" is used by the Michigan festival but not by other women's music festivals in the United States. The respelling of words ending in "-man" or "-men" emerges in lesbian discourses as just one of the issues addressed by those engaged in the study of "lavender languages." See William Leap, "Studying Lesbian and Gay Languages: Vocabulary, Text-Making, and Beyond," in *Out in Theory: The Emergence of Lesbian and Gay Anthgopology*, ed. Ellen Lewin and William L. Leap (Urbana: University of Illinois Press, 2002). Bonnie Morris's Appendix B, "A Lexicon of Festivalese," in *Eden Built by Eves* contributes to the ethnography of communication in women's music communities as well. At the same time, I concur with William Leap, who suggests that lesbian-related text making reflects issues of "opportunity, inequality, and privilege that need careful analysis in lesbian/gay contexts" (138).

8 Many fans of the Grammy-award-winning sextet (formerly a quintet) are unaware of the ensemble's frequent appearances over the years at women's music festivals. During the course of my research beginning in 1992, this was especially true of the ensemble's Washington, DC, base.

9 By "keeper of the flame," DeMore refers to tropes of African American heritage and the freedom struggle.

10 I conducted interviews with some, but not all, of these musicians. This list does not include the names of all members of ensembles who have performed at women's music festivals; rather, these performers are primarily headliners. I have omitted from this list musicians like Elizabeth Cotton and the late African American folksinger Odetta, who performed at early women's music festivals but who would not be considered a part of the women's music scene.

11 This book does not include interviews with sign language interpreters.

12 Verta Taylor and Leila J. Rupp, "Women's Culture and Lesbian Feminist Activism: A Reconsideration of Cultural Feminism," *Signs* 19, no. 1 (1993): 32–61.

13 Important sources for analyses of black women's activism as feminists in the second wave include Kimberly Springer, *Living for the Revolution* (Durham, N.C.: Duke University Press, 2005), and Benita Roth, *Separate Roads to Feminism: Black, Chicana, and White Feminist Movements in America's Second Wave* (Cambridge, U.K.: Cambridge University Press, 2003). Joy James devotes some attention to black women in feminist organizations, white and black, in *Shadowboxing*.

14 Ray Charles, "Hit the Road Jack," (ABC 415), 1961, written by Percy Mayfield and recorded by Ray Charles.

15 Whittier, *Feminist Generations*, 2.

16 Ibid., 21.

17 Ibid., 171, cites Barry D. Adam, *The Rise of a Gay and Lesbian Movement* (Boston: Twayne, 1987).

18 See Andrea Densham, "The Marginalized Uses of Power and Identity: Lesbians' Participation in Breast Cancer and AIDS Activism," in Cathy Cohen, Kathleen B. Jones, and Joan C. Tronto, eds., *Women Transforming Politics* (New York: New York University Press, 1997).

19 Whittier, *Feminist Generations*, 21.

20 Robin D. G. Kelley, *Freedom Dreams,* cited in Springer, *Living for the Revolution,* 168.
21 James, *Shadowboxing,* 83.
22 Whittier, *Feminist Generations,* 21.
23 Ellen Koskoff, *Women and Music in Cross-Cultural Perspective* (1987; Urbana: University of Illinois Press, 1989). For an early discussion of the additive approach, see Elizabeth V. Spelman, *Inessential Woman: Problems of Exclusion in Feminist Thought* (Boston: Beacon Press, 1988).
24 Sherrie Tucker, *Swing Shift: "All-Girl" Bands of the 1940s* (Durham, NC: Duke University Press, 2000).
25 Here, I give a nod to Lucius Outlaw Jr., *Critical Social Theory in the Interest of Black Folks* (Lanham, Md.: Rowman and Littlefield, 2005).
26 Whittier, *Feminist Generations,* 251.
27 I thank anthropologist Beverly Davenport for sharing with me her presuppositions about black women in women's music.
28 See James, *Shadowboxing,* 109.
29 For valuable leads in this direction see James, *Shadowboxing,* xiii and 108–10; and Patricia Collins, *Fighting Words: Black Women and the Search for Justice* (Minneapolis: University of Minnesota Press, 1998), 54. The correlation of feminist identity with physical appearance has also been discussed by contemporary white feminist scholars. In many cases, young women are characterized as regarding feminists as "unattractive." For a clear example of this, see Gayle Kimball, ed., *Women's Culture in a New Era* (Lanham, Md.: Scarecrow Press, 2005), xxi. See also Kobena Mercer, "Black Hair/Style Politics," in *Welcome to the Jungle: New Positions in Black Cultural Studies* (New York: Routledge, 1994).

CHAPTER 1: DIARY OF A MAD BLACK WOMAN FESTIGOER

1 By riffing on the title of Perry's film in the title of this chapter, I am doing only that; by no means is it my intent to draw additional comparisons between the complicated, and at times troubling, filmic narrative and the contents of this chapter. Perry riffs on author Sue Kaufman's novel, *Diary of a Mad Housewife* (2005), published originally in the late 1960s. The novel was made into a film of the same name by director Frank Perry (no relation to Tyler Perry) and released in 1970.
2 Perry's plays have grossed over $100 million. Audiences are predominantly black working-class women; some have used the word *Christian* to describe this consumer base, but the specificity suggested by the word *Protestant,* if not *evangelical Protestant,* is more apt.
3 This was true until August 2006 when the Michigan festival changed its policy, admitting any person who identifies as a woman.
4 Michael Awkward, *Negotiating Difference: Race, Gender, and the Politics of Positionality* (Chicago: University of Chicago Press, 1995), 15.
5 See Valerie Smith, *Not Just Race, Not Just Gender: Black Feminist Readings* (New York: Routledge, 1998), and Hazel V. Carby, *Reconstructing Womanhood: The Emergence of the Afro-American Woman Novelist* (New York: Oxford University Press, 1987).
6 See Ellen Lewin and William Leap, eds., "Introduction," *Out in Theory: the Emergence of Lesbian and Gay Anthropology* (Urbana: University of Illinois Press), 12. This has been not only my experience but also the experience of my straight colleagues in ethnomusicology who conduct research on the role of music in gay and lesbian community formation.
7 Stuart Hall, "What Is This 'Black' in Black Popular Culture," in *Representing Blackness: Issues in Film and Video,* ed. Valerie Smith. (New Brunswick, N.J.: Rutgers University

Press, 1997). Hall's essay was originally published in Gina Dent, ed., *Black Popular Culture* (Seattle: Bay Press, 1992), 123–33.

8 John Langston Gwaltney, *Drylongso: A Self-Portrait of Black America* (New York: Random House, 1980). By the latter phrase, I mean gay and lesbian scholars conducting ethnography in gay and lesbian communities. The wording becomes redundant, but it is important to be clear, since straight scholars also do work in gender and sexuality studies.

9 Irma McClaurin traces the lineage of "autoethnography" in *Black Feminist Anthropology: Theory, Politics, Praxis, and Poetics* (New Brunswick, N.J.: Rutgers University Press, 2001), 65.

10 Ethnomusicologist Carol E. Robertson includes a case study of her participant observation with this particular chorus in an essay titled "Power and Gender in the Musical Experiences of Women," in Koskoff, *Women and Music.* In the early years, lesbian ensembles frequently went under the name of "feminist" or "women's" choruses. The Gay and Lesbian Association of Choruses was founded in 1982. See the association's Web site at www.galachoruses.org, accessed on May 29, 2009.

11 See Angela Davis, *Blues Legacies and Black Feminism* (New York: Pantheon Books, 1998).

12 Howlin' Wolf's "Built for Comfort" can be found on the album *Howlin' Wolf: His Best (The Chess 50th Anniversary Collection),* Chess, 1997.

13 This sentiment is given voice by Ray Kinsella, the protagonist played by actor Kevin Costner in Phil Alden Robinson's *Field of Dreams.* Although this is the way viewers remember the line in the film, the voice Kinsella hears actually says, "If you build it, he will come." The Terence Mann character reinforces this by saying, "People will come, Ray."

14 These names have changed over time, and in this account I have used the names that are current as this book goes to press.

15 Gayatri Spivak, "Subaltern Studies: Deconstructing Historiography," in *In Other Worlds: Essays in Cultural Politics* (New York: Meuthuen, 1987).

16 Although scholars have debated the content of Truth's speech, that is not my concern here. As the African American historian Nell Painter has pointed out, the exact content will probably never be known, since there is no written transcript of the speech. In this speech, in which Truth proclaims that she, too, as a black woman, counts as a female, the part that is most salient for my purposes is her purported baring of her breasts. See Nell Irwin Painter, *Sojourner Truth: A Life, A Symbol* (New York: W. W. Norton, 1997).

17 The actress Lucy Lawless played Xena, and Renee O'Conner played her sidekick, Gabrielle; the popular show ran from 1995 to 2001.

18 For an entertaining twist on the theme of black women as consumers of psychic services, see Tina "Knowedgeable" Peden, "Black Women, Stop Hogging All the Psychic Hotline Infomercial Hosting Jobs!" at www.buzzle.com/editorials/9-11-2005-76547.asp, accessed May 20, 2009.

19 I first heard this widely circulated joke about Ike Turner made by white comedian Christopher Titus, whose cd *Normal Rockwell Is Bleeding* can be purchased at http://www.comedycentral.com/comedians/browse/t/christopher_titus.html.

20 Holly Near, *Imagine My Surprise,* Redwood Records, 1978.

21 In this case, I am referring only to the black women I interviewed. While it is true that pregnancy or motherhood is not necessarily evidence of intimate relationships with men, the majority of the black women musicians and festigoers I interviewed who had children had them while in earlier heterosexual relationships. For a discussion of

the discourse of lesbian motherhood, see Julie M. Thompson, *Mommy Queerest: Contemporary Rhetorics of Lesbian Maternal Identity* (Amherst: University of Massachusetts Press, 2002).

22 Lillian Faderman, *Odd Girls and Twilight Lovers* (New York: Penguin, 1991).

23 In women's music discourse, the term is used in a romantic, reverent tone. In earlier years, Native American women pointed out the ethnocentrism of both white and black women as they participated in workshops on "unlearning racism" and appropriated Native American rituals and musical tropes at the same time.

24 Philip Deloria, *Playing Indian* (New Haven, Conn.: Yale University Press, 1998).

25 Michigan's Women of Color tent was founded in 1983, according to Morris, *Eden Built by Eves*, 160. See Amoja Three Rivers and Blanche Jackson, *Cultural Etiquette: A Guide for the Well-Intentioned* (Gladstone, Va.: Market Wimmin, 1991). With Jackson, Three Rivers founded Market Wimmin, a "cultural crafts and merchandising business."

26 Spillane's understanding was that the White Women's Patio was a new initiative sponsored by the 1995 festival. In contrast, the program booklet for the 1992 festival states that the Women of Color tent would have an open house ("all womyn welcome") for one hour each day so that women (all women, but especially white women) could ask questions along the lines of "Who are those womyn and what goes on in that tent anyway? Are white womyn really welcome?" The 1992 festival booklet makes no mention of other special-interest tents (such as Womyn Over 40, Young Womyn's Program, Jewish Womyn's Networking, and the Quilting Bee Tent, which were uncontested) offering comparable open houses so that members could explain their purpose to others. Given the complex web of identity politics I have outlined, having a separate event for white women, such as the White Women's Patio, makes sense.

27 Powell and I met at the West Coast Women's Music and Comedy Festival in 1995.

28 Here, I borrow the phrase from ethnomusicologist Deborah Wong, *Speak It Louder: Asian Americans Making Music* (New York: Routledge, 2004). Scholars such as Catherine Saalfield and the late Ray Navarro write convincingly about the ways colors function symbolically for communities of color, lesbians, and gay men. See their "Shocking Pink Praxis: Race and Gender on the ACT UP Frontlines," in *Inside/Out: Lesbian Theories, Gay Theories*, ed. Diana Fuss (New York: Routledge, 1991).

29 See Kay Mills, *This Little Light of Mine: The Life of Fannie Lou Hamer* (Lexington: University Press of Kentucky, 2007). The civil rights leader, born in 1918, died in 1977.

30 James, *Shadowboxing*, 33, 101.

31 My use of "unpacking my bags at this location" is a nod to an essay in Homi K. Bhabha, *The Location of Culture* (London: Routledge, 1994).

32 See Christopher Small, *Music of the Common Tongue: Survival and Celebration in African American Music* (Hanover, N.H.: University Press of New England, 1998).

33 See, for example, Gregory P. Beehler, Bridget M. McGuinness, and John E. Verta, "Polluted Fish, Sources of Knowledge, and the Perception of Risk: Contextualizing African American Anglers' Sport Fishing Practices," *Human Organization* 60, no. 3 (2001): 288–97.

34 They actually use the word in ways that are more complicated than that, but the use I have offered suits my purposes here.

35 Judith Butler, *Undoing Gender* (New York: Routledge, 2004). See also Paul Gilroy, *The Black Atlantic* (Cambridge, Mass.: Harvard University Press, 1993), and Roth, *Separate Roads*.

36 See Collins, *Fighting Words*, and Judith Butler, *Bodies That Matter: On the Discursive Limits of "Sex"* (New York: Routledge, 1993).

37 For studies of the vaudeville blueswomen, see Daphne Harrison, *Black Pearls: Blues*

Queens of the 1920s (New Brunswick, N.J.: Rutgers University Press, 1988). See also Hazel V. Carby, "'It Jus Be's Dat Way Sometimes': The Sexual Politics of Women's Blues," *Radical America* 20, no. 4 (June-July 1986), and Davis, *Blues Legacies.*

38 The limits of metaphors of the family have been articulated by Collins in *Fighting Words* and Wendy Brown in *States of Injury: Power and Freedom in Late Modernity* (Princeton, N.J.: Princeton University Press, 1995).

39 Howard Becker, *Tricks of the Trade: How to Think about Your Research While You Are Doing It* (Chicago: University of Chicago Press, 1998).

40 Here, I draw on the now-classic argument that Clifford Geertz makes between studying villages and studying *in* villages in *The Interpretation of Cultures: Selected Essays* (New York: Basic Books, 1973).

41 James, *ShadowBoxing,* 84–88.

42 In arriving at this decision, I have been influenced by writings of theorist Michelle Wallace as well as writings by bell hooks and Michael Awkward. See Michael Awkward, "Negotiations of Power," in *Negotiating Difference: Race, Gender, and the Politics of Positionality* (Chicago: University of Chicago Press, 1995). See also bell hooks, "Facing Difference: The Black Female Body," in *Art on My Mind: Visual Politics* (New York: New Press, 1995), and Michelle Wallace, "Modernism, Post-Modernism, and the Problem of the Visual in Afro-American Culture," in *Out There: Marginalization and Contemporary Culture,* ed. Russell Ferguson, Martha Gever, Trinh T. Minh-Ha, Cornel West (Cambridge, Mass.: MIT Press, 1990).

43 Charles Nero, "Why Are the Gay Ghettoes White?" in *Black Queer Studies: A Critical Anthology,* ed. E. Patrick Johnson and Mae G. Henderson (Durham, N.C.: Duke University Press).

44 Weston, *Families We Choose.*

45 Gloria Hull, Patricia Bell Scott, and Barbara Smith, eds., *All the Women Are White, All the Blacks Are Men, but Some of Us Are Brave: Black Women's Studies* (Old Westbury, N.Y.: Feminist Press, 1982).

46 Paula Stewart Brush, "Problematizing the Race Consciousness of Women of Color," *Signs* 27, no. 1 (2001). The reference to "jes' grew" is my own shout out to Ishmael Reed's *Mumbo Jumbo* (New York: Bantam Books, 1972). Reed borrows the term from James Weldon Johnson's earlier writing concerning the history of ragtime songs.

47 The phrase "coming to voice" is a metaphor for social power as well as a referent for more concrete discussions of vocality. Leslie C. Dunn and Nancy A. Jones, *Embodied Voices: Representing Female Vocality in Western Culture* (Cambridge, U.K.: Cambridge University Press, 1994), is an example of the type of work scholars have carried out in regard to the latter; this study emanates from understandings culled from notions of "coming to voice" as akin to representation and social power.

CHAPTER 2: RECONNAISSANCE

1 The dates of the runs of the festivals are as follows: National Women's Music Festival, 1974-present; Michigan Womyn's Music Festival, 1976–present; West Coast Women's Music and Comedy Festival, 1980–1992; Wiminfest, 1981–2006; Gulf Coast Womyn's Festival, 1989–present; Sistahfest, 1990–present; Northampton Lesbian Festival, 1990–1995; Serafemme, 2005–present.

2 Various levels of responsibility ensue from different levels of involvement in festival life; I include festival organizers under the rubric of attendees.

3 Renato Rosaldo, *Culture and Truth: The Remaking of Social Analysis* (Boston: Beacon Press, 1989).

4 Andy Bennett and Richard A. Peterson, *Music Scenes: Local, Translocal, and Virtual* (Nashville: Vanderbilt University Press, 2004), 6, 9, 10; emphasis mine.
5 Michael H. Agar, *The Professional Stranger: An Informal Introduction to Ethnography* (New York: Academic Press, 1980).
6 Kristina Minister, "A Feminist Frame for the Oral History Interview," in *Women's Words: The Feminist Practice of Oral History*, ed. Sherna Berger Gluck and Daphne Patai (New York: Routledge, 1991), 36–37.
7 Gwaltney, *Drylongso*. See Akhill Gupta and James Ferguson, *Anthropological Locations: Boundaries and Grounds of a Field Science* (Berkeley: University of California Press, 1997); see also Tony Larry Whitehead and Mary Ellen Conaway, ed., *Self, Sex, and Gender in Cross-Cultural Fieldwork* (Urbana: University of Illinois Press, 1986); Faye Harrison, ed., *Decolonizing Anthropology: Moving Further toward an Anthropology for Liberation* (Washington, D.C.: American Anthropology Association, 1991); and Dell Hymes, ed., *Reinventing Anthropology* (1969; New York: Vintage Books, 1974).
8 Mitchell Duneier, *Sidewalk* (New York: Farrar, Straus and Giroux 1999), 14.
9 Philip V. Bohlman, "Becoming Ethnomusicologists," *Newsletter of the Society for Ethnomusicology* 41, no. 2 (2007): 1.
10 The subtitle of this section harks back to David N. Baker, Lida M. Belt, and Herman Hudson, *The Black Composer Speaks* (Metuchen, N.J.: Scarecrow Press, 1978).
11 See Hymes, ed., *Reinventing Anthropology;* Talal Asad, ed., *Anthropology and the Colonial Encounter* (London: Ithaca Press, 1973).
12 Robin D. G. Kelley discusses the work of early black Communists in Alabama in *Hammer and Hoe: Alabama Communists during the Great Depression* (Chapel Hill: University of North Carolina Press, 1990).
13 F. Harrison, *Decolonizing Anthropology*, 90.
14 Suzanne Cusick, "On a Lesbian Relation with Music: A Serious Effort Not to Think Straight," in Philip Brett, *Queering the Pitch: The New Gay and Lesbian Musicology* (New York: Routledge, 1994), 70.
15 Collins, *Fighting Words*, 46.
16 Greg Tate, *Flyboy in the Buttermilk: Essays on Contemporary America* (New York: Simon and Schuster, 1992). Tate uses the phrase "flyboy in the buttermilk" to refer to the highly regarded black visual artist Jean Michel Basquiat, who died in 1988 at the age of twenty-seven. See James Baldwin's essay in his compilation of essays by the same name, *The Price of the Ticket: Collected Nonfiction, 1948–1985* (New York: St. Martin's, 1985).
17 Baldwin's story appeared in the October 1958 edition of *Harper's* magazine in an essay originally titled "The Hard Kind of Courage." The word *flyboy* was also a name that some attributed to air personnel during World War II, although some enlisted men reported never having heard the term during the time of their service.
18 Robin Leidner's "On Whose Behalf? Feminist Ideology and Dilemmas of Constituency," in Barbara Ryan, ed., *Identity Politics in the Women's Movement* (New York: New York University Press 2001), 52.
19 I was surprised to learn that these larger festivals do not keep records of demographics in terms of race, especially since they claim to be interested in diversity.
20 John Urry, *The Tourist Gaze: Leisure and Travel in Contemporary Societies* (London: Sage, 1990), 3.
21 See Jane Desmond, *Staging Tourism: Bodies on Display from Waikiki to Sea World* (Chicago: University of Chicago Press, 1999), xx.
22 Ann duCille, "The Occult of True Black Womanhood: Critical Demeanor and Black

Feminist Studies," *Signs* 19, no. 3 (1994): 591–629. The essay is reprinted in Ryan, *Identity Politics.*

23 Undoubtedly, DuCille signifies on the well-known song by Richard Rodgers and Lorenz Hart, "Bewitched, Bothered, and Bewildered." Lena Horne and Ella Fitzgerald are just two of the song stylists who popularized this tune from Rodgers and Hart's *Pal Joey.*

24 Terence Turner, cited in Maureen Mahon, *Right to Rock: The Black Rock Coalition and the Cultural Politics of Race* (Durham, N.C.: Duke University Press, 2004), 23.

25 Michelle Kisliuk, "(Un)doing Fieldwork: Sharing Songs, Sharing Lives," in Gregory F. Barz and Timothy J. Cooley, *Shadows in the Field: New Perspectives for Fieldwork in Ethnomusicology* (New York: Oxford University Press, 1997), 26; Mahon, *Right to Rock,* 23.

26 Collins, *Fighting Words.*

27 Ibid., 215. It is important to note that in *Fighting Words,* Collins revisits the black woman standpoint that she outlined in *Black Feminist Thought* in light of what she calls the "new politics of containment" that black women experience. Patricia Hill Collins, *Black Feminist Thought: Knowledge, Consciousness, and the Politics of Empowerment* (Boston: Unwin Hyman, 1990).

28 Collins, *Fighting Words,* 228.

29 Interview with Melanie DeMore, Oakland, California, November 23, 1995. In addition to being a solo performer, DeMore is a longtime member of Linda Tillery and the Cultural Heritage Choir.

30 Springer, *Living for the Revolution,* 151.

31 Ibid.

32 Here, I use the term *feminist movement* strategically. This book recognizes multiple feminisms and several women's movements.

33 Lilith Fair, subtitled "A Celebration of Women in Music," debuted in George, Washington, and ran for four tours from 1997 to 1999. McLachlan stated that she wanted to end Lilith while the tour was still on top. (For news of the tour's future, see http://www.billboard.com/bbcom/news/lilith-fair-to-return-in-2010–1003967171.story.) On June 21, 2005, the Lilith Fair Web site (www.lilithfair.com) posted an e-mail written by a woman who had attended the fair's last show, in Edmonton. The attendee writes that the fair "gave me an opportunity to experience something I was never able to find while growing up in the late sixties and seventies: a venue for females from every walk of life to gather together, to celebrate our humanity." I shared this e-mail with a friend who was active in the women's movement, and she retorted, "Where was *she*?" It might be argued that the writer's unfamiliarity with all-women environments—particularly with women's music festivals—foreshadows the containment of the genre I discuss in this chapter.

34 Joan Morgan, *When Chickenheads Come Home to Roost: My Life as a Hip-Hop Feminist* (New York: Simon and Schuster, 1999).

35 "Ladies First" can be found on *All Hail the Queen,* Tommy Boy Records, 1989.

36 "The Ru Report #168," The Crusade.net, http://thecrusade.net/2005/06/the-ru-report-168.

37 I would suggest two additional examples of links between market-driven initiatives and black lesbian invisibility in popular culture: First is the fact that popular black artists such as India.Arie and Toni Braxton have appeared on the cover of *LN* (Lesbian News) more often than black performers affiliated with the women's music festival circuit; second is that during the years I prepared this book, Patti LaBelle performed more frequently at gay Pride marches than did the performers covered in this study. Granted, LaBelle was the leading top-tier black entertainer to lend her support to the movement to raise HIV-AIDS awareness and to eradicate the disease. Still, an explora-

tion of the tension between black lesbian invisibility and the need for producers to cater to popular demand, real or perceived, is not tangential, since this book is based on the supposition that women's music has been contained and that black women artists have not been excluded from its effects. I do not portend to have the answers; I only point to mechanisms that, while seemingly progressive, function in ways that contribute to the continued marginalization of the musicians of this study.

38 Christopher Waterman, "Race Music: Bo Chatmon, '*Corrine Corrina*,' and the Excluded Middle," in Ronald M. Radano and Philip V. Bohlman, eds., *Music in the Racial Imagination* (Chicago: University of Chicago Press, 2000), 167.

39 Telephone interview with Rhonda Benin, December 5, 1995.

40 Feminism and Hip Hop Conference, sponsored by Center for Race, Politics, and Culture, University of Chicago, April 7–9, 2005.

41 See Rebecca Walker, *To Be Real* (New York: Anchor Books, 1995), a collection of essays by young women concerning their engagement with feminism.

CHAPTER 3: AFTER THE GOLDEN AGE

1 Whittier, *Feminist Generations*, 57.

2 Taylor and Rupp, "Women's Culture," 38.

3 In 1989 Olivia ceased operations as a record label and morphed into a more lucrative lesbian-oriented travel and cruise company. For more information on Goldenrod and Ladyslipper, see www.goldenrod.com/custom/herstory.htm and www.Ladyslipper.org, respectively.

4 African American neo-folksinger Tracy Chapman performed at Sisterfire in 1984 and at the Michigan festival in 1986 and 1987. In an interview with Bonnie Morris, white women's music founder Margie Adam says that not everyone expected these artists to look back and thank them, herself included. See Morris, *Eden Built by Eves*, 105.

5 This is a concern that also resonates for Sherrie Tucker in her study of all-girl swing bands of the 1940s. See "Introduction," *Swing Shift*.

6 *Radical Harmonies*, directed by Dee Mosbacher; coproduced by Margie Adam, June Millington, Boden Sandstrom (San Jose, Calif.: Wolfe Video, 2004). See Eileen Hayes, "Radical Harmonies" (film review), *Ethnomusicology* 48, no. 2 (2004): 312–14.

7 Morris, *Eden Built by Eves*, xiii. One of the most important and early dissertations on women's music is Cynthia Lont, *Between Rock and a Hard Place: A Model of Subcultural Persistence and Women's Music*, PhD diss., University of Iowa, 1984.

8 Linda Tillery invokes the term "queen mother" in Morris, *Eden Built by Eves*, 108.

9 Cris Williamson, *Changer and the Changed*, Olivia Records, 1975, reissued by Wolf Moon Records, 1993.

10 "*Radical Harmonies*," Woman Vision, http://www.womanvision.org/radical-harmonies.html, accessed June 29, 2009.

11 See Nelson George, *The Death of Rhythm and Blues* (New York: Pantheon Books, 1988); Brian Ward, *Just My Soul Responding: Rhythm and Blues, Black Consciousness, and Race Relations* (Berkeley: University of California Press, 1998); and Michael Eric Dyson, *Race Rules: Navigating the Color Line* (New York: Random House, 1996).

12 Kathleen Stewart, "Nostalgia—A Polemic," *Cultural Anthropology* 3, no. 3 (1988): 227–41.

13 Ibid., 227.

14 The year 1997 marked the end of phase one of my research.

15 Telephone interview with Judy Dlugacz, president of Olivia Records, November 19, 2005. Dlugacz was twenty years old when she and nine other women borrowed four thousand dollars and formed Olivia Records. During its twenty years of operation, Olivia

produced more than forty albums and sold more than one million records. National Women's Music Festival, program booklet, 1992, 8.

16 In suggesting that there are two different political generations in women's music, I am following the lead of sociologist Nancy Whittier, who in *Feminist Generations* uses political generations as an organizational framework in her study of radical feminists in Columbus, Ohio.

17 Whittier, *Feminist Generations,* 81.

18 For treatment of intergenerational viewpoints about black feminism, see Morgan, *When Chickenheads Come Home.*

19 Johnson figures as a member of the next generation. The song "Amazon Woman Rise" appears on *Nedra,* Big Mouth Girl Records, 2005. For an in-depth discussion of women's spirituality and the emergence of the opening ceremony, see Boden Sandstrom, "Performance, Ritual, and Negotiation of Identity in the Michigan Womyn's Music Festival," PhD diss., University of Maryland, 2002.

20 Telephone interview with Nedra Johnson, July 26, 2006.

21 Telephone interview with Malika, September 14, 2005.

22 Whittier, *Feminist Generations,* 4, 18.

23 Linda Alcoff, "Cultural Feminism versus Post-Structuralism: The Identity Crisis in Feminist Theory," *Signs* 13, no. 3 (1988): 408.

24 Vicki Randle, quoted in Laura Post, *Backstage Pass: Interviews with Women in Music* (Norwich, Vt.: New Victoria), 1997.

25 Interview with Mary Watkins, Oakland, California, November 27, 1995. *Something Moving,* Olivia Records, 1978. For a discussion of Watkins's music and career beyond her involvement in women's music, see Helen Walker-Hill, *From Spirituals to Symphonies: African-American Women Composers and Their Music* (Westport, Conn.: Greenwood Press, 2002).

26 Interview with Tara Jenkins, musician, 1995.

27 DeMore interview.

28 Michigan Womyn's Music Festival, program booklet, 1992, 22.

29 Telephone interview with Sandra Washington, December 3, 1995. Washington presents her comments in present tense, even though by the time of our interview, the Washington Sisters had ceased performing on the women's music festival circuit. More recent footage of a Washington Sisters performance, filmed at a concert held for the making of the documentary, appears in *Radical Harmonies.*

30 Jenkins interview.

31 In African American speech communities, "down low" means that the information or behavior is considered off the record, a secret, or confidential.

32 Sue Fink, quoted in Morris, *Eden Built by Eves,* 15. The statement is also found in "Sue Fink interviewed by Toni Armstrong Jr.," in Julia Penelope and Susan Wolfe, *Lesbian Culture: Lesbian Culture: An Anthology* (Freedom, Calif.: Crossing Press, 1993), 396.

33 Lillian Faderman, cited in Morris, *Eden Built by Eves,* 29 and 30. The passage is taken from Faderman, *Odd Girls,* 222.

34 Tillery, quoted in Morris, *Eden Built by Eves,* 108.

35 Eileen M. Hayes, "Not Your Mother's Racial Uplift: Sweet Honey in the Rock, Journey, and Representation: Sweet Honey in the Rock: Raise Your Voice," in *Women and Music: A Journal of Gender and Culture* 10 (Winter 2006): 71–79.

36 White musician and women's music founder Margie Adam recounts taking a hiatus from women's music in 1984 and returning in 1991. Upon her return, she found that women were no longer as turned on politically as they had been. As she recounts to

Bonnie Morris, "As a political activist who had stepped back in, it seemed to me that lesbians had taken their feminist energies into the gay male political arena to work on AIDS. I'm sure they expected to feminize the men. But I feel that an unintended consequence is that it shifted the energy of radical feminists away from the ongoing struggle for women's liberation in this country and around the world." Adam, quoted in Morris, *Eden Built by Eves,* 104. Adam's observation is borne out by numerous scholars.

37 Telephone interview with Judith Casselberry, January 10, 1996. The tension that attends being asked to rank or prioritize one's identities is captured by Gregory Connerly in "Are You Black First or Are You Queer?" in *The Greatest Taboo: Homosexuality in Black Communities,* ed. Delroy Constantine-Simms (Los Angeles: Alyson Books, 2000).

38 See www.lauralove.net and www.vickirandle.com. Some of the black musicians who identify as biracial seem to have made conscious attempts to assert their black identity through the crafting of their biographical narrative.

39 Musicologist and jazz studies scholar Sherrie Tucker experienced a similar "quietness" in regard to an avowed lesbian identity on the part of members of all-swing girl bands of the 1940s. See her "When Subjects Don't Come Out," in *Queer Episodes in Music and Modern Identity,* ed. Sophie Fuller and Lloyd Whitesell (Urbana: University of Illinois Press, 2000).

40 The NBJC is a national advocacy civil rights organization dedicated to "empowering Black same-gender-loving, lesbian, gay, bisexual, and transgendered people" based in Washington, DC. See http://www.nbjcoalition.org/about, accessed June 2, 2009. Likewise, the National Black Lesbian Conference, sponsored by the Zuna Institute, a national advocacy organization for black lesbians, has not changed its name to reference queer identities. See http://www.zunainstitute.org, accessed June 2, 2009.

41 Addressing the gap between queer theory and lesbian and gay studies, Ellen Lewin and William Leap also discuss the use of identity labels in *Out in Theory,* 6–10. I am cognizant that my decision to use the word *lesbian* instead of *queer* might lessen my cache in some queer studies circles, both black and white.

42 A male colleague referred to a musician who takes up casual work of this sort as a "gig rat"; women I spoke with used other terms that were even less complimentary.

43 See Eve Sedgwick's influential "Epistemology of the Closet," in *The Lesbian and Gay Studies Reader,* ed. Henry Abelove, Michèle Aina Barale, and David M. Halperin (New York: Routledge, 1993).

44 Patricia Hill Collins, *Black Sexual Politics: African Americans,Gender, and the New Racism* (New York: Routledge, 2004). Collins cites writer Keith Boykin in supporting this perspective.

45 Interview with Tanya Ray, organizer, 2006.

46 Interview with Monica Falls, musician, 2005.

47 Collins, *Fighting Words,* 38.

48 Interview with Chandra Foley, musician, 1995.

CHAPTER 4: NAPPY (AND DEEP) ROOTS

1 For a discussion of the folk music revival of the 1960s and its aftermath in the singer/songwriter era, see Gillian Garr, *She's a Rebel: The History of Women in Rock and Roll* (New York: Seal Press, 1992). My thanks to Christopher Waterman for helping me distill this complex history, details of which would appear later in Waterman and Larry Starr's *American Popular Music: From Minstrelsy to MTV* (New York: Oxford University Press, 2003). For a discussion of African American music organized diachronically

and by theme, see Portia K. Maultsby and Mellonee V. Burnim, eds., *African American Music: An Introduction* (New York: Routledge, 2006).

2 Greg Tate, ed., *Everything but the Burden: What White People Are Taking from Black Culture* (New York: Random House, 2003), 10.

3 Waterman, "Race Music," 177.

4 Bernice Johnson Reagon, *We Who Believe in Freedom: Sweet Honey in the Rock. Still on the Journey* (New York: Anchor Books, 1993), 13.

5 Paula Giddings, *When and Where I Enter: The Impact of Black Women on Race and Sex in America* (New York: Bantam Books, 1984), 282.

6 Reagon, *We Who Believe,* 16.

7 Ibid., 18.

8 Ibid., 32. Sweet Honey members at this time included Bernice Johnson Reagon, Evelyn Maria Harris, Laura Sharp, and Yasmeen Williams.

9 Ibid., 32.

10 Ibid., 33.

11 Roth, *Separate Roads,* 117.

12 Reagon, *We Who Believe,* 16.

13 Ibid., 28.

14 E-mail communication from Bernice Johnson Reagon to the author, January 5, 2004.

15 For more about Sisterfire, see Amy Horowitz, "Some Factors in the Equation," in Reagon, *We Who Believe,* 191–94. See also Eileen M. Hayes, "Black Women and Women's Music," in *Black Women and Music: More Than the Blues,* ed. Eileen M. Hayes and Linda F. Williams (Urbana: University of Illinois Press, 2007), 166–67.

16 Horowitz, in "Some Factors in the Equation," 193.

17 Cynthia Lont, "Women's Music: No Longer a Small Private Party," in *Rockin' the Boat: Mass Music and Mass Movements,* ed. Reebee Garofalo (Boston: South End Press, 1992), 245.

18 Reagon, *We Who Believe,* 34.

19 Sara Evans, *Personal Politics: The Roots of Women's Liberation in the Civil Rights Movement and the New Left* (New York: Vintage, 1979), 105.

20 Ibid.

21 Philip S. Foner, *Women and the American Labor Movement: From World War I to the Present* (New York: Free Press, 1980), 489, cited in Giddings, *When and Where I Enter.*

22 James, *Shadowing,* 77.

23 Combahee River Collective, "A Black Feminist Statement," quoted in James, *Shadowboxing,* 77.

24 The collective published "A Black Feminist Statement" in Zillah R. Eisenstein, ed., *Capitalist Patriarchy and the Case for Socialist Feminism* (New York: Monthly Review Press, 1979). Reprinted in Beverly Guy-Sheftall, ed., *Words of Fire: An Anthology of African-American Feminist Thought* (New York: New Press, 1995), and in Barbara Smith, ed., *Home Girls: A Black Feminist Anthology* (New York: Kitchen Table: Women of Color Press, 1983).

25 See Giddings, *When and Where I Enter.* According to Joy James, members of Combahee included Barbara Smith, Gloria Hull, and Margo Okazawa-Rey (*Shadowboxing,* 77). Benita Roth writes that additional CRC members included Demita Frazier, Sharon Page Ritchie, and Cheryl Clarke (*Separate Roads,* 121).

26 Combahee River Collective, "A Black Feminist Statement," in Barbara Smith, ed., *Home Girls: A Black Feminist Anthology* (1983; New Brunswick, N.J.: Rutgers University Press, 2000), 264–74. Quotation on 269.

27 Referring to Eisenstein, *Capitalist Patriarchy.*

28 See the introduction to B. Smith, ed., *Home Girls*.

29 Karen Kahn, *Frontline Feminism, 1975–1995: Essays from* Sojourner*'s First 20 Years* (San Francisco: Aunt Lute Books, 1995).

30 Ibid., 7.

31 Adrienne Rich, "Compulsory Heterosexuality and Lesbian Existence," in *Blood, Bread, and Poetry: Selected Prose, 1978–1985* (New York: W.W. Norton, 1986); reprinted in Abelove et al., *Lesbian and Gay Studies Reader*. Another early discussion of "women-identified" identities is carried out by contributors to *Women-Identified Women*, a collection edited by Trudy Darty and Sandee Potter (Palo Alto, Calif.: Mayfield, 1984).

32 See Kate Brandt's interview with Armstrong titled "Midwife to the Culture: Hot Wire," in Armstrong, *Happy Endings: Lesbian Writers Talk about Their Lives* (Tallahassee, Fla.: Naiad Press, 1993), 165.

33 See the discussion Keil carries out in "People's Music Comparatively: Style and Stereotype, Class and Hegemony," *Dialectical Anthropology* 10 (1985): 119–30.

34 Faye D. Ginsburg, *Contested Lives: The Abortion Debate in an American Community* (Berkeley: University of California Press, 1989), 137.

35 In this section, I tried to highlight musicians whose reflections do not appear elsewhere in the book.

36 Taylor and Rupp, "Women's Culture," 38.

37 Casselberry interview. As I mentioned earlier, insiders to the women's music scene often indicate festivals by location rather than by name.

38 DeMore interview. At the time of our interview, DeMore was forty-one.

39 Taylor and Rupp, "Women's Culture," 38. I have taken Taylor and Rupp's statement and made it past tense in light of the fact that for many the era of a "women's community" in the sense that it flourished in the 1980s and earlier has passed.

40 Ibid., 34.

41 DeMore interview. Journalists and life partners Phyllis Lyon and Del Martin founded *The Ladder*, which, according to gay historian John D'Emilio, "offered American lesbians, for the first time in history, the opportunity to speak with their own voices." In June 2008, Lyon and Martin were the first same-sex couple to marry in San Francisco. See Rodger Streitmatter, "About Phyllis Lyon and Del Martin," The National Lesbian and Gay Journalists Association, http://www.nlgja.org/awards/hof_lyon_martin.htm, accessed June 2, 2009.

42 DeMore's mention of the Bay Area Lesbian Choral Ensemble is an important note, because although gay and lesbian choruses have since consolidated into GALA (Gay and Lesbian Association of Choruses), in the early 1970s feminist choirs were independent of men's choruses. DeMore's work as a conductor of a lesbian chorus contributes to the recovery of lesbian chorus history.

43 Benin interview. At the time of our interview in 1995, Rhonda Benin was forty.

44 Telephone interview with Emma Jean Foster, December 1, 1995. Foster described the ensemble, affiliated with the Glide Memorial United Methodist Church in San Francisco, as comprised primarily of gay men and lesbians. According to Foster, most of Glide's membership "is of European descent." Glide Memorial, at Ellis and Taylor Streets in San Francisco, sponsors numerous ongoing social service programs. The most famous, after the food program, is the recovery and daily support circles for substance abusers. Readers may remember Glide Memorial as the church depicted in director Gabriele Muccino's *The Pursuit of Happyness* (Columbia Pictures), the 2006 film about the poverty-to-riches saga of African American businessman Chris Gardner, played by actor Will Smith. The Glide Memorial Church Web site is www.glide.org.

45 Interview with Ubaka Hill. This was during the early 1980s. At the time, she was a member of an ensemble called Spirit of Life, a predominantly male group of contemporary jazz musicians. (Hill played percussion and did primary vocals.) Prior to this, Hill worked as a program director for a nonprofit organization in East Harlem. For more information on the DrumSong Institute, see www.ubakahill.com.

46 In addition to Edwina Lee Tyler, other prominent black women hand drummers who play or have played the women's music festival circuit—and, arguably even more often, the women's drumming circuit—include Nurudafina Pel Pina, Regina Wells, Joan Ashley, Debra Kenya McGee, Phyllis Burrell and other members of ASE, Caru Thompson, and Afia Walking Tree.

47 At the time of our interview, on June 6, 2003, at the National Women's Music Festival, Wahru Cleveland was in her fifties.

48 Interview with Jacque Jones, musician, 1995.

49 See Sally R. Munt, ed., *Butch/Femme: Inside Lesbian Gender* (London: Cassell, 1997), and Laura Harris, ed., *Femme: Feminists, Lesbians, and Bad Girls* (New York: Routledge, 1997).

CHAPTER 5: "IDEAL RELATIONSHIPS"

1 Christopher Small, "Why Doesn't the Whole World Love Chamber Music?" *American Music* 19, no. 3 (2001): 344.

2 Sue Fink, quoted in Penelope and Wolfe, *Lesbian Culture,* 397.

3 Eileen M. Hayes, "Black Women and Women's Music," in Hayes, *Black Women and Music,* 158n24. In an early attempt to define women's music, writer Karen Petersen suggested that gender concerns (and implicitly gender concerns without regard for ethnic identity) were foremost. This does not appear to be true in the music of black musicians. See Karen Petersen, "An Investigation into Women-Identified Music in the United States," in Koskoff, *Women and Music in Cross-Cultural Perspective,* 207.

4 Classical music would figure as a minority genre in this environment.

5 Barbara Rose Lange, "'What was that Conquering Magic?': The Power and Discontinuity in Hungarian Gypsy *Nóta,*" *Ethnomusicology* 41, no. 3; and Deborah Hernandez, *Bachata: A Social History of a Dominican Popular Music* (Philadelphia: Temple University Press, 1995).

6 Telephone interview with Rae Baskin, July 11, 2005.

7 Likewise, performances of music scored for instruments only require a different set of criteria for evaluation.

8 Nanette de Jong, "Women of the AACM: Four Narratives," in Hayes and Williams, *Black Women and Music.*

9 The Northampton Lesbian Festival was produced by WOW Productions. It ran from 1990 to 1995.

10 Telephone interview with Rae Lewis, May 2005.

11 Morris, *Eden Built by Eves,* 9, 103. See also Barbara Bradby, "Lesbians and Popular Music: Does It Matter Who Is Singing?" in G. Griffin, ed., *Outwrite: Lesbianism and Popular Culture* (London: Pluto Press, 1993). See also Hayes, "Women-Identified Music," in Maultsby and Burnim, *African American Music,* 555.

12 At Serafemme: A Women of Color Music Festival, an event that I discuss in chapter 6, the degree to which musicians performed "blackness" did not emerge as an issue.

13 Here, it might be useful to differentiate between producers (the CEO of the festivals)—such as Robin Tyler of the former West Coast Women's Music and Comedy Festival or Lisa Vogel, head of the Michigan festival—and organizers or volunteers who work

diligently throughout the year organizing the event. Producers, as opposed to organizers, have the final say on all matters.

14 bell hooks, "Performance Practice as a Site of Opposition," in *Let's Get It On: The Politics of Black Performance,* Catherine Ugwu, ed. (Seattle: Bay Press, 1995), 219.

15 Brown, *States of Injury,* 61.

16 Ellen Lewin, *Inventing Lesbian Cultures in America* (Boston: Beacon Press, 1996).

17 See Ryan, "Introduction," in *Identity Politics* 1, and 326. See also Brown, *States of Injury,* 59.

18 Brown, *States of Injury,* 59.

19 Interview with June Millington, Bodega, California, January 1995. Eileen M. Hayes, "Black Women Performers of Women-Identified Music: 'They Cut Off My Voice; I Grew Two Voices,'" PhD diss., University of Washington, 1999.

20 Although I tend throughout this book to use the formulation "lesbian feminists," I do this mainly as a shorthand. I am well aware that some women identify as lesbian, others as feminists, others as lesbian feminists, a few as radicals, and so on.

21 Private communication with Toni Armstrong Jr., Camp Sister Spirit (Gulf Coast Womyn's Festival), summer 1995.

22 Mark Slobin, *Subcultural Sounds: Micromusics of the West* (Hanover, Mass.: University Press of New England, 1993), 20.

23 Boden Sandstrom, "Women's Music: Passing the Legacy," in Kimball, *Women's Culture,* 111–12.

24 Kay Weaver and Martha Wheelock, *One Fine Day,* VHS, 1984, www.ishtarfilms.com, accessed June 3, 2009. *One Fine Day* was shown annually during the period the research for this book was conducted.

25 James Scott, *Domination and the Arts of Resistance: Hidden Transcripts* (New Haven, Conn.: Yale University Press, 1990).

26 Roth, *Separate Roads,* 3.

27 The Web site images change yearly.

28 Yvonne Welbon, *Living with Pride: Ruth C. Ellis @ 100,* VHS, Our Film Works, 1999. I use the term "same-gender-loving" here because "lesbian" was not a term commonly used during the period in which Ellis grew up. In the film, she mentions the point at which she began trying to use the word "lesbian," although, she says, it never really fit within her speaking pattern in a way that was comfortable.

29 See the late Terri Jewell's interview with Ellis (known as "Miss Ruth") in *Does Your Mama Know?* ed. Lisa C. Moore (Austin, Tex.: RedBone Press, 1997). At the dinner sponsored by the Women of Color series at the NWMF one year, Ellis introduced herself to me, offering that, in her nineties, she was probably the "oldest black lesbian" I knew. My reply was, "Yes, ma'am, you're right." Ellis was 101 when she passed away October 5, 2000.

30 The pose seems derivative from the filmed celebration of Lorde's life (*A Litany for Survival: The Life and Work of Audre Lorde,* directed by Ada Gay Griffin and Michelle Parkerson, Third World Newsreel, 1995) created for the "I Am Your Sister" conference in 1990. This photo, widely circulated and now famous in women's studies circles, depicts Lorde with outstretched hands, palms facing forward, with her arms raised over her head. See www.nedrajohnson.com/images/audre_poster.jpg.

However, the inclusion of Ruth Ellis's photo on the Web site raises an interesting issue. What about the photos of white lesbians her age? Are there not any? Has the story of Ellis inspired others to identify and celebrate elder white lesbians who also could become famous not only for being themselves in festival environments but also for serving as a focal point for lesbian and gay activities in earlier decades?

31 Benita Roth makes this observation in *Separate Roads,* xi.
32 Roth, *Separate Roads,* 77.
33 This point amplifies one that Angela Davis makes in her appearance in Marlon Riggs's *Black Is, Black Ain't,* cited in Morris, *Eden Built by Eves,* 156.
34 See Sue Ann Pressley, "Three Held in Black Man's Dragging Death," *Times Picayune,* June 10, 1998. Available at http://www.yale.edu/glc/archive/990.htm, accessed June 3, 2009. Given the surveillance that black people—particularly young black men—experience in department stores or other retail establishments, as discussed by Patricia Hill Collins in *Black Sexual Politics: African Americans, Gender, and the New Racism* (New York: Routledge, 2004), 78, it doesn't seem as though indoor spaces are safe ones necessarily either.
35 Karen Williams, *Human Beings: What a Concept,* Uproar, 1998.
36 Witold Rybczynski, *Waiting for the Weekend* (New York: Penguin Books, 1992).
37 Noella Santos, "A Do-Something Vacation," *Texas AAA* (2007): 28–31.
38 Faderman, *Odd Girls,* 222.
39 At one point, Northampton, Massachusetts, was said to boast one of the most educated and affluent (white) lesbian populations in the United States.
40 Interview with Marietta Beamer, organizer, Northampton Lesbian Festival, 2004.
41 I admit to a similar filtering of race and space whenever I patronize a restaurant and am seated, as some women dining alone often are, by the doors to the kitchen.
42 Bonnie Morris recounts this incident in *Eden Built by Eves,* 40–41. My intent is not to repeat incidents that Morris reports, but this one is particularly illustrative of the types of cultural "collisions" (race/space) that have occurred in the context of women's music festivals. Tyler reports that thirty-five hundred were in attendance at the 1981 festival. Tyler organized the main stage for the March on Washington, DC, in 1979, 1987, 1993, and 2000. She also now runs an upscale lesbian-oriented travel company, Robin Tyler Tours. No women I interviewed mentioned this incident.
43 Robin Tyler, quoted in Morris, *Eden Built by Eves,* 40.
44 Following bell hooks, I omit the use of "the" before "lesbian feminist movement." The omission of "the" has the same effect of adding an "s" to "movement."
45 Hazel V. Carby, "The Multicultural Wars," in Gina Dent, ed., *Black Popular Culture* (Seattle: Bay Press, 1992).
46 Brian Lanker, *I Dream a World: Portraits of Black Women Who Changed America* (New York: Stewart, Tabori and Chang, 1999).

CHAPTER 6: REDISTRICTING

1 The concert roster was comprised entirely of women of color.
2 According to musician Melanie DeMore, a women of color music festival was held in Austin, Texas, during the early 1980s.
3 Interview with Marquita Thomas, Los Angeles. May 2005.
4 For more on Hanifah Walidah, see Queer Cultural Center, "Straight Black Folks' Guide to Gay Black Folks: Hanifah Walidah's One-Woman Show," www.queerculturalcenter.org/pages/Qfestival03/hanifa.html. The debut of the New York actress' show was received "with standing ovations and amazing reviews." Three years after our interview, Thomas announced that a number of artists who had performed at Serafemme would appear at the Michigan festival in 2008. See OutandAbout Newsletter, August 4, 2008, http://visitor.constantcontact.com/manage/optin/ea?v=001bWApi8U865uQTyW3XtHeBg%3D%3D.
5 In 1980 Tyler founded the West Coast Women's Music and Comedy Festival, which

in 2005 was held outside of Yosemite National Park, California. Tyler also founded the Southern Women's Music and Comedy Festival in north Georgia in 1984.

6 GLAAD (Gay and Lesbian Alliance Against Defamation) and the June Mazer Archives, an important lesbian archive based in Los Angeles, offered to cosponsor Serafemme. Thomas said that the festival budget for the first year was five thousand dollars.

7 For more on the Dyke Marches for visibility across the country, see "Herstory," Dyke March Los Angeles, http://www.dykemarchla.com/history/OurHistory.html, accessed June 4, 2009.

8 "Get Here If You Can" was Adams's standout track from her debut album, *Circle of One*. The song was penned and performed earlier by Brenda Russell.

9 Interview with Miss Money.

10 Jewelle Gomez, *Forty-three Septembers* (Ann Arbor, Mich.: Firebrand Books, 1993), 170.

11 Ibid. Audre Lorde, *Zami: A New Spelling of My Name* (Freedom, Calif.: Crossing Press, 1982). According to Lorde, *Zami* is part history, myth, and autobiography.

12 Miss Money refers to Beyoncé Knowles, Eve (Eve Jihan Jeffers, a rapper and star of the TV show *Eve*), the singer Ashanti (Ashanti Shequoiya Douglas), and Trina (Katrina Laverne Taylor), known for her renditions of songs such as "No Panties," and "69 Ways." All of these artists have "sexy" looks (stereotypical for women in the industry), with hair weaves, makeup, and so on.

13 *Hustle and Flow*, directed by Craig Brewer, Crunk Pictures, 2005.

14 The Houston Women's Festival was founded in 1995 and does not appear in Bonnie Morris's list of women's music festivals. Morris's focus is residential festivals; the Houston event is one day only. See Houston Women's Music Festival, http://hwfestival.org, accessed June 4, 2009.

15 Karrine Steffans, *Confessions of a Video Vixen* (New York: Amistad, 2005).

16 See Collins's discussion of surveillance in *Fighting Words*, 32–43. To be sure, black women are also pulled over by the police while driving, and black men are also scrutinized in retail establishments; this does not, however, detract from the gendered and class quality of the surveillance. Also see Ellis Cose, *The Rage of a Privileged Class* (New York: Harper Collins, 1993), and Joe Feagin and Melvin P. Sikes, *Living with Racism: The Black Middle-Class Experience* (Boston: Beacon Press, 1994).

17 Interestingly, Miss Money's comment recalls black jazz musician Trudy Pitts's statement that being female was inconsequential but being black is not. See Linda Williams's "Black Women, Jazz, and Feminism," in Hayes and Williams, *Black Women and Music*.

18 I recall news events that illustrate this point, the second of which is an ongoing case. See "Black Lesbian Firefighter Wins Harassment Lawsuit," in the *Dallas Morning News*, July 5, 2007. Available at http://www.advocate.com/news_detail_ektid47151.asp. The other miscarriage of justice is described in Anemona Hartocollis, "Four Women Are Sentenced in Attack on Man in Village," *New York Times*, June 15, 2007. See http://www.nytimes.com/2007/06/15/nyregion/15attack.html, accessed June 4, 2009.

19 Linda Hillier, Ellen's Coming Out Page, http://www.geocities.com/Hollywood/1777/ellycome.html, accessed May 26, 2009. I'm not sure if Money was referring to Ellen's current TV talk show or to her sitcom, which began in 1994. Ellen's character uses the word "gay" on ABC's *Prime Time Live*. For coverage of "The Puppy Episode," as the airport incident was called, see Malinda Lo, "Back in the Day: Coming Out with Ellen," April 2005, http://www.afterellen.com/column/2005/4/backintheday.html, accessed May 26, 2009.

20 ULOAH underwent a change in leadership the following year and therefore cancelled Sistahfest 2006.

21 Benita Roth, "Race, Class, and the Emergence of Black Feminism in the 1960s and 1970s," *Womanist Theory and Research* 2, no. 1 (1999): 1–4. Available at http://www.uga.edu/~womanist/roth3.1.htm, accessed June 4, 2009.

22 Yvonne Retter, "Lesbian (Feminist) Los Angeles, 1970–1990: An Exploratory Ethnohistory," 1995, www.usc.edu/libraries/archives/queerfrontiers/queer/papers/retter.html, accessed May 26, 2009. Retter's article begins to do for Los Angeles what Kennedy and Davis's study does for pre-Stonewall lesbian culture in Buffalo, New York.

23 Goddard gives the founding date of February 1988. The Black and Gay Leadership Forum was founded in 1988 and dissolved in 2003. See Keith Boykin, "Black Gay Leadership Group Vanishes: Americans Mark the 1963 March on Washington as the National Black Lesbian and Gay Leadership Forum Dies," August 21, 2003, Gay Mundo. Available at Gully Online Magazine, http://www.thegully.com/essays/gaymundo/030821_gay_black_1963march.html, accessed June 3, 2009. According to Boykin, the forum began as a conference for black gays and lesbians. It was founded in Los Angeles by Phill Wilson (now head of the Black AIDS Institute) and Ruth Waters. Boykin served as executive director of the forum from 1995 to 1998. In 1995 the forum organized a "historic" black gay contingent in the Million Man March called for by the Rev. Louis Farrakhan. The following year, according to Boykin's report, it led the media effort against anti-gay gospel recording artists Angie and Debbie Winans of the famed Winans family.

24 Interview with Rachel Rahman, organizer, Sistahfest, 2005.

25 B. Smith, *Home Girls.*

26 Interview with Delores Goddard, organizer, Sistahfest, 2005.

27 Although Goddard misspeaks with her reference to the LA Women's Music Festival—she meant the West Coast Women's and Comedy Festival, produced by white Jewish comedian and activist Robin Tyler (the last one was produced in 1995)—as this book goes to press there is a festival that goes by that name. See "About Us," LA Women's Music Festival, http://www.lawmf.com/about.html. Although the Web site's headline reads "Female on Fire," it does not mention that the festival emphasizes feminism or that it is open only to women. Instead, it states that the event "provides unparalleled exposure for unsigned and independent female artists by offering them performance opportunities in the epicenter of the music industry." The LAWMF is emblematic of those events that draw on codes of the lesbian feminist festivals but that actually demonstrate an ambivalent relationship to feminism.

28 Indeed, Sistahfest 2005 had only one musical performance in its lineup, and that was on the last evening. There were no concert programs.

29 See NIA Collective, http://www.niacollective.org. NIA is an "annual gathering" of black lesbians in Northern California. NIA observed its twentieth anniversary in 2007.

30 White anthropologist Kath Weston refutes this idea in *Render Me, Gender Me: Lesbians Talk Sex, Class, Color, Nation, Studmuffins* (New York: Columbia University Press, 1996).

31 By "androgynous" it appears that Goddard means not occupying either butch or femme subject positions.

32 Telephone interview with Naya'Hri Suhalia, July 11, 2005. At the time of our interview, Suhalia was twenty-five.

33 Ursula Le Guin, *The Disposessed* (New York: Avon, 1974), 44, quoted in Kamala Visweswaran, "Feminist Ethnography as Failure," in *Fictions of Feminist Ethnography* (Minneapolis: University of Minnesota Press, 1994).

34 Camp Hess Kramer turned fifty years old in 2002. See Wilshire Boulevard Temple Camps, http://www.wbtcamps.org, accessed June 4, 2009.

35 Octavia Butler died on February 24, 2006, in Seattle.

36 I would mention the lesbian newsletter *Lesbian Connection* here, but it wasn't clear to me that a lot of the women I met were familiar with it.

37 Juneteenth is also known as Freedom Day or Emancipation Day. Although the Emancipation Proclamation was announced in September 1862 and went into effect on January 1, 1863, the state of Texas did not enforce the law until June 19, 1865. William Wiggins, *O Freedom! Afro-American Emancipation Celebration* (Knoxville: University of Tennessee Press, 1990).

38 David W. Samuels, *Putting a Song on Top of It* (Tucson: University of Arizona Press, 2004).

39 Reagon's address took place at the 1981 West Coast Women's Music and Comedy Festival. See Bernice Reagon Johnson, "Coalition Politics: Turning the Century," in *Home Girls*, 356–68.

40 My subtitle (YES I Am!) recalls the album that catapulted Melissa Etheridge into fame, *Yes I Am* (Island Records, 1993).

41 Gay and Lesbian Advocates and Defenders Media Program for People of Color. Seehttp://archive.glaad.org/poc/index.php, accessed June 4, 2009.

42 The single was released by Motown at the end of 2005. It also appears on her album *Testimony* Vol. 1, Life & Relationship (2006).

43 In Spielberg's film, Shug Avery sings the song to Celie. *The Color Purple*, directed by Steven Spielberg, Amblin Entertainment, 1985.

44 Jewelle Gomez's critique that the lesbian content of *The Color Purple* has been frequently effaced by critics appears in her *Forty-three Septembers*. For an early work on black women's film spectatorship, see Jacqueline Bobo, *Black Women as Cultural Readers* (New York: Columbia University Press, 1995).

45 "Miss Celie's Blues," lyrics by Lionel Ritchie, music by Quincy Jones and Rod Temperton. Kobena Mercer writes that Temperton also wrote Michael Jackson's "Off the Wall" and "Thriller." See Mercer, "Monster Metaphors: Notes on Michael Jackson's *Thriller*," in *Welcome to the Jungle*, 38.

46 Samuels, *Putting a Song on Top of It*, 147.

47 *Comedy Jam* is a BET (Black Entertainment Television) production featuring both upcoming and veteran stand-up comics.

CHAPTER 7: LEGACY

1 Linda Tillery's comment appears in Morris, *Eden Built by Eves*, 109.

2 The original version of "Amazon Women Rise" appears on *Lavender Concentrate*, a 1977 compilation of songs and recitations by women's music artists and feminist poets. On Johnson's album, the track is referred to as "Amazon." *Nedr*, Big Mouth Girl Records, BMI 1997–2005.

3 Verta Taylor and Leila T. Rupp have identified feminist ritual as one of four elements of lesbian feminist culture that promoted survival of the women's movement during periods of waning activity. The others are female values, separatism, and the primacy of women's relationships. See Taylor and Rupp, "Women's Culture," 34.

4 "*Radical Harmonies*," Woman Vision, http://www.womanvision.org/radical-harmonies.html, accessed June 29, 2009.

5 In 2001 the IMA purchased property in western Massachusetts as the site for a permanent facility. See "IMA Update: From the Executive Director's Chair," January 15, 2009, http://ima.org/pages/newsletter.html, accessed May 27, 2009.

6 Millington interview. My interview with Millington also occurred at a time when musicians of color were coming to terms with the fact that the heyday of women's music had passed and they had not yet been accorded their due in women's music circles.

7 This chapter is based on interviews with a handful of musicians of the next generation. Others of this cohort include Doria Roberts, Kim Archer, Miss Money, and Sphear. At age forty-two at the time of this interview, Johnson is older than other musicians I have identified as members of the next generation, but the type of politics she mobilizes in women's music are clear departures from those of the first generation. While some might view musician Toshi Reagon as a bridge, both musically and politically, to the next generation, the latter is not consistent with the understanding about political generations that I advance in earlier chapters.

8 This Southern Women's Festival, produced by Pat Cobb, differs from the one Robin Tyler produced years ago.

9 When I asked Means her age, she responded, "Age is the last thing that I am not out about, but I probably will be soon."

10 Although the identification of a performer with the material performed is a hallmark of popular music, it is typical for songwriters to collaborate with others on lyrics. Johnson had help composing the song ("talkin' shit" included) from Erica Lindsay and Kathleen Sandwald in addition to Sossity Chiricuzio. An artist by the name of Natasha handles the vocals on this track.

11 In the actual lyrics, the protagonist (singer) says to her lover (the "female" voice on the track), "If you didn't want me to come over, why did you swallow that wine like it was my fingers?"

12 "Gettin' Jiggy Wit It" dates from Will Smith's *Big Willie Style,* Sony, 1997. Howard Johnson's band is comprised of six tuba players, a rhythm section, and Johnson the younger. During the 1970s, Johnson was a member of the *Saturday Night Live* show band.

13 The Unity Fellowship Church movement was established by Carl Beam in 1990 to reach out specifically to black and lesbian churchgoers. See Unity Fellowship Church, www.unityfellowshipchurch.org/site2009, accessed May 27, 2009. I attended services of the Unity Fellowship congregation in Los Angeles.

14 See J. L. King, *On the Down Low: A Journey into the Lives of "Straight" Black Men Who Sleep with Men* (New York: Broadway Books, 2004). King discusses MSM, or men having sex with men but not identifying as gay. The influence of an earlier feminist spirituality movement can also be felt in Johnson's song text.

15 Pamela Means, *Single Bullet Theory,* Wirl Records, 2003, and *Jazz Project, Vol. 1,* Wirl Records, 2007. The unattributed phrase, "folk-politico-rocktress," comes from the artist's promotional postcard for the *Jazz Project* album. This type of attribution that recognizes or fuses a number of musical styles is quite common in the promotion of black women's music artists.

16 An entrepreneur and philanthropist who made her fortune manufacturing black hair care products, Mrs. Charles Joseph Walker, known as Madam C. J. Walker, was reportedly the first self-made female millionaire. Contrary to the beliefs of some, C. J. Walker did not invent the straightening comb, which had been in use since the last quarter of the nineteenth century, but, rather, she popularized its use among black women. See the Web site of Walker's heir and biographer, A'lelia Bundles at www.madamcjwalker.com, accessed June 6, 2009. See also Noliwe M. Rooks, *Hair Raising: Beauty, Culture, and African American Women* (New Brunswick, N.J.: Rutgers University Press, 1996).

17 See Reginald McKnight's "Confessions of a Wannabee Negro," in *Lure and Loathing:*

Essays on Race, Identity, and the Ambivalence of Assimilation, G. Early, ed. (New York: Penguin, 1993).

18 See http://www.myspace.com/malika1922.

19 As this book goes to press, Malika received her master's degree in music education.

20 See the work of noted theorist, Clenora Hudson-Weems, the author of numerous books, including *Africana Womanism: Reclaiming Ourselves* (Troy, Mich.: Bedford Publishing, 1994).

21 Malika's mention of buying crystals from the vendors' booths reminded me of a workshop at Michigan 17 called "Advanced Crystals: So You've Got a Crystal, Now What?" Michigan Womyn's Music Festival, program booklet, 1992, 62.

22 Parkerson and Griffin, *Litany for Survival.* Lorde died at the age of fifty-eight on November 17, 1992, after a long battle with breast cancer. Her memorial service was held at the Cathedral of Saint John the Divine in Harlem. Mourners included Angela Davis, Sonia Sanchez, Blanche Weisen Cook, and Barbara Smith, among others. See Melinda Goodman, "A Tribute to Audre Lorde," http://www.colorado.edu/journals/standards/V5N1/Lorde/goodman.html, accessed May 28, 2009.

23 Audre Lorde, *The Cancer Journals,* special edition (San Francisco: Aunt Lute Books, 2006).

24 See Alice Walker, *In Search of Our Mother's Gardens: Womanist Prose* (San Diego: Harcourt Brace Jovanovich, 1983).

25 The present text does not explore meanings that performers and festigoers read into "biracial" black identities, nor does it discuss the meanings that music consumers adhere to them. Musicians identifying as black and biracial include Pamela Means, Vicki Randle, and Laura Love.

26 The 81.55 percent figure comes from the Brookings Institution, "Detroit in Focus: A Profile from Census 2000," November 2003. Available at www.brookings.edu/reports/2003/11_livingcities_detroit.aspx, accessed May 28, 2009.

27 See the Web site of the International Federation of Black Prides, http://www.ifbprides.org, accessed May 28, 2009. The Black Pride march was founded in Washington, DC, in 1990. See DC Black Pride, www.dcblackpride.org, accessed May 28, 2009.

28 Judith Butler, *Bodies That Matter: On the Discursive Limits of "Sex."* New York: Routledge, 1993, 233.

29 According to Malika, Ladyfests cater to people from age sixteen "to probably age thirty-five or fortyish."

30 Cathy Cohen, *The Boundaries of Blackness: AIDS and the Breakdown of Black Politics* (Chicago: University of Chicago Press, 1999), 27.

31 Springer, *Living for the Revolution,* 166, 177, 122–30.

32 I borrow from the title of Gage Averill's dissertation, "Haitian Dance Band Music: The Political Economy of Exuberance," University of Washington, 1987, a study that served as the foundation for his book *A Day for the Hunter, A Day for the Prey: Popular Music and Power in Haiti.* Chicago: University of Chicago Press, 1997.

CHAPTER 8: WORKING FOR THE WEEKEND

1 All names of interviewees in this chapter are pseudonyms except Linda Tillery.

2 Given the low likelihood that I would meet by happenstance black women who had served in these capacities, I sought referrals from board officers or staffers of festival organizations with whom I made contact.

3 While there are several predominantly white lesbian/bisexual coming out narratives, Lisa Moore's *Does Your Mama Know?* brings together new and previously published

narratives, interviews, and poetry by black lesbian authors in a volume organized around the theme of coming out. Precursors include the Black Women's Issue of *Conditions: A Feminist Magazine of Writing by Women with a Particular Emphasis on Writing by Lesbians* (*Conditions: Five,* no. 2 [1979]). The special issue contained a range of writings by black feminists. See Gay/Lesbian Related Events—Historical Time Line—Gay Firsts, http://www.glinn.com/news/tline1.htm, accessed June 6, 2009. *Conditions* ceased publication in 1990. In contrast to *Conditions: Five,* there is no reference to "black feminist" in the introduction, on the book cover, or in the table of contents of Moore's volume.

4 Beamer interview. Neither black musicians nor festigoers mentioned their former husbands or male partners often. Neither did festigoers mention their children frequently, although, admittedly, I did not ask about them. In retrospect, it is clear that some women had offspring, because in recent private communications a few have mentioned their now-adult children. At the time of our interview, Beamer was local to the area and requested anonymity because she was involved in a pending court case over the custody of her children, who were not living with her at the time. Also at the time of our conversation, Marietta was not out to her family, which included her mother, one sister, and two "conservative" brothers.

5 Lewin and Leap, introduction, *Out in Theory,* 10.

6 For information on the domestic partnership legislation drive Beamer describes, see Gay & Lesbian Pride & Politics, http://www.lib.neu.edu/archives/voices/gl_domestic2.htm, accessed June 6, 2009.

7 Interview with Karla Gee, tech crew, August 7, 2006. Gee requested anonymity; at the time of our conversation she was taking a break from the festival circuit. Gee mentions the festival's various locations. According to Morris, NWMF was held at Illinois State University from 1974 to 1980; at Indiana University, Bloomington, from 1982 to 1997; and at Ball State University in Muncie, Indiana, in 1998. Since 1999 the festival has been held at various locations in Illinois, Indiana, and Wisconsin. See Morris, *Eden Built by Eves,* 25.

8 Interview with Cal Mitchell, organizer, summer 2006.

9 Mountain Moving Coffeehouse for Womyn, http://www.angelfire.com/il2/mmch/index.html, accessed May 27, 2009. According to the Web site, black singer/songwriter Deidre McCalla performed on that day.

10 Whittier, *Feminist Generations.*

11 Wiminfest ceased operating as a festival in 2005. Roberts has a master's degree in women's studies and a master's in public health. She did social science health research for years. At the time of our interview, she was working from home so that she could be with her son.

12 See www.sarahickman.com (accessed on June 7, 2008) and www.toriamos.com (accessed on July 23, 2009).

13 Part of the late 1980s crossover of more "androgynous" neo-folk stars such as Tracy Chapman, the Indigo Girls eventually signed with Epic Records. What exactly observers mean when they refer to "androgynous" stars is a topic worthy of discussion.

14 Arlene Stein, "Androgyny Goes Pop: But Is It Lesbian Music?" in *Sisters, Sexperts, Queers: Beyond the Lesbian Nation* (New York: Penguin Books, 1993), 97. To be clear, Stein includes only the Indigo Girls, Tracy Chapman, and Michelle Shocked in this list.

15 Bradby, "Lesbians and Popular Music," 155. Bradby's study of the reception of U.S. women's music in an Irish context reveals that during the heyday of women's music, consumers listened to both women's music and mainstream rock and pop.

16 Linda Tillery, *Secrets,* Redwood Records, 1985.

17 Interview with Linda Tillery, Oakland, California, January 1, 1995.
18 Few have problematized their personal listening habits in regard to this contradiction as well as Gwendolyn Pough in "Hip-Hop Soul Divas and Rap Music: Critiquing the Love That Hate Produced," in Hayes and Williams, eds., *Black Women and Music.*
19 Ethnomusicologist Boden Sandstrom, who has written extensively on the Michigan Womyn's Music Festival, confirms that Me'shell Ndegéocello never performed at MWMF. Private communications, July 2, 2007.
20 James distinguishes between different types of black feminisms in *Shadowboxing,* 74–92.
21 As Cal Mitchell recalls, the year was 1998.
22 Even identifying as a woman of color is not an indicator of one's political viewpoint.
23 See Collins, *Fighting Words,* 203–11.
24 Collins discusses macro and meso levels in *Fighting Words,* 226–27.
25 Interview with Jay Howard, organizer, July 21, 2006.
26 Gee interview.
27 Tricia Rose, *Black Noise: Rap Music and Black Culture in Contemporary America* (Hanover, N.H.: Wesleyan University Press, 1994). Rose describes her interaction with a then-young MC Lyte, who, when asked if she identified as a feminist, responded no. Rose then took the extra step of asking the rapper, known at the time for her 1988 hit release "Paper Thin," if she knew what a feminist was.
28 Brown, *States of Injury,* 61.
29 Ibid.
30 Weston, *Render Me, Gender Me,* 8. Weston also refutes the idea that it is shortsighted to say that butch/femme subject positions are no longer considered viable subject positions.
31 Tracy Morgan, "Butch-Femme and the Politics of Identity," in Stein, ed., *Sisters, Sexperts,* 35–46.
32 Lisa Walker, *Looking Like What You Are: Sexual Style, Race, and Lesbian Identity* (New York: New York University Press, 2001).
33 Here, Mitchell uses the term "radar" where others might use the term "gaydar," a play on the words "gay radar."
34 Brown, *States of Injury,* 23.

CHAPTER 9: GUYS LIKE US

1 This chapter was written in light of the press release, issued in summer 2006, that transgender persons would no longer be barred from the festival. See "Michigan Womyn's Music Festival Ends Policy of Discrimination against Trans Women: After 15 Years of Controversy, Supporters Welcome Trans Women to "The Land," Camp Trans press release, August 24, 2006. Available at http://www.ifge.org/Article273.phtml, accessed May 27, 2009.
2 These festivals were Wiminfest and NWMF. Videotaping or recording by audience members was not allowed at either event.
3 E-mail communication with representatives from the predominantly white protest group Camp Trans also yielded no responses from black persons.
4 It is important that I make clear at the outset that these performances occurred in different venues, that only one drag king was available for an interview, and that I was unable to locate black women spectators to interview.
5 For treatment of the topic in a European context, see Zachary I. Nataf, *Lesbians Talk Transgendered* (London: Scarlet, 1994).
6 *The Aggressives,* directed by Daniel Peddle. Secret Gallery, 2005.

7 Judith Halberstam, *Female Masculinity* (Durham, N.C.: Duke University Press, 1998), 41.

8 Judith "Jack" Halberstam, *The Drag King Book* (London: Serpent's Tail, 1999), 105.

9 See Michelle Parkerson's film *Storme: The Lady of the Jewel Box* at Women Make Movies, http://www.wmm.com/filmcatalog/pages/c217.shtml. During the course of my research, I met only one black woman who had seen Stormé perform in Harlem during the early 1960s. See also Elizabeth Drorbaugh's discussion of this black drag king performer in "Sliding Scales: Notes on Stormé DeLarverie and the Jewel Box Revue, the Cross-Dressed Woman on the Contemporary Stage, and the Invert," in *Crossing the Stage*, Lesley Ferris, ed. (London: Routledge, 1993). See also Bud Coleman's recollections captured in "The Jewel Box Revue: America's Longest-Running, Touring Drag Show," *Theatre History Studies* (June 1997): 79–92. For a discussion of Gladys Bentley, an earlier cross-dressing performer, see Carmen Mitchell, "Creations of Fantasies/Constructions of Identities: The Oppositional Lives of Gladys Bentley," in *The Greatest Taboo: Homosexuality in Black Communities*, ed. Delroy Constanine-Simms (Los Angeles: Alyson Books, 2001).

10 See *Traps: African American Men on Gender and Sexuality*, ed. Rudolph P. Byrd and Beverly Guy-Sheftall (Bloomington: Indiana University Press, 2001). See also Devon Carbado, *Black Men on Race, Gender, and Sexuality* (New York: New York University Press, 1999).

11 See Donna Troka, Kathleen Lebesco, and Jean Noble, ed. *The Drag King Anthology*, (New York: Harrington Park Press, 2000), 4.

12 Kim Surkan, "Drag Kings in the New Wave: Gender Performance and Participation," in Troka, Lebesco, Noble, eds. *Drag King Anthology*. Surkan writes that "by engaging the 'audience' in drag, the Extravaganza 'Science Fair' successfully referenced drag kings' shared history with early American freak shows in a clever and critical way" (161). The last two items (facial hair and condom) come from pg. 176.

13 Ibid., 177.

14 Donna Jean Troka, "The History of the First International Drag King Extravaganza," IDKE Board, http://www.idke.info/about_us.html#history, accessed May 26, 2009. The IDKE was founded by Donna Jean Troka, Julie Applegate, Si'le Singleton, and Shani Scott. The first extravaganza was held in October 1999.

15 Feinberg gave the keynote at Wiminfest. Personal communication, Lena McQuade, Wiminfest board member. See Leslie Feinberg, *Stone Butch Blues* (Ithaca, N.Y.: Firebrand Books, 1993).

16 Figuring in the momentum are studies by an earlier generation of gay and lesbian anthropologists, including Esther Newton, *Mother Camp: Female Impersonators in America* (Chicago: University of Chicago Press, 1972).

17 The Albuquerque King's Club of Alberquerque, New Mexico, has performed at Wiminfest for four years. At Wiminfest 2003 the AKC performed in a banquet room in the hotel reserved for festival attendees.

18 Colleen Ayoup and Julie Podmore, "Making Kings," in Troka et al., *Drag King Anthology*, 69.

19 Telephone interview with Kory Chandler, May 15, 2005. Chandler is the owner of a custom picture-framing shop. "Toma" and "Seymore Johnson" are pseudonyms.

20 "Sharp" is a pseudonym.

21 Halberstam, an English professor and a queer cultural critic, describes her research in "Mackdaddy, Superfly, Rapper: Gender, Race, and Masculinity in the Drag King Scene," *Social Text* 15, no. 52/53 (1997): 104–31. One of these performers, Dréd, appears in filmmaker Gabrielle Baur's *Venus Boyz*, Clockwise Productions, 2002. After the filming

of *Venus Boyz*, Diyaa MilDred Gerestant moved from New York City to Santa Monica, California. See Amy Jo Goddard, "Staging Activism: New York City Performing Artists as Cultural Workers," in *Social Justice: A Journal of Crime, Conflict, and World Order*, March 22, 2007, http://goliath.ecnext.com/coms2/summary_0199-7185652_ITM, accessed June 9, 2009.

22 Halberstam, "Mackdaddy," 12.

23 Halberstam identified that this was also true of Dréd (in "Mackdaddy").

24 Neither does Dréd of *Venus Boyz* attempt to pass as a man offstage. According to the documentary, she describes herself as very feminine, and, indeed, when she is not performing, that is how she appears (in the film).

25 Tara Pauliny, "Erotic Arguments and Persuasive Acts: Discourses of Desire and the Rhetoric of Female-to-Male Drag," in Troka et al., *Drag King Anthology*, 231.

26 Ayoup and Podmore, "Making Kings," 67.

27 From the NWMF 2003 program booklet (for the 29th Annual NWMF), we learn that H.I.S. Kings was named after the three original Kings—Helen, Ivett, and Sue (15).

28 Robin Deisher, *XY:DRAG*, Reel Keen Films, 2001.

29 NWMF 2003 program booklet, 29.

30 NWMF 2003 program booklet.

31 Interview with Kelly Marshall, festival attendee, NWMF, 2003. At the time of our interview, Marshall worked at Goldenrod, one of the country's largest and longest-lasting distributors of women's music.

32 See Judith Butler, *Gender Trouble: Feminism and the Subversion of Identity (Thinking Gender)* (New York: Routledge, 1990).

33 Noted author and activist Riki Wilchins is founding executive director of the Gender Public Advocacy Coalition (GenderPAC), the national gender rights organization.

34 Feinberg's books include *Stone Butch Blues: A Novel* (1993), *Trans Liberation: Beyond Pink or Blue* (1998), and *Transgender Warriors: Making History from Joan of Arc to Dennis Rodman* (1996). She is interviewed in *Outlaw*, a video by Alisa Lebow. DocuDrag Productions, 1994.

35 See Kate Bornstein, *Gender Outlaw: On Men, Women, and the Rest of Us* (New York: Routledge, 1994).

36 Daniela Sea plays Moira Sweeney, who transitions to "Max." The character Kit Porter is played by the actress Pam Grier, well known to African American audiences as a 1970s star of blaxploitation films and more recently as the star of the Quentin Tarantino film *Jackie Brown*.

37 This phenomenon reminds me of the 1990s, when, if popular culture discourse is held to reflect social science fact, it was "chic" to be lesbian.

38 bell hooks's discussion of Spike Lee's *Do the Right Thing* comes to mind. See bell hooks, *Black Looks: Race and Representation* (Boston: South End Press, 1992).

39 See Jessica Munns and Penny Richards's *The Clothes That Wear Us: On Dressing and Transgressing in Eighteenth-Century Culture* (Newark: University of Delaware Press, 1999), 16.

40 Butler, *Bodies That Matter*, 125.

41 Carole-Anne Tyler, "Boys Will Be Girls: The Politics of Gay Drag," in Fuss, *Inside/Out*, 61.

42 Pauliny, "Erotic Arguments," 231.

43 The Michigan Womyn's Music Festival is not the only cultural event for women that specifies that women must be born female. According to an article in *USA Today*, "The USGA put the 'female at birth' clause in its entry forms in 1989, while the

LPGA Tour added the restriction in 1991." "Transsexual to Compete in Women's Australian Open," March 4, 2004, http://www.usatoday.com/sports/golf/2000–03–03-transsexual-competes_x.htm, accessed June 5, 2009.

44 "A Fest in Distress," Bitch: Feminist Response to Pop Culture, *Bitch*, no. 17 (Summer 2002), roundtable discussion. Available at http://eminism.org/michigan/20020700-bitch.txt, accessed May 26, 2009.

45 This statement is taken from the Web site for Ladyfest South 2007, http://www.ladyfestsouth.org, accessed on May 26, 2009.

46 Joshua Gamson, "Messages of Exclusion: Gender, Movements, and Symbolic Boundaries," in *Identity Politics in the Women's Movement* (New York: New York University Press, 2001), 215. See Janice G. Raymond's *The Transsexual Empire* (Boston: Beacon Press, 1979).

47 Gamson, "Messages of Exclusion," 216. Here, Gamson draws on Nancy Jean Burkholder, "A Kinder, Gentler Festival?" in *TransSisters* 2 (November/December 1993): 4–5, and Lisa M. Keen, "Michigan Festival Expels Transsexual in Middle of the Night," in *Washington Blade* 13 (September 1991): 17.

48 See "Frequently Asked Questions on Michigan/Trans Controversy: Protests," Michigan/Trans Controversy Archive, http://eminism.org/michigan/faq-protest.html, accessed May 26, 2009.

49 Ibid, 2.

50 "What We Do," Camp Trans 2009: Room for All Kinds of Womyn, http://www.camp-trans.org/pages/whatwedo.html, accessed July 31, 2009.

51 See http://www.camp-trans.org/pages/ct-history.html.

52 Gamson, "Messages of Exclusion," 220.

53 Anthony Cohen, *The Symbolic Construction of Community* (London: Tavistock, 1985), 20.

54 The statement in quotes reflects notions of the inside/outside as articulated by Diane Fuss, Stuart Hall, and numerous others. Here, Gamson ("Messages of Exclusion," 212) cites Shane Phelan, *Identity Politics: Lesbian Feminism and the Limits of Community* (Philadelphia: Temple University Press, 1993), and Verta Taylor and Nancy Whittier, "Collective Identity in Social Movement Communities: Lesbian Feminist Mobilization," in *Frontiers in Social Movement Theory*, ed. Alan D. Morris and Carol M. Mueller (New Haven, Conn.: Yale University Press, 1992).

55 Gamson, "Messages of Exclusion," 212. Italics in original.

56 Ibid., 213.

57 Ibid., 218.

58 I use "might" advisedly because the fact that transexuals and transgenders are admitted to a women-born women's music festival does not necessarily mean they will feel welcomed or indeed experience a welcoming environment under all circumstances.

59 Gamson, "Messages of Exclusion," 218.

60 Ibid., 221.

61 Ibid., 219.

62 Interview with Penny Jameson, festival attendee, Boston, MA, February 2005. According to many transgender scholars and scholars of transgender culture and identity politics, the preferred term is "sex-reassignment" surgery.

63 Riki Wilchins, quoted in Nataf, *Lesbians Talk Transgender*, 31.

64 Halberstam, *Female Masculinity*, 159.

65 Cathy Cohen, *The Boundaries of Blackness: AIDS and the Breakdown of Black Politics* (Chicago: University of Chicago Press, 1999).

66 Halberstam, *Female Masculinity*, 161.

67 I also have not attended Camp Trans.

68 Gee references the popular television character portrayed by actress Barbara Billingsley on *Leave It to Beaver*, a show that was regarded as the epitome of 1950s/early 1960s middle-class domesticity. *Leave It to Beaver* premiered in 1957; the original series ceased occupying prime-time hours in 1963.

69 Interview with Klarete Hudley, festival attendee, National Women's Music Festival, 2005.

70 Two reflections on the limits of the family trope in black political discourse are exemplified by Paul Gilroy (*Black Atlantic*, 98–99) and Patricia Hill Collins (*Fighting Words*, 219–28). Stuart Hall, "When Was the Post-Colonial: Thinking at the Limit," in Iain Chambers and Lidia Curti, ed., *The Post-Colonial Question: Common Skies, Divided Horizons* (London: Routledge, 1996).

71 In *Black Sexual Politics* Collins does not provide a separate index listing for gay, bisexual, and transgender. Rather, LGBT topics are glossed under the subheading "lesbian."

72 Even the language I am using here is problematic, as it presupposes a "we" on the "inside" and a "them" on the "outside."

73 As Halberstam relates, some transsexual men do not consider themselves "men," even after having surgery. She suggests that "their retention of the FTM label suggests the emergence of a new gender position marked by this term," *Female Masculinity*, 154.

74 Ibid, 160.

75 David Valentine, "We're 'Not about Gender': The Uses of 'Transgender,'" in Lewin and Leap, *Out in Theory*, 222.

76 Ibid., 225.

77 Ibid.

78 Halberstam, *Female Masculinity*, 159.

79 Ibid., 144.

80 See FORGE, www.forge-forward.org, accessed June 5, 2009. FORGE is an acronym that stands for "For Ourselves: Reworking Gender Expression."

81 Judith Halberstam writes of the problematics of bathroom encounters and of the bathroom as a barometer of gender identification in *Female Masculinity*, 20–29, as do a number of queer theorists; the topic is frequently mentioned in transgender narratives.

82 Brochure of the National Center for Transgender Equality. See National Center for Transgender Equality, http://www.nctequality.org/About/about.html, accessed May 26, 2009.

83 Transgender Law Center newsletter, Fall 2004, 1. The center can be reached at www.transgenderlawcenter.org, accessed June 5, 2009.

84 Collins cites data from the 2000 U.S. Census, particularly a study by Tavia Simmons and Martin O'Connell. Collins, *Black Sexual Politics*, 270.

85 Telephone conversation, April 2005, with a policy analyst at the National Gay and Lesbian Task Force concerning the data for black same-sex households.

86 Collins expands on these points in *Black Sexual Politics*, ch. 8, notes 40–42. Numerous authors have discussed the political valences of the mainstreaming of gay politics or of attempts to "normalize" gay and lesbian identities. There is an underlying message here about desexualizing the representation of these relationships for the general public's benefit.

87 Juan Battle, Cathy J. Cohen, et al., "Say It Loud, I'm Black and I'm Proud: Black Pride Survey 2000," report from the Policy Institute of the National Gay and Lesbian Task Force (2002), 4. Available at http://www.thetaskforce.org/downloads/reports/reports/SayItLoudBlackAndProud.pdf, accessed May 27, 2009.

88 A list of Black Pride events can be found at International Federation of Black Prides, www.ifbprides.org, accessed June 6, 2009.
89 Battle et al., "Say It Loud," 10. These statistics are also from the Task Force report cited by Collins, *Black Sexual Politics*, 342.
90 Collins, *Black Sexual Politics*, 270.
91 David van Leer, "Visible Silence: Spectatorship in Black Gay and Lesbian Film," in V. Smith, *Representing Blackness*. I have also been inspired by bell hooks's collection of film criticism, *Reel to Real: Race, Sex, and Class at the Movies* (New York: Routledge, 1996).
92 The question might arise as to how I knew that most women in attendance were lesbian. Beyond casual or assertive claims to "gaydar," rarely have I seen this question addressed in either the humanities or social science literatures. Beyond the inexactitude of "gaydar," I looked for and sought contextual clues. In a society segregated by race, and with a media that is overwhelmingly directed toward the heterosexual mainstream, it seems intuitive that the showing of a film about black lesbians held at a center for gay and lesbians of color (specifically black and Latino) would draw an audience of primarily black lesbians. Had the presenters wanted or anticipated an audience of white gays and lesbians, they would have scheduled the film for one of the venues that white gays and lesbians frequent. During the course of my research, a showing of a film by the highly respected black gay British filmmaker Issac Julien was an example of a film by a black filmmaker that was shown in a different venue that attracted predominantly white gay and lesbian audience members. The showing of *The Aggressives* was also cosponsored by ULOAH.
93 YES! summer events have included movie night, a breakfast club, basketball, and a leadership retreat.
94 *Paris Is Burning*, directed by Jennie Livingston, Off White Productions, Inc., 1990. See bell hooks's essay, "Is Paris Burning?" in *Black Looks*, and Judith Butler's essay "Gender and Appropriation in *Paris Is Burning*," in *Bodies That Matter*.
95 Van Leer, "Visible Silence," 158.
96 *The Aggressives* has no voice-over narration.
97 Likewise, none of the women mention taking male hormones, a fact that contrasts notably with presentations of the white FtMs at the gender queer workshop I attended at Transgender Unity, a festival of Transgender Pride, held in Los Angeles in the summer of 2005.
98 See Cindy Patton, "Embodying Subaltern Memory: Kinesthesia and the Problematics of Gender and Race," in *The Madonna Connection: Representational Politics, Subcultural Identities, and Cultural Theory*, ed. Cathy Schwichtenberg (Boulder: Westview Press, 1993).
99 It is not at all clear that the narrators identify as "queer." Their self-disclosures in terms of sexual identity alternate between lesbian and gay.
100 F. Gary Gray, *Set It Off*, New Line Cinema, 1996.
101 Van Leer, "Visible Silence," 167.
102 Lisa Walker, "How to Recognize a Lesbian: The Cultural Politics of Looking Like What You Are," *Signs* 18, no. 4 (1993).
103 Van Leer, "Visible Silence," 160.
104 Caren Kaplan, quoted in Visweswaran, *Fictions of Feminist Ethnography*, 110.

DREAMGIRLS

1 The film is based loosely on groups affiliated with Motown, the book for the original *Dreamgirls* was by Tom Eyen; the music by Henry Krieger.

DISCOGRAPHY OF BLACK MUSICIANS IN WOMEN'S MUSIC

Abena, Nurudfina Pili. *Drum Call*. Ladyslipper, 1994.
Allen, Lillian. *Dub Poet: The Poetry of Lillian Allen*, 1983.
———. *Revolutionary Tea Party*, 1986.
———. *Conditions Critical*. Redwood Records, 1988.
———. *Freedom & Dance*. Festival Records, 1999.
Archer, Kim. *They Say I'm Crazy*, 2003.
Avery, Gwen. *Sugar Mama*, 2000.
Bagby, Rachel. *Reach Across the Lines*, 2006.
Benin, Rhonda. *A Matter of the Heart*, 2006.
Burrell, Elouise. "It's Alright." Scintilla.
———. "Thinkin' about S.E.X." Scintilla, 1984.
———. "Cream Always Rises to the Top." Scintilla.
Casselberry/Dupreé. *City Down*. Iceberg Records, 1987.
———. *Hot Corn in the Fire*. Ladyslipper, 1994.
DeMore, Melanie. *Share My Song, and Come Follow Me*, 1993.
Foster, Emma Jean. *Stand Tall and Be Happy*, 2002.
Hill, Ubaka. *Shapeshifters*. Ladyslipper, 1995.
———. *Dance the Spiral Dance*, 1998.
———. *Beyond the Wind*, 2006.
In Process . . . *Mission Love*, 2003.
———. *In Process*, 2002.
Johnson, Nedra. *Nedra*. Big Mouth Girl Records, 2005.
Love, Laura. *You Ain't Got No Easter Clothes*. Koch Records, 2004.
———. *Z Therapy*. Octoroon Biography, 1990.
———. *Pangaea*. Octoroon Biography, 1992.
———. *Helvetica Bold*. Octoroon Biography, 1996.
———. *The Laura Love Collection*. Putumayo, 1995.
———. *Octoroon*. Fontana Island, 1997.
———. *Fourteen Days*. Zoe Records, 2000.

Malika. *Myriad,* 2004.
McCalla, Deidre. *Playing for Keeps.* Maidenrock Records, remastered 2003.
———. *Everyday Heroes & Heroines.* Olivia, 1992.
———. *With a Little Luck.* Olivia, 1987.
———. *Don't Doubt It.* Olivia, 1985.
Means, Pamela. *Pamela Means Jazz Project.* Wirl, 2006.
———. *Single Bullet Theory,* 2003.
———. *Pearls,* 2000.
———. *Cobblestones,* 1998.
———. *Bone Spurs,* 1995.
Miss Money. *The Love of Money,* 2006.
Nolan, Faith. *Faith Nolan Live,* 2003.
———. *Let It Shine,* 2002.
———. *Faith Nolan Compilation, 1986–1996,* 1996.
———. *Hard to Imagine,* 1996.
———. *Freedom to Love,* 1989.
———. *Sistership,* 1987.
———. *Africville,* 1986.
Randle, Vicki. *Sleep City,* 2007.
Reagon, Toshi. *Toshi,* 2002.
———. *The Righteous Ones,* 1999.
———. *The Rejected Stone,* 1994.
———. *Justice,* 1990.
Roberts, Doria. *Radio Doria.* Hurricane Doria Records.
———. *Restoration,* 1999.
Sweet Honey in the Rock. *Sweet Honey in the Rock.* Flying Fish, 1979.
———. *B'lieve I'll Run On.* Redwood, 1978.
———. *Good News.* Flying Fish, 1981.
———. *We All Everyone of Us.* Flying Fish, 1983.
———. *The Other Side.* Flying Fish, 1985.
———. *Breaths.* Flying Fish, 1985.
———. *Live at Carnegie Hall.* Flying Fish, 1988.
———. *All for Freedom.* Music for Little People, 1989.
———. *In This Land.* Earthbeat! 1992.
———. *Still on the Journey.* Earthbeat! 1993.
———. *I Got Shoes.* Music for Little People, 1994.
———. *Sacred Ground.* Earthbeat! 1996.
———. *Selections.* Rounder, 1997.
———. *Still the Same Me.* Rounder Kids, 2000.
———. *The Women Gather.* Earthbeat! 2003.
———. *Alive in Australia.* Freedom Song Productions, 2003.
———. *Endings and Beginnings.* Sweet Honey in the Rock, 2004.
———. *Raise Your Voice.* Music for Little People, 2005.
Tillery, Linda. *Sweet Linda Divine.* CBS, 1970.
———. *Linda Tillery.* Olivia Records, 1978.
———. *Secrets.* Redwood Records, 1985.
———. *Shake It to the One That You Love the Best.* 1989.
Linda Tillery and the Cultural Heritage Choir. *Front Porch Music.* Rhino, 1997.
———. *Good Time, A Good Time.* Tuizer Music, 1997.
———. *Say Yo' Business: Live!* Rhino, 2001.

Tyler, Edwina Lee. *Drum Drama*. Percussion Piquant.
Walking Tree, Afia. *Soul Affirmationz,* 2000.
The Washington Sisters. *Understated,* 1987.
———. *Take Two,* 1991.
Watkins, Mary. *Something Moving*. Olivia Records
———. *Winds of Change*. Palo Alto, 1981.
———. *Spirit Song*. Redwood, 1985.
———. *The Soul Kings*. Wenefil, 1992.
———. *Touch, Heal, and Deliver*. DDS, 1995.
———. *Prayer for Peace*. Shotsky Music, 2003.
Williams, Karen. *Human Beings: What a Concept*. Uproar Entertainment, 1998.
Women of the Calabash. *The Kwanzaa Album*. Bermuda Reef Records, 1999.

BIBLIOGRAPHY

Abelove, Henry, Michèle Aina Barale, and David M. Halperin, eds. *The Lesbian and Gay Studies Reader.* New York: Routledge, 1993.

Adam, Barry D. *The Rise of a Gay and Lesbian Movement.* Boston: Twayne, 1987.

Agar, Michael H. *The Professional Stranger: An Informal Introduction to Ethnography.* New York: Academic Press, 1980.

Alcoff, Linda. "Cultural Feminism versus Post-Structuralism: The Identity Crisis in Feminist Theory." *Signs: Journal of Women in Culture and Society* 13, no.3 (1988): 405–36.

Armstrong, Toni, Jr. "An Endangered Species: Women's Music by, for, and about Women," *Hot Wire: The Journal of Women's Music and Culture* 5 (1989).

———. "Midwife to the Culture: Hot Wire." In *Happy Endings: Lesbian Writers Talk about Their Lives and Work,* edited by Kate Brandt. Tallahassee, Fla.: Naiad Press, 1993.

———. "The Great White Folk Music Myth." In Penelope and Wolfe, *Lesbian Culture.*

Asad, Talal, ed. *Anthropology and the Colonial Encounter.* London: Ithaca Press, 1973.

Averill, Gage. "Haitian Dance Band Music: The Political Economy of Exuberance." PhD diss. University of Washington, 1987.

———. *A Day for the Hunter, A Day for the Prey: Popular Music and Power in Haiti.* Chicago: University of Chicago Press, 1997.

Awkward, Michael. *Negotiating Difference: Race, Gender, and the Politics of Positionality.* Chicago: University of Chicago Press, 1985.

Ayoup, Colleen, and Julie Podmore. "Making Kings." In Troka et al., *Drag King Anthology.*

Baker, David N., Lida M. Belt, and Herman Hudson. *The Black Composer Speaks.* Metuchen, N.J.: Scarecrow Press, 1978.

Baldwin, James. "The Hard Kind of Courage." *Harper's,* October 1958, 61–65.

———. *The Price of the Ticket: Collected Nonfiction, 1948–1985.* New York: St. Martin's, 1985.

Battle, Juan, Cathy J. Cohen, Dorian Warren, Gerard Fergerson, and Suzette Audam. *Say It Loud: I'm Black and I'm Proud.* New York: Policy Institute of the National Gay and Lesbian Task Force, 2002.

Becker, Howard S. *Tricks of the Trade: How to Think about Your Research*
Doing It. Chicago: University of Chicago Press, 1998.
Beehler, Gregory P., Bridget M. McGuinness, and John E. Verta. "Polluted
of Knowledge, and the Perception of Risk: Conceptualizing African Amer
Sport Fishing Practices." *Human Organization* 60, no. 3 (2001): 288–97.
Bennett, Andy, and Richard A. Peterson. *Music Scenes: Local, Translocal, and Vir*
ville: Vanderbilt University Press, 2004.
Bhabha, Homi K. *The Location of Culture.* London: Routledge, 1994.
"Black Lesbian Firefighter Wins Harassment Lawsuit." *Dallas Morning News.* July 5, 2
Blount, Marcellus, and George P. Cunningham. *Representing Black Men.* New York: R
ledge, 1996.
Bobo, Jacqueline. *Black Women as Cultural Readers.* New York: Columbia University Press,
1995.
Bohlman, Philip V. "Becoming Ethnomusicologists." *Newsletter of the Society for Ethnomusicology* 41, no. 2 (2007): 1.
Bornstein, Kate. *Gender Outlaw.* New York: Routledge, 1994.
Boykin, Keith. "Black Gay Leadership Group Vanishes: Americans Mark the 1963 March on Washington as the National Black Lesbian and Gay Leadership Forum Dies," August 21, 2003, Gay Mundo. Available at Gully Online Magazine, http://www.thegully.com/essays/gaymundo/030821_gay_black_1963march.html, accessed June 3, 2009.
Bradby, Barbara. "Lesbians and Popular Music: Does It Matter Who Is Singing?" In *Outwrite: Lesbianism and Popular Culture,* edited by G. Griffin. London: Pluto Press, 1993.
Brett, Philip, ed. *Queering the Pitch: The New Gay and Lesbian Musicology.* New York: Routledge, 1994.
Brown, Wendy. *States of Injury: Power and Freedom in Late Modernity.* Princeton, N.J.: Princeton University Press, 1995.
Brush, Paula Stewart. "Problematizing the Race Consciousness of Women of Color." *Signs* 27, no. 1 (2001): 171–98.
Burkholder, Nancy Jean. "A Kinder, Gentler Festival?" *TransSisters* 2 (November/December 1993): 4–5.
Butler, Judith. *Bodies That Matter: On the Discursive Limits of "Sex."* New York: Routledge, 1993.
———. "Gender and Appropriation in *Paris Is Burning.*" In *Bodies That Matter.*
———. *Gender Trouble: Feminism and the Subversion of Identity (Thinking Gender).* New York: Routledge, 1990.
———. *Undoing Gender.* New York: Routledge, 2004.
Byrd, Rudolph P., and Beverly Guy-Sheftall, eds. *Traps: African-American Men on Gender and Sexuality.* Bloomington: University of Indiana Press, 2001.
Carbado, Devon W., ed. *Black Men on Race, Gender, and Sexuality.* New York: New York University Press, 1999.
Carby, Hazel V. "'It Jus Be's Dat Way Sometimes': The Sexual Politics of Women's Blues." *Radical America* 20, no. 4 (June-July 1986): 9–22. Reprinted in *Unequal Sisters* (first edition), edited by V. Ruiz and E. DuBois. New York: Routledge, 1990.
———. "The Multicultural Wars." In Dent, *Black Popular Culture.*
———. *Reconstructing Womanhood: The Emergence of the Afro-American Woman Novelist.* New York: Oxford University Press, 1987.
Cohen, Anthony. *The Symbolic Construction of Community.* London: Tavistock, 1985.
Cohen, Cathy. *The Boundaries of Blackness: AIDS and the Breakdown of Black Politics.* Chicago: University of Chicago Press, 1999.

Kathleen B. Jones, and Joan C. Tronto, eds. *Women Transforming Politics.* ew York University Press, 1997.

. "The Jewel Box Revue: America's Longest-Running, Touring Drag Show." *tory Studies* 17 (June 1997): 79–91.

icia Hill. *Black Feminist Thought: Knowledge, Consciousness, and the Politics of ment.* Boston: Unwin Hyman, 1990.

Black Sexual Politics: African Americans,Gender, and the New Racism. New York: edge, 2004.

—. *Fighting Words: Black Women and the Search for Justice.* Minneapolis: University of innesota Press, 1998.

mbahee River Collective. "A Black Feminist Statement." In *Capitalist Patriarchy and the Case for Socialist Feminism,* ed. Zillah R. Eisenstein. New York: Monthly Review Press, 1979.

Connerly, Gregory. "Are You Black First or Are You Queer?" In Constantine-Simms, *Greatest Taboo.*

Constantine-Simms, Delroy, ed. *The Greatest Taboo: Homosexuality in Black Communities.* Los Angeles: Alyson Books, 2000.

Cose, Ellis. *The Rage of a Privileged Class.* New York: Harper Collins, 1993.

Cusick, Suzanne. "On a Lesbian Relation with Music: A Serious Effort Not to Think Straight." In Brett et al., *Queering the Pitch.*

Darty, Trudy, and Sandee Potter, eds. *Women-Identified Women.* Palo Alto, Calif.: Mayfield, 1984.

Davis, Angela. *Blues Legacies and Black Feminism.* New York: Pantheon Books, 1998.

De Jong, Nanette. "Women of the AACM: Four Narratives." In Hayes and Williams, *Black Women and Music.*

Deloria, Philip. *Playing Indian.* New Haven, Conn.: Yale University Press, 1998.

Densham, Andrea. "The Marginalized Uses of Power and Identity: Lesbians' Participation in Breast Cancer and AIDS Activism." In Cohen et al., *Women Transforming Politics.*

Dent, Gina. *Black Popular Culture.* Seattle: Bay Press, 1992.

Desmond, Jane. *Staging Tourism: Bodies on Display from Waikiki to Sea World.* Chicago: University of Chicago Press, 1999.

Drorbaugh, Elizabeth. "Sliding Scales: Notes on Stormé DeLarverie and the Jewel Box Revue, the Cross-Dressed Woman on the Contemporary Stage, and the Invert." In *Crossing the Stage,* edited by Lesley Ferris. London: Routledge, 1993.

Du Cille, Ann. "The Occult of True Black Womanhood: Critical Demeanor and Black Feminist Studies." *Signs* 19, no.3 (1994): 591–629.

Duneier, Mitchell. *Sidewalk.* New York: Farrar, Straus and Giroux, 1997.

Dunn, Leslie C., and Nancy A. Jones. *Embodied Voices: Representing Female Vocality in Western Culture.* Cambridge, UK: Cambridge University Press, 1994.

Dyson, Michael Eric. *Race Rules: Navigating the Color Line.* New York: Random House, 1996.

Eisenstein, Zillah R., ed. *Capitalist Patriarchy and the Case for Socialist Feminism.* New York: Monthly Review Press, 1979.

Evans, Sara. *Personal Politics: The Roots of Women's Liberation in the Civil Rights Movement and the New Left.* New York: Vintage, 1980.

Faderman, Lillian. *Odd Girls and Twilight Lovers.* New York: Penguin, 1991.

Feagin, Joe, and Melvin P. Sikes. *Living with Racism: The Black Middle-Class Experience.* Boston: Beacon Press, 1994.

Feinberg, Leslie. *Stone Butch Blues: A Novel.* Ithaca, NY: Firebrand Books, 1993.

———. *Transgender Warriors: Making History from Joan of Arc to Dennis R*
Beacon Press, 1996.
———. *Trans Liberation: Beyond Pink or Blue.* Boston: Beacon Press, 1998.
Ferris, Leslie, ed. *Crossing the Stage.* London: Routledge, 1993.
Foner, Philip S. *Women and the American Labor Movement: From World War I*
New York: Free Press, 1980.
Fuss, Diana, ed. *Inside/Out: Lesbian Theories, Gay Theories.* New York: Routledge
Gamson, Joshua. "Messages of Exclusion: Gender, Movement, and Symbolic Boun
In Ryan, *Identity Politics.*
Garr, Gillian G. *She's a Rebel: The History of Women in Rock and Roll.* New York: Seal P
1992.
Geertz, Clifford. *The Interpretation of Cultures: Selected Essays.* New York: Basic Books, 1973.
George, Nelson. *The Death of Rhythm and Blues.* New York: Pantheon Books, 1988.
Giddings, Paula. *When and Where I Enter: The Impact of Black Women on Race and Sex in America.* New York: Bantam Books, 1984.
Gilroy, Paul. *The Black Atlantic: Modernity and Double Consciousness.* Cambridge, Mass.: Harvard University Press, 1993.
Ginsburg, Faye D. *Contested Lives: The Abortion Debate in an American Community.* Berkeley: University of California Press, 1989.
Goddard, Amy Jo. "Staging Activism: New York City Performing Artists as Cultural Workers." *Social Justice: A Journal of Crime, Conflict, and World Order* 34, no. 1 (2007): 97–116.
Gomez, Jewelle. *Forty-three Septembers.* Ann Arbor, MI: Firebrand Books, 1993.
Gupta, Akhill, and James Ferguson. *Anthropological Locations: Boundaries and Grounds of a Field Science.* Berkeley: University of California Press, 1997.
Guy-Sheftall, Beverly, ed. *Words of Fire: An Anthology of African-American Feminist Thought.* New York: New Press, 1995.
Gwaltney, John Langston. *Drylongso: A Self-Portrait of Black America.* New York: Random House, 1980.
Halberstam, Judith "Jack." *The Drag King Book.* Photos by Del LaGrace Volcano. London: Serpent's Tail, 1999.
———. *Female Masculinity.* Durham, N.C.: Duke University Press, 1998.
———. "Mackdaddy, Superfly, Rapper: Gender, Race, and Masculinity in the Drag King Scene." *Social Text* 15, no. 52/53 (1997): 104–31.
Hall, Stuart. "What Is This 'Black' in Black Popular Culture?" In *Representing Blackness: Issues in Film and Video,* edited by Valerie Smith. New Brunswick, N.J.: Rutgers University Press, 1997. First published in Dent, *Black Popular Culture.*
———. "When Was the Post-Colonial: Thinking at the Limit." In Iain Chambers and Lidia Curti, *The Post-Colonial Question: Common Skies, Divided Horizons.* London: Routledge, 1996.
Harris, Laura, ed. *Femme: Feminists, Lesbians, and Bad Girls.* New York: Routledge, 1997.
Harrison, Daphne. *Black Pearls: Blues Queens of the 1920s.* New Brunswick, N.J.: Rutgers University Press, 1988.
Harrison, Faye, ed. *Decolonizing Anthropology: Moving Further toward an Anthropology for Liberation.* Washington, DC: American Anthropology Association, 1991.
Hartocollis, Anemona. "Four Women Are Sentenced in Attack on Man in Village." *New York Times.* June 15, 2007.
Hayes, Eileen M., and Linda F. Williams, eds. *Black Women and Music: More Than the Blues.* Urbana: University of Illinois Press, 2007.

Women and Women's Music." In Hayes and Williams, eds., *Black Women*

Women Performers of Women-Identified Music: 'They Cut Off My Voice; Voices.'" PhD diss., University of Washington, 1999.

Your Mother's Racial Uplift: Sweet Honey in the Rock, Journey, and Repre-: Sweet Honey in the Rock: Raise Your Voice," in *Women and Music: A Journal r and Culture* 10 (Winter 2006): 71–79.

"Radical Harmonies." (film review) *Ethnomusicology* 48, no. 2 (2004): 312–14.

—. "Women-Identified Music." In Maultsby and Burnim, *African American Music.*

andez, Deborah. *Bachata: A Social History of a Dominican Popular Music.* Philadelphia: Temple University Press, 1993.

ooks, bell. *Black Looks: Race and Representation.* Boston: South End Press, 1992.

———. "Facing Difference: The Black Female Body." In *Art on My Mind: Visual Politics.* New York: New Press, 1995.

———. "Is Paris Burning?" In *Black Looks, Race, and Representation.* Boston: South End Press, 1992.

———. "Performance Practice as a Site of Opposition." In *Let's Get It On: The Politics of Black Performance,* edited by Catherine Ugwu. Seattle: Bay Press, 1995.

———. *Reel to Real: Race, Sex, and Class at the Movies.* New York: Routledge, 1996.

Hudson-Weems, Clenora. *Africana Womanism: Reclaiming Ourselves.* Troy, Mich.: Bedford Publishing, 1994.

Hull, Gloria, Patricia Bell Scott, and Barbara Smith. *All the Women Are White, All the Blacks Are Men, but Some of Us Are Brave: Black Women's Studies.* Old Westbury, N.Y.: Feminist Press, 1982.

Hymes, Dell. *Reinventing Anthropology.* 1969. New York: Vintage Books, 1974.

James, Joy. *Shadowboxing: Representations of Black Feminist Politics.* New York: St. Martin's, 1999.

Johnson, Patrick E., and Mae G. Henderson, eds. *Black Queer Studies: A Critical Anthology.* Durham, N.C.: Duke University Press, 2005.

Kahn, Karen. *Frontline Feminism, 1975–1995: Essays from* Sojourner*'s First 20 Years.* San Francisco: Aunt Lute Books, 1995.

Keen, Lisa M. "Michigan Festival Expels Transsexual in Middle of the Night." *Washington Blade* 13 (September 1991): 17.

Keil, Charles. "People's Music Comparatively: Style and Stereotype, Class and Hegemony." *Dialectical Anthropology* 10 (1985).

Kelley, Robin D. G. *Freedom Dreams: The Black Radical Imagination.* Boston: Beacon Press, 2002.

———. *Hammer and Hoe: Alabama Communists during the Great Depression.* Chapel Hill: University of North Carolina Press, 1990.

Kimball, Gayle, ed. *Women's Culture in a New Era.* Lanham, Md.: Scarecrow Press, 2005.

———. "Women's Musical Composition": An Interview with Kay Gardner. In Kimball, *Women's Culture.*

King, J. L. *On the Down Low: A Journey into the Lives of "Straight" Black Men Who Sleep with Men.* New York: Broadway Books, 2004.

Kisliuk, Michelle R. "(Un)doing Fieldwork: Sharing Songs, Sharing Lives." In Gregory F. Barz and Timothy J. Cooley, *Shadows in the Field: New Perspectives for Fieldwork in Ethnomusicology.* New York: Oxford University Press, 1997.

Koskoff, Ellen. *Women and Music in Cross-Cultural Perspective.* 1987. Urbana: University of Illinois, 1989.

Lange, Barbara Rose. "'What was that Conquering Magic . . .': The Power a
in Hungarian Gypsy *Nóta*." *Ethnomusicology* 41, no. 3 (1994): 517–37.
Lanker, Brian. *I Dream a World: Portraits of Black Women Who Changed Ame*
Stewart, Tabori and Chang, 1999.
Leap, William Leap, "Studying Lesbian and Gay Languages: Vocabulary, Text
Beyond." In Lewin and Leap, *Out in Theory*.
Leidner, Robin. "'On Whose Behalf?': Feminist Ideology and Dilemmas of Con
In Ryan, *Identity Politics*.
Lewin, Ellen. *Inventing Lesbian Cultures in America*. Boston: Beacon Press, 1996.
Lewin, Ellen, and William Leap, eds. *Out in Theory: The Emergence of Lesbian and Gay
thropology*. Urbana: University of Illinois Press, 2002.
Lont, Cynthia. *Between Rock and a Hard Place: A Model of Subcultural Persistence and Women
Music*. PhD diss. University of Iowa, 1984.
———. "Women's Music: No Longer a Small Private Party." In *Rockin' the Boat: Mass Music and Mass Movements*, ed. Reebee Garofalo. Boston: South End Press, 1992.
Lorde, Audre. *The Cancer Journals*. Special edition. San Francisco: Aunt Lute Books, 2006.
———. *Zami: A New Spelling of My Name*. Freedom, Calif.: Crossing Press, 1982.
Mahon, Maureen. *Right to Rock: The Black Rock Coalition and the Cultural Politics of Race*. Durham, N.C.: Duke University Press, 2004.
Maultsby, Portia K., and Mellonee V. Burnim, eds. *African American Music: An Introduction*. New York: Routledge, 2006.
McClaurin, Irma. *Black Feminist Anthropology: Theory, Politics, Praxis, and Poetics*. New Brunswick, N.J.: Rutgers University Press, 2001.
McKnight, Reginald. "Confessions of a Wannabee Negro." In *Lure and Loathing: Essays on Race, Identity and the Ambivalence of Assimilation*, edited by G. Early. New York: Penguin Press, 1993.
Mercer, Kobena. "Black Hair/Style Politics." In *Welcome to the Jungle: New Positions in Black Cultural Studies*. New York: Routledge, 1994.
"Michigan Womyn's Music Festival Ends Policy of Discrimination against Trans Women: After 15 Years of Controversy, Supporters Welcome Trans Women to 'The Land.'" Camp Trans press release. August 24, 2006. http://www.ifge.org/Article273.phtml.
Michigan Womyn's Music Festival. Program booklet, 1992.
Mills, Kay. *This Little Light of Mine: The Life of Fannie Lou Hamer*. Lexington: University Press of Kentucky, 1994.
Minister, Kristina. "A Feminist Frame for the Oral History Interview." In *Women's Words: The Feminist Practice of Oral History*, edited by Sherna Berger Gluck and Daphne Patai. New York: Routledge, 1991.
Mitchell, Carmen. "Creations of Fantasies/Constructions of Identities: The Oppositional Lives of Gladys Bentley." In Constantine-Simms, *Greatest Taboo*.
Moore, Lisa C. *Does Your Mama Know? An Anthology of Black Lesbian Coming Out Stories*. Austin, Tex.: RedBone Press, 2004.
Morgan, Joan. *When Chickenheads Come Home to Roost: My Life as a Hip-Hop Feminist*. New York: Simon and Schuster, 1999.
Morgan, Tracy. "Butch-Femme and the Politics of Identity." In Stein, *Sisters, Sexperts*, 1993.
Morris, Bonnie J. *Eden Built by Eves: The Culture of Women's Music Festivals*. New York: Alyson Books, 1999.
Munns, Jessica, and Penny Richards, eds. *The Clothes That Wear Us: On Dressing and Transgressing in Eighteenth-Century Culture*. Newark: University of Delaware Press, 1999.
Munt, Sally R., ed., *Butch/Femme: Inside Lesbian Gender*. London: Cassell, 1997.

. *Lesbians Talk Transgendered.* London: Scarlet, 1994.
n's Music Festival. Program booklet, 1992.
m booklet, 2003.
I. "Why Are the Gay Ghettoes White?" In Johnson and Henderson, *Black* *es.*
her. Foreword. In Lewin and Leap, *Out in Theory.*
other Camp: Female Impersonators in America. Chicago: University of Chicago , 1972.
w, Lucius T., Jr. *Critical Social Theory in the Interests of Black Folks.* Lanham, Md.: owman and Littlefield, 2005.
nter, Nell Irwin. *Sojourner Truth: A Life, A Symbol.* New York: W. W. Norton, 1997.
atton, Cindy. "Embodying Subaltern Memory: Kinesthesia and the Problematics of Gender and Race." In *The Madonna Connection: Representational Politics, Subcultural Identities, and Cultural Theory,* edited by Cathy Schwichtenberg. Boulder: Westview Press, 1993.
Pauliny, Tara. "Erotic Arguments and Persuasive Acts: Discourses of Desire and the Rhetoric of Female-to-Male Drag." In Troka et al., *Drag King Anthology.*
Peden, Tina. "Black Women, Stop Hogging All the Psychic Hotline Infomercial Hosting Jobs!" www.buzzle.com/editorials/9-11-2005-76547.asp.
Penelope, Julia, and Susan Wolfe, eds. *Lesbian Culture: An Anthology.* Freedom, Calif.: Crossing Press, 1993.
Petersen, Karen. "An Investigation of Women-Identified Music in the United States." In Koskoff, *Women in Cross-Cultural Perspective.*
Post, Laura. *Backstage Pass: Interviews with Women in Music.* Norwich, Vt.: New Victoria, 1997.
Pough, Gwendolyn. "Hip-Hop Soul Mate? Hip-Hop Soul Divas and Rap Music: Critiquing the Love That Hate Produced." In Hayes and Williams, *Black Women and Music.*
Pressley, Sue Ann. "Three Held in Black Man's Dragging Death." *Times Picayune.* June 10, 1998. Available at http://www.yale.edu/glc/archive/990.htm.
Radano, Ronald M., and Philip V. Bohlman, ed. *Music in the Racial Imagination.* Chicago: University of Chicago Press, 2000.
Raymond, Janice G. *The Transsexual Empire: The Making of the She-Male.* Boston: Beacon Press, 1979.
Reagon, Bernice Johnson. "Coalition Politics: Turning the Century." In Smith, *Home Girls.*
———. *We Who Believe in Freedom: Sweet Honey in the Rock . . . Still on the Journey.* New York: Anchor Books, 1993.
Reed, Ishmael. *Mumbo Jumbo.* New York: Bantam Books, 1972.
Rich, Adrienne. "Compulsory Heterosexuality and Lesbian Existence." In *Blood, Bread, and Poetry: Selected Prose, 1978–1985.* New York: W. W. Norton, 1986. Rprt. in Abelove et al., *Lesbian and Gay Studies Reader.*
Robertson, Carol E. "Power and Gender in the Musical Experiences of Women." In Koskoff, *Women and Music.*
Rooks, Noliwe. *Hair Raising: Beauty, Culture, and Africa American Women.* New Brunswick, N.J.: Rutgers University Press, 1996.
Rosaldo, Renato. *Culture and Truth: The Remaking of Social Analysis.* Boston: Beacon Press, 1989.
Rose, Tricia. *Black Noise: Rap Music and Black Culture in Contemporary America.* Hanover, N.H.: Wesleyan University Press, 1994.
Roth, Benita. "Race, Class, and the Emergence of Black Feminism in the 1960s and 1970s." *Womanist Theory and Research* 2, no. 1 (1999): 1–4.

———. *Separate Roads to Feminism: Black, Chicana, and White Feminist Moven* *Second Wave*. Cambridge, UK: Cambridge University Press, 2003.

Ryan, Barbara, ed. *Identity Politics in the Women's Movement*. New York: versity Press, 2001.

Rybczynski, Witold. *Waiting for the Weekend*. New York: Penguin Books, 19

Saalfield, Catherine, and Ray Navarro. "Shocking Pink Praxis: Race and Gende UP Frontlines." In Fuss, *Inside/Out*.

Samuels, David W. *Putting a Song on Top of It*. Tucson: University of Arizona Press,

Sandstrom, Boden. "Performance, Ritual, and Negotiation of Identity in the Mic Womyn's Music Festival." PhD diss. University of Maryland, 2002.

———. "Women's Music: Passing the Legacy." In Kimball, *Women's Culture*.

Santos, Noella. "A Do-Something Vacation." *Texas AAA* (2007): 28–31.

Scott, James C. *Domination and the Arts of Resistance: Hidden Transcripts*. New Haven, Conn.: Yale University Press, 1990.

Sedgwick, Eve. "Epistemology of the Closet."In Abelove et al., *Lesbian and Gay Studies Reader*.

Slobin, Mark. *Subcultural Sounds: Micromusics of the West*. Hanover, Mass.: University Press of New England, 1993.

Small, Christopher. *Music of the Common Tongue: Survival and Celebration in African American Music*. Hanover, N.H.: University Press of New England, 1998.

———. "Why Doesn't the Whole World Love Chamber Music?" *American Music* 19, no. 3 (2001): 340–59.

Smith, Barbara, ed. *Home Girls: A Black Feminist Anthology*. New York: Kitchen Table: Women of Color Press, 1983.

———, ed., *Home Girls: A Black Feminist Anthology*. New Brunswick, N.J.: Rutgers University Press, 2000.

Smith, Valerie. *Not Just Race, Not Just Gender: Black Feminist Readings*. New York: Routledge, 1998.

———, ed. *Representing Blackness: Issues in Film and Video*. New Brunswick, N.J.: Rutgers University Press, 1997.

Spelman, Elizabeth. *Inessential Woman: Problems of Exclusion in Feminist Thought*. Boston: Beacon Press, 1988.

Spivak, Gayatri Chakravorty. "Subaltern Studies: Deconstructing Historiography." In *In Other Worlds: Essays in Cultural Politics*. New York: Methuen, 1987.

Springer, Kimberly. *Living for the Revolution: Black Feminist Organizations, 1968–1980*. Durham, N.C.: Duke University Press, 2005.

Steffans, Karrine. *Confessions of a Video Vixen*. New York: Amistad, 2005.

Stein, Arlene, ed. "Androgyny Goes Pop: But Is It Lesbian Music?" In *Sisters, Sexperts*.

———. *Sisters, Sexperts, Queers; Beyond the Lesbian Nation*. New York: Penguin Books, 1993.

Stewart, Kathleen. "Nostalgia—A Polemic." *Cultural Anthropology* 3, no. 3 (1988): 227–41.

Streitmatter, Rodger. "About Phyllis Lyon and Del Martin," The National Lesbian and Gay Journalists Association, http://www.nlgja.org/awards/hof_lyon_martin.htm.

Surkan, Kim. "Drag Kings in the New Wave: Gender Performance and Participation." In Troka et al., *Drag King Anthology*.

Tate, Greg, ed. *Everything but the Burden: What White People Are Taking from Black Culture*. New York: Random House, 2003.

———. *Flyboy in the Buttermilk: Essays on Contemporary America*. Foreword by Henry Louis Gates Jr. New York: Simon and Schuster, 1992.

nd Leila J. Rupp. "Women's Culture and Lesbian Feminist Activism: A
on of Cultural Feminism." *Signs* 19, no. 1 (1993): 32–61.

ie M. Thompson. *Mommy Queerest: Contemporary Rhetorics of Lesbian Ma-*
y. Amherst: University of Massachusetts Press, 2002.

Amoja, and Blanche Jackson. *Cultural Etiquette: A Guide for the Well-Inten-*
dstone, Va.: Market Wimmin, 1991.

na, Kathleen Lebesco, and Jean Noble, eds. *The Drag King Anthology*. New York:
gton Park Press, 2000.

, Sherrie. *Swing Shift: "All-Girl" Bands of the 1940s*. Durham, N.C.: Duke University
ess, 2000.

—. "When Subjects Don't Come Out." In *Queer Episodes in Music and Modern Iden-tity*, edited by Sophie Fuller and Lloyd Whitesell. Urbana: University of Illinois Press, 2002.

Tyler, Carole-Ann. "Boys Will Be Girls: The Politics of Gay Drag." In Fuss, *Inside/Out*.

Urry, John. *The Tourist Gaze: Leisure and Travel in Contemporary Societies*. London: Sage, 1990.

Valentine, David. "We're 'Not about Gender': The Uses of 'Transgender.'" In Lewin and Leap, *Out in Theory*.

Van Leer, David. "Visible Silence: Spectatorship in Black Gay and Lesbian Film." In V. Smith, *Representing Blackness*.

Visweswaran, Kamala. *Fictions of Feminist Ethnography*. Minneapolis: University of Minnesota Press, 1994.

Walker, Alice. *The Color Purple: A Novel*. New York: Harcourt Brace Jovanovich, 1982.

———. *In Search of Our Mothers' Gardens: Womanist Prose*. San Diego: Harcourt Brace Jovanovich, 1983.

Walker, Lisa. "How to Recognize a Lesbian: The Cultural Politics of Looking Like What You Are," *Signs* 18, no. 4 (1993): 866–90.

———. *Looking Like What You Are: Sexual Style, Race, and Lesbian Identity*. New York: New York University Press, 2001.

Walker, Rebecca. *To Be Real: Telling the Truth and Changing the Face of Feminism*. New York: Anchor Books, 1995.

Walker-Hill, Helen. *From Spirituals to Symphonies: African-American Women Composers and Their Music*. Westport, Conn.: Greenwood Press, 2002.

Wallace, Michelle. "Modernism, Post-Modernism, and the Problem of the Visual in Afro-American Culture." In *Out There: Marginalization and Contemporary Cultures*, ed. Russell Ferguson, Martha Gever, Trinh T. Minh-Ha, Cornel West. Cambridge, Mass.: MIT Press, 1990.

Ward, Brian. *Just My Soul Responding: Rhythm and Blues, Black Consciousness, and Race Relations*. Berkeley: University of California Press, 1998.

Waterman, Christopher A. "Race Music: Bo Chatmon, '*Corrine Corrina*,' and the Excluded Middle." In Radano and Bohlman, *Music in the Racial Imagination*.

Waterman, Christopher A., and Larry Starr. *American Popular Music: From Minstrelsy to MTV*. New York: Oxford University Press, 2003.

Weston, Kath. *Families We Choose: Lesbians, Gays, Kinship*. 1991. New York: Columbia University Press, 1997.

———. *Render Me, Gender Me: Lesbians Talk Sex, Class, Color, Nation, Studmuffins*. New York: Columbia University Press, 1996.

Whitehead, Tony Larry, and Mary Ellen Conaway, eds. *Self, Sex, and Gender in Cross-Cultural Fieldwork*. Urbana: University of Illinois Press, 1986.

Whittier, Nancy. *Feminist Generations: The Persistence of the Radical Wo*
Philadelphia: Temple University Press, 1995.
Wiggins, William. *O Freedom! Afro-American Emancipation Celebration.* Knox
of Tennessee Press, 1990.
Williams, Linda F. "Black Women, Jazz, and Feminism." In Hayes and W
Women and Music.
Wong, Deborah. *Speak It Louder: Asian Americans Making Music.* New York:
2004.

FILMS

Baur, Gabriel. *Venus Boyz.* Clockwise Productions, 2002.
Brewer, Craig. *Hustle and Flow.* Crunk Pictures, 2005.
Gray, F. Gary. *Set It Off.* New Line Cinema, 1996.
Livingston, Jennie. *Paris Is Burning.* Off White Productions, Inc., 1990.
Mosbacher, Dee. *Radical Harmonies.* DVD. Produced by Margie Adam, June Millington, Boden Sandstrom. Wolfe Video, 2001.
Muccino, Gabriele. *The Pursuit of Happyness.* DVD. Columbia Pictures, 2006.
Parkerson, Michelle. *Storme: The Lady of the Jewel Box,* 1987.
Parkerson, Michelle, and Ada Gay Griffin. *A Litany for Survival: The Life and Work of Audre Lorde.* Third World Newsreel, 1995.
Peddle, Daniel. *The Aggressives.* Secret Gallery, 2005.
Spielberg, Steven. *The Color Purple.* Amblin Entertainment, 1985.
Welbon, Yvonne. *Living in Pride: Ruth C. Ellis @100.* Our Film Works, 1999.

PERSONS INTERVIEWED

The following list of musicians, organizers, and producers includes named individuals who provided material used in this book. It does not represent a complete list of everyone I interviewed during the course of my research. Depending on the context, at times I have included the individual's name; elsewhere in the text I might reference the comments of that same person with a pseudonym. Musicians who wished to remain anonymous are not included in this list. In most cases, festival workers and attendees are referred to by pseudonym in the text. Frequently, I have referred to individuals named by interviewees by pseudonym also, especially if I did not interview them.

Allen, Lillian. Telephone interview by author. December 12, 1995.
Archer, Kim. Telephone interview by author. August 1, 2006.
Avery, Gwen. Telephone interview by author. December 4, 1995.
Bagby, Rachel. Telephone interview by author. 1995.
Baskin, Rae. Telephone interview by author. July 11, 2005.
Benin, Rhonda. Telephone interview by author. December 5, 1995.
Burrell, Elouise. Telephone interview by author. January 1995.
Casselberry, Judith. Telephone interview by author. January 10, 1996.
Chandler, Kory. Telephone interview by author. May 15, 2005.
Cleveland, Wahru. Interview by author. Kent State University. June 6, 2003.
Cooke, India. Interview by author. Oakland, California. November 26, 1995.
DeMore, Melanie. Interview by author. Oakland, California. November 23, 1995.
Dlugacz, Judy. Telephone interview by author. November 19, 2005.

ean. Telephone interview by author. December 1, 1995.
ephone interview by author. January 24, 1996.
. Telephone interview by author. July 26, 2006.
helle. Interview by author. Washington, DC. October 1992.
elephone interview by author. May 2005.
phone interview by author. September 14, 2005.
eidre. Telephone interview by author. November 1, 1995.
Debra Kenya. Telephone conversation with author. August 17, 2007.
oney. Telephone interview by author. November 7, 2005.
ngton, June Millington. Interview by author. Bodega, California. January 1995.
ans, Pamela. Telephone inteview by author. January 24, 2007.
ogers, Pamela. Interview by author. Washington, DC. October 1992.
Suhalia, Naya'Hari. Telephone interview by author. July 11, 2005.
Thomas, Marquita. Interview by author. Los Angeles. May 2005.
Tillery, Linda. Interview by author. Oakland, California. January 1, 1995.
Washington, Sandra. Telephone interview by author. December 3, 1995.
Washington, Sharon. Telephone interview by author. December 4, 1995.
Watkins, Mary. Interview by author. Oakland, California. November 27, 1995.
Wells, Regina. Telephone interview by author. November 11, 1995.

Interviews with Women Given Pseudonyms

Beamer, Marietta, organizer, Northampton Lesbian Festival, 2004.
Falls, Monica, musician, 2005.
Foley, Chandra, musician, 1995.
Gee, Karla, tech crew, August 7, 2006.
Goddard, Delores, organizer, Sistahfest, 2005.
Howard, Jay, organizer, July 21, 2006.
Hudley, Klarete, NWMF, 2005.
Jameson, Penny, festival attendee, Boston, February 2005.
Jenkins, Tara, musician, 1995.
Jones, Jacque, musician, 1995.
Marshall, Kelly, festival attendee, NWMF, 2003.
Mitchell, Cal, organizer, summer 2006.
Rahman, Rachel, organizer, Sistahfest, 2005.
Ray, Tanya, organizer, 2006.
Roberts, Trade, organizer, June 7, 2005.

WEB SITES

http://detroit.areaconnect.com/statistics.htm (Accessed on July 5, 2008).
http://dykemarchla.com/history/herstory.html (Accessed on July 11, 2007).
http://eminism.org/michigan/faq-protest.html (Accessed on June 28, 2008).
http://faculty.washington.edu/qtaylor/speeches/truth.htm (Accessed on June 28, 2008).
http://glaad.org (Accessed on July 11, 2008).
http://glide.org/timeline.aspx (Accessed on July 11, 2008).
http://Jewishjournal.com/home/preview.php (Accessed on July 14, 2007).
http://library.duke.edu/digitalcollections/rbmscValfa2/inv/ (Accessed on July 7, 2007).
http://stonewallvets.org/stormedelarverie.htm (Accessed on July 7, 2007).
http://witchvox.com (Accessed on May 18, 2008).
http://www.afterellen.com/archive/ellen/column/2005 (Accessed on August 13, 2007).
http://www.angelfire.com/il2/mmch/index.html (Accessed on July 5, 2008).

http://www.askmen.com/women/singer_150/169b_trina.html (Accessed
http://www.blackgoddessrecords.com/ (Accessed on July 5, 2008).
http://www.bloomingtonnormalcvb.org (Accessed on June 25, 2007).
http://www.buzzle.com/editorials/9–11–2005 (Accessed on June 28, 200
http://www.camptrans.org (Accessed on June 28, 2008).
http://www.colorado.edu/journals/standards/V5N1/Lorde/goodman.html (
July 18, 2007).
http://www.forge-forward.org (Accessed on June 28, 2008).
http://www.galachoruses.org (Accessed on May 29, 2009).
http://www.gay.com (Accessed on June 28, 2008).
http://www.geocities.com/Hollywood/1777/ellycome.html (Accessed on May 26, 200
http://www.goldenrod.com/custom/herstory.htm (Accessed June 7, 2009).
http://www.hollynear.com (Accessed on June 28, 2008).
http://www.hwfestival.org/main.html. (Accessed on July 11, 2008).
http://www.idke.info (Accessed on July 5, 2007).
http://www.ladyfestsouth.org (Accessed on June 28, 2008).
http://www.lawmf.com/aboutus.html. (Accessed on July 14, 2007).
http://www.lilithfair.com (Accessed June 7, 2009).
http://www.madamcjwalker.com/ (Accessed on July 5, 2008).
http://www.nctequality.org (Accessed on June 28, 2008).
http://www.niacollective.org (Accessed on July 11, 2008).
http://www.queerculturalcenter.org/pages/festival03/hanifa.html, (Accessed July 7, 2007).
http://www.soapboxinc.com (Accessed June 7, 2009).
http://www.swc-cfc.gc.ca/pubx/pubspr/revisiting/revisiting_/_e.html (Accessed on July 7, 2007).
http://www.synthiasaintjames.com/metroame.htm (Accessed on July 2, 2007).
http://www.thirdworldnewsreel.org/record (URL no longer active).
http://www.transgenderlawcenter.org (Accessed on June 28, 2008).
http://www.unityfellowshipchurch.org/news (URL no longer active).
http://www.usc.edu/libraries/archives/queerfrontiers/queer/papers/retter.html (Accessed on July 7, 2007).
http://www.venusboyz.com/intwe.html (Accessed on June 28, 2008).
http://www.wbtcamps.org (Accessed on July 11, 2008).
http://www.yale.edu/glc/archive/990.htm (Accessed on June 27, 2007).

INDEX

EILEEN M. HAYES is an associate professor of music and the chair of the division of music history, theory, and ethnomusicology at the University of North Texas. She is the coeditor of *Black Women and Music: More than the Blues*.

MERICAN MUSIC IN GLOBAL PERSPECTIVE

men and Music: More than the Blues—*Edited by Eileen M. Hayes* *inda F. Williams*

blin' on My Mind: New Perspectives on the Blues—*Edited by* *David Evans*

ollow Your Heart: Moving with the Giants of Jazz, Swing, and Rhythm and Blues—*Joe Evans with Christopher Brooks*

Songs in Black and Lavender: Race, Sexual Politics, and Women's Music—*Eileen M. Hayes*

THE UNIVERSITY OF ILLINOIS PRESS
IS A FOUNDING MEMBER OF THE
ASSOCIATION OF AMERICAN UNIVERSITY PRESSES.

1325 SOUTH OAK STREET
CHAMPAIGN, IL 61820-6903
WWW.PRESS.UILLINOIS.EDU